Tolley's
Tax Planning for
Family Companies

by

Gerry Hart FTII, ATT
The Tax Team Ltd

Peter Rayney FCA, FTII
of Moores Rowland, Chartered Accountants

Tolley Publishing Company Ltd

un A United News & Media publication

Published by
Tolley Publishing Company Limited
Tolley House
2 Addiscombe Road
Croydon
Surrey
CR9 5AF
0181–686 9141

Typeset in Great Britain by
Letterpart Limited
Reigate, Surrey

Printed in Great Britain by
BPC Wheatons Ltd, Exeter

ISBN 0 85459 675–5

Preface

There are few areas of taxation which do not impinge upon the activities of a family company at one time or another. This book consequentially covers a wide variety of tax planning matters, but where it is different is that we consider each topic from the separate viewpoints of the company itself, the shareholders who work for the company (usually as directors), the non-working shareholders and in some instances the employees.

Only by taking that approach can the complete picture be seen. Clearly there will be occasions when what is tax effective for the company itself (and then directly or indirectly for the shareholders) will not necessarily be effective for the shareholders in their capacity as individual taxpayers. This conflict need not always present a major problem, but proper regard must be had to the interests of all parties in their differing capacities before embarking upon any tax planning exercise.

This approach is taken by us throughout the book, and each Chapter ends with a summary of the main planning points by reference to the tax position of the different parties. As such, it is intended that this book will give the complete picture on family company tax planning for professional advisers such as tax consultants, accountants and solicitors, and to the owners and financial directors of family companies themselves. That is certainly the aim, drawing upon the authors' combined experience in dealing with such companies and providing many worked examples illustrating their practical operation in a host of typical situations (all references to characters in the examples are entirely fictitious).

The book naturally enough starts with consideration of the family company, its structure and its operation. Consideration is then given to the corporate structure, followed by an overview of appropriate tax strategy. We look at specific areas affecting a family company, such ways in which funds can be extracted from the company; remuneration strategies; benefits and expenses; the company car (an area where the personal tax position of a working shareholder may well conflict with the tax position of the company); and full consideration of the particular pension scheme opportunities available to family companies. Employee share incentives are discussed including the ways in which extra shares can be found to eventually pass to employees who are not members of the family.

It is true to say that for any size of company the individual circumstances and mode of operation must be fully considered. With a family company, there is more to it than that and in particular the various methods of rewarding a key executive are fully considered by reference to all factors.

Preface

Succession planning remains a big issue for many long established family companies and we therefore cover the relevant tax and commercial angles extensively in *Passing on the Family Company*. However, it must be recognised that the next generation may not have the desire or possibly the ability to take over the running of the business, in which case a sale of the company or a management buy-out (perhaps though a purchase of own shares) must be contemplated. All these areas and the related planning issues are examined.

Valuing a family company is a minefield when either passing on a family company or selling it to outsiders. The principles of commercial and fiscal share valuations are therefore discussed in some detail.

We also cover other important tax aspects of family companies, including financing issues, expanding the business by way of acquisitions, reconstructions where a separation of shareholders is required, and how to wind-up the company in a tax-efficient manner as well as securing the best possible relief for any losses.

It is hoped that this book will be an indispensable guide for those involved in advising and running family companies. The authors will be pleased to receive any comments or suggestions for future editions.

We would like to thank our respective secretaries, Elaine Brazier and Tina Bayley, for their help and assistance in typing the manuscripts. We also owe a considerable debt of gratitude to the commitment and professionalism of the publishing and editorial team at Tolley and their encouragement, with particular thanks to Julie Watterston for her excellent editorial work.

Finally, we both would like to thank our respective families for their tolerance and support whilst 'wholly and exclusively and necessarily' working on this book!

Gerry Hart
Peter Rayney

Contents

Contents

Contents

10. Raising Funds

Contents

Contents

Table of Cases

Table of Statutory Instruments

Table of Statutes

Chapter 1

Introduction

There seems little point in attempting to strictly define what is meant by a 'family company' for the purposes of this book. By doing so, there would be a danger of some of the tax planning techniques not being given sufficient coverage. Furthermore, the driving forces behind one family company might well be a lot different from another and it would be disingenuous to restrict ourselves to a rigid definition.

In general terms, we could simply say that a family company is one where over 50% of the voting control is in the hands of members of a family. That gives a fairly wide definition and it must be appreciated that many of the techniques covered in this book will apply to companies where although there are family connections they are not sufficient to give voting control.

There used to be a definition of a 'family company' in the tax legislation, by reference to various capital gains tax reliefs (viz retirement relief, hold-over relief on gifts of business assets, and roll-over relief on business assets). These reliefs have now been changed to a definition of a 'personal company', which merely requires entitlement to exercise at least 5% of the voting rights of an unquoted company and cannot be regarded as comparable to a family company. [*TCGA 1992, 6 Sch 1(2)*].

There is an important term used in tax legislation which effectively covers family companies, and that is the term 'close company'. The importance of that definition is not as great as it used to be, but nevertheless there are a number of special tax provisions which only apply to a 'close company' and these are covered in this book. Essentially, a close company is one which is controlled by its directors or by five or fewer participators. This means that although most family companies will be close companies, not all close companies will be family companies. [*ICTA 1988, s 414*].

This book assumes that the limited company is the most suitable vehicle for the business and examines the tax planning techniques that are available to the family company through each stage of its development.

This book looks at tax planning strategies for the family company, and it must be appreciated that there are a number of special factors which apply to family companies where any plan of action is being proposed —

whether the plan is related to tax or any other topic. Concentrating as we do on tax matters, the special features and relationships within a family company must not be overlooked. Otherwise, putting forward what seem to be sound tax planning techniques could sooner or later create resistance or major problems.

It is always true to say, no matter who the taxpayer may be, that the tax tail should not wag the commercial dog. Tax is an important factor in the decision-making processes but it should not be considered in isolation. Some of us can no doubt remember when the top rate of tax was 98% (the chances of ever going back to those days are thankfully remote to the extreme) and if you are considering spending £1,000, then with a tax rate of 50% it is still going to cost you at least £500 net of tax.

Some planning techniques will centre around the structure of the company and others will be brought about by that company's activity. Essentially there are two types of activity that a family company can carry out, either 'trading' or 'investment'. Various reliefs will be available that are attached to these activities. Such reliefs will of course be available to all companies but will be of particular interest to family companies where there is an in-built facility to match reward with ownership.

With the family company, as already mentioned there are particular characteristics which must be taken into account in determining a tax planning strategy. There are several books which look at the particular dynamics of a family company (both the good points and the bad), and below is merely a summary of the factors involved.

(*a*)   There is usually a stronger commitment by the family members, compared with executives in other companies, although there can be some family members who for one reason or another do not pull their weight. This particular aspect can therefore be both a strength and a weakness.

(*b*)   Employees of a family company often have a loyalty which can prove invaluable.

(*c*)   The family company can have a well-established and special way of running its business. Whilst this can often be a good point, it does mean that they can be left behind when it comes to necessary changes. This is particularly true in terms of technological changes, and family companies can lag behind.

(*d*)   Whilst a family company will often be preparing long-term plans, they are not always adhered to. There is of course nothing wrong with a degree of flexibility where a long-term plan is changed in the light of events (and hopefully in anticipation of events), but sometimes this suggests the lack of a structure within any long-term plan.

(*e*)   Certainly the decision-making process can be a lot quicker with a family company. This in itself can be a tremendous advantage in terms of the business environment and the relationship with the employees. The use of committees in decision-making can be a major problem, and one which is usually avoided within a family company.

(*f*)   When looking at the individual family members, there can be problems. This is particularly the case if there is a leading member of the family who is running the business with no clear succession route. This in itself can create friction between various members of the family, and as a result the business can suffer.

(*g*)   A family company can have particular problems when business is booming. It may not have the required capital base to fund the expansion which it has not specifically planned for but which has occurred by accident rather than design. There can also be a problem with the family company when it comes to an economic recession, as it may not be in a sound position to take the necessary decisions to restructure its business in the light of a downturn in activities.

A family company can be an invigorating environment, and it is one which has a major role to play in the business world. The successful family company will have seen a number of changes in recent years (e.g. the rise of the existence of non-executive directors in a family company and the increase in the demands for a specialised service or product). With proper tax planning strategies being adopted, the family company can look forward to continuing success.

Chapter 2

Strategies for Extracting Funds from the Company

Should surplus profits be retained or extracted?

2.1   Family companies can now freely decide how much of their profits should be returned to the shareholders or retained within the business. The 'working' shareholders will need to extract a basic level of income from the company to satisfy their personal requirements. Since 1988, the comparatively lower income tax rates have also encouraged companies to extract surplus profits. However, the recession of the early 1990s caused a number of companies to reduce the return available to their shareholders. Companies which have relied on bank borrowing or institutional finance will also have been prescribed financial limits on the amount of dividends and other payments made to the proprietor.

2.2   If the company can afford it, shareholders should consider the potential benefits of extracting profits from the company now. These include:

(*a*)   the current low income tax cost of extracting the funds. The tax cost of extracting cash from family companies is probably as low as it will ever be and there are signs that tax rates may well increase in the future, particularly if there is a change of Government. If the company requires funds for working capital, the amount extracted by the proprietor-shareholders can be lent back to the company on loan account, which can then be repaid at a later date tax free;

(*b*)   the potential double charge to tax which arises where profits retained in the company are invested in appreciating assets:

   (i)   the appreciation in asset values could potentially be taxed both in the company and when the value is realised by the shareholders, perhaps on a sale or liquidation of the company. However, if the company is eventually sold for a price based on a multiple of earnings, the value of the shares may bear little relationship to the level of retained profits;

   (ii)   the impact of this so called double charge has been reduced in recent years by the ability to rebase asset values to March

4

1982 and indexation of gains for CGT purposes and the ability to extract capital gains by dividend and offset the relevant ACT. Furthermore, the double charge effect would not be a problem where the company's shares are to be passed down as a 'family heirloom' on death.

In practice, a balanced approach between retention and extraction of profits will generally be required.

Extracting funds or value from the company

2.3 It is possible to extract funds or value from the company in a number of ways, although (*a*) to (*c*) below are usually available only for those shareholders which work in the company as a director or employee. The most important methods of extracting value are listed below (the references indicate where a detailed discussion of the topic may be found in this book):

(*a*) directors' remuneration or bonuses and paying salaries to other family members (see 2.12, 2.17–2.19);

(*b*) provision of benefits-in-kind (see 6.1–7.16);

(*c*) pension contributions (see 9.1–9.28);

(*d*) dividends (see 8.1–8.23);

(*e*) selling assets to the company for value (see 2.21);

(*f*) loans or advances from the company (subject to *Companies Act* rules) (see 2.23);

(*g*) charging interest on loans to the company (see 2.22, 10.5–10.8);

(*h*) charging rent on personally owned property which is used in the company trade (see 2.20);

(*i*) purchase of own shares (see 12.23–12.28);

(*j*) liquidation of the company (see 15.1–15.24).

The tax cost of the various methods of extraction will vary and it is important to determine the tax efficiency for each method of extracting funds/value.

On an ongoing basis, the working shareholders may well, in addition to drawing a normal salary, decide whether to extract surplus profits by means of a bonus or dividend. This aspect is considered in further detail in 2.7 to 2.16. In addition, the director-shareholders will often ensure that adequate provision is made to their future pension and benefits-in-kind are provided. Directors may also consider extracting funds on loan account, but this too involves a tax cost.

Capital receipts v income receipts

2.4   The purchase of own shares, liquidation or sale of a company are effectively exit-routes for the shareholder when he wishes to leave the company, retire or realise capital value.

In the current fiscal climate, it may often be beneficial to structure one of these transactions to provide the shareholder with an income receipt rather than a capital receipt. In many cases, a pre-determined split between income and capital may be required to give maximum tax efficiency. Although both income and capital are taxed at the same nominal rates, the effective tax rate may vary due to the impact of the tax credit carried with dividend income, the base cost of the shares (which may perhaps be based on March 1982 values), indexation relief, the annual CGT exemption and other reliefs.

2.5   In the context of a purchase by the company of its own shares, it is usually possible to structure the transaction either as a capital gains receipt within *ICTA 1988, s 219*, or as a distribution. Similarly, if the company is about to be wound-up, value can be extracted by means of an income dividend if the amount is paid prior to liquidation. Any amount distributed during the winding up would be a capital distribution (liable to CGT) for the shareholder. On the sale of the company, it may be possible to substitute dividend income for sale proceeds, by means of a pre-sale dividend.

2.6   It is particularly important to compare the tax liabilities under the income and capital route well in advance of these transactions in order to determine the most tax efficient route. Any planning steps which are then necessary to characterise the transaction as income can then be implemented with minimal risk of Inland Revenue attack under the '*Furniss v Dawson*' doctrine.

Bonus v dividends

2.7   Although the working shareholders can reward themselves in a number of ways, the main choice often lies between whether to pay a bonus or dividend. The controlling shareholder will often draw remuneration in excess of the upper earnings limit for NIC purposes. No additional employee's NIC cost would arise on paying a bonus but it would currently attract additional employer's NIC at 10.2%. Consideration might be given to paying remuneration through one of the remaining commodity schemes to avoid the NIC cost (see 6.4).

If the company pays tax at the small companies rate of 25%, it can often be beneficial to extract surplus funds by means of a dividend as the NIC cost is avoided. The substitution of dividends for remuneration is not regarded as an abnormal pay practice for NIC purposes (*Social Security* and *Benefits Act 1992, para 4(c), 1 Sch* and *Contribution Regs 21* and *22*, NIC Brief February 1994).

The *FA 1993* reduction in the tax credit carried with dividends to 20% has made the bonus v dividend decision more marginal. The best way to compare the tax treatment of extracting surplus profits as a bonus or a dividend is through the use of a worked example.

Example 1

Bonus v dividend comparison (CT at 25%)

Greaves Limited will have surplus profits available of £100,000 for the year ended 31 March 1996, which could be paid to its sole shareholder, Mr Jimmy, as a bonus or dividend. Mr Jimmy has already drawn a salary of £30,000 (i.e. in excess of the NIC upper earnings limit), and he pays income tax at 40%. Greaves Limited is subject to corporation tax at 25%.

The relevant tax and NIC effects are compared below.

			Bonus £	£	Dividend £
Available profits			100,000		100,000
Less Employer's NIC @ 10.2%			(9,256)		
Corporation tax @ 25%					(25,000)
			90,744		75,000
Income tax thereon					
Bonus	£90,744	@40%	(36,298)		
Dividend:					
Cash	£75,000				
Tax credit					
(20/80)	18,750				
Gross	93,750	@ 40%		(37,500)	
Less Tax credit				18,750	(18,750)
Net cash available			54,446		56,250
Tax and NIC liabilities					
Employer's NIC			9,256		
Corporation tax					25,000
PAYE			36,298		
Higher rate assessment					18,750
			45,554		43,750

Tax saved by dividend = £1,804 (£45,554 less £43,750).

2.8   The above example illustrates that it is still marginally beneficial to extract surplus profits as a dividend where the company is paying
tax at the small companies rate, subject to the other factors in 2.15.
Shareholders paying tax at the basic rate of 25% will obtain the full
benefit of the tax credit (see 8.3–8.4). The reduced rate of ACT on the
dividend is only relevant in so far as it affects the timing of the payment
of corporation tax.

2.9   Where the company's profit suffers tax at the main rate of 33%
or the marginal rate of 35%, the advantage switches in favour of
bonuses. This is because the benefit of the higher corporation tax relief
for the bonus (and employer's NIC) outweighs the additional NIC cost
(see Example 2).

Example 2

Bonus v dividend comparison (CT at 33%)

Assume the same facts as in Example 1, except that Greaves Limited
pays corporation tax at the main rate of 33%.

		Bonus £	£	*Dividend* £
Available profits		100,000		100,000
Less Employer's NIC @ 10.2%		(9,256)		
Corporation tax @ 33%				(33,000)
		90,744		67,000
Income tax thereon				
Bonus	£90,744 @ 40%	(36,298)		
Dividend:				
Cash	£67,000			
Tax credit				
(20/80)	16,750			
Gross	83,750 @ 40%		(33,500)	
Less Tax credit			16,750	(16,750)
Tax				
Net cash available		54,446		50,250
Tax and NIC liabilities				
Employer's NIC		9,256		
Corporation tax				33,000
PAYE		36,298		
Higher rate assessment				16,750
		45,554		49,750

Tax saved by paying bonus = £4,196 (£49,750 less £45,554).

Companies with tax losses

2.10   If the company has tax losses, the payment of a bonus will increase the tax adjusted trading loss. If there is scope to carry back the loss against the three previous years, corporation tax relief is effectively obtained. The rate of relief would depend on the level of prior year profits.

Under Pay and File, repayment interest would accrue on tax repaid for the previous year 9 months after the end of that period. Tax repayments for the earlier two years only attract repayment interest 9 months after the end of the loss making accounting period. Where losses are carried back against pre-Pay and File periods i.e. accounting periods ending on or before 30 September 1993, similar rules apply but the repayment supplement only accrues 21 months after the end of the relevant period.

In contrast, a dividend would not create an additional loss. However, as there is no current year tax liability, surplus ACT would arise on the dividend. Surplus ACT could be relieved by carrying it back against the company's tax liabilities for the previous six years. When surplus ACT is carried back against a pre-Pay and File period, it is unlikely that there would be any repayment supplement as it accrues 21 months after the surplus ACT period end. [*ICTA 1988, s 825(4)*]. Surplus ACT recovered in a pay and file period will be augmented by repayment interest from 9 months after the end of the accounting period in which the surplus ACT arose. [*ICTA 1988, s 826(7)*].

The bonus v dividend equation would therefore depend, amongst other things, on the effective rate of company tax relief and the amount of repayment interest supplement.

When should comparison be made

2.11   To obtain maximum flexibility, the above arithmetical comparisons between extracting profits as a bonus or dividend should be made before the company's year end. This means that reliable management accounting figures should be available. One particular reason is that if a dividend is necessary, it is better to pay a dividend before the year end. This would enable the ACT to be recovered as quickly as possible. However, it is possible to obtain corporation tax relief for a bonus provided in the statutory accounts (if it is paid within 9 months of the year end).

Detailed implications of paying a bonus

Corporation tax relief

2.12   In the case of a trading company, the remuneration or bonus should be deductible against profits. It is quite rare for an Inspector to challenge the level of remuneration paid to working director-shareholders. In contrast, the Inland Revenue often seek to limit the tax deduction for directors' fees paid by investment companies to a very modest amount (see 4.18). In such cases extracting funds via a dividend is likely to be more tax efficient.

If the Inspector challenges the corporation tax deduction for the remuneration and denies relief for the amount considered to be excessive, this amount will still be subject to income tax and NIC. However, by concession, the Inland Revenue are prepared to refund the income tax paid on this amount, provided the excess amount is formally waived by the director and the amount is actually reimbursed to the company (see ICAEW Tax Faculty Technical Release TAX 11/93). However, any NIC liability will still stand as the Contributions Agency do not apply this concession.

Relief for accrued remuneration

2.13 A special rule applies to remuneration which is accrued or unpaid at the end of a company's accounting period, such as a provision for a bonus. Such remuneration can only be deducted against the company's taxable profits for that period if it is paid within 9 months after the period end. [*FA 1989, s 43(1)(2)*]. The date when remuneration is deemed to be paid is defined in *ICTA 1988, s 202B* (this rule also applies for PAYE purposes (see 5.2)).

In the case of directors, the date of payment will often be the time when payment is actually made or when the director becomes legally entitled to the amount (although the statutory definition also includes other events). Unless a director has a service agreement, his remuneration can only be determined when it is approved by the shareholders at the company's annual general meeting, which will normally be the date on which the company's annual accounts are signed. However, where appropriate, reliance can be placed on the decision in *Re Duomatic (1969) 1 All ER 161*. This case decided that where the directors agree in their capacity as shareholders the amount to be paid to them, this agreement will have the same effect as a resolution passed at the annual general meeting. Consequently where the annual general meeting is likely to occur after the end of the 9-month period, it should still be possible to trigger a 'payment' of the bonus within the 9-month period by agreement of the director-shareholders, which should be formally minuted.

If the shareholder-director is fortunate enough to have a healthy credit balance on his loan/current account, he can draw amounts from the account during the accounting period without attracting any PAYE charges. The loan/current account can then be topped up by a bonus following the year end and the exercise repeated next year.

The tax deduction rules for accrued bonus/remuneration may be used to obtain earlier corporation tax relief for amounts to be paid in the nine months following the year end. Provided the statutory accounts have not been signed-off, a provision can be made for bonuses paid (or to be paid) within nine months of the year end.

When providing for accrued directors' remuneration in the accounts, it is normal practice to provide also for the PAYE and NIC (including employer's NIC) contribution liabilities in the accounts to which the remuneration relates. If this practice is not adopted, the amount would be provided gross and when the directors' final remuneration is approved (at the AGM, if not earlier), the net remuneration would then be credited to the relevant director's accounts. At that date, the PAYE and NIC contributions must then be accounted for (ICAEW Tax Faculty Guidance Note TAX 11/93).

PAYE and cashflow

2.14   The payment of the bonus will of course attract a PAYE/NIC liability. The director/shareholder will therefore only receive the net amount. In contrast, if a dividend is paid, he will receive the full cash amount and will not have to pay the higher rate tax until a later date. For dividends paid in 1995/96, the due date will be 1 December 1996. For 1996/97 dividends, the due date under the transitional self-assessment rules will be 31 January 1998. From 1997/98 payments of tax will be made in accordance with the new self-assessment regime, which requires interim tax payments to be made on 31 January in the tax year and on 31 July following the tax year (based on the previous year's tax liability) with a final payment being due on the following 31 January.

It may be beneficial to defer the payment of a dividend from March to 6 April, as this will currently defer the higher rate liability (as well as deferring the payment of the ACT). However, this would not be attractive if, for example, the company has a 31 March year end since this will delay the company's recovery of the ACT by up to 12 months. The tax cash flow implications therefore need to be considered, which will vary according to the individual circumstances of each case. When interest costs have been taken into account, this may affect the 'bonus v dividend' equation considered above.

Bonus v dividend — other factors

2.15   The 'bonus v dividend' decision will often be influenced by a number of other factors, the main ones being set out below:

(*a*)   the level of pension provision directors can make is directly linked to their earnings. Consequently, a certain level of remuneration is required to make adequate provision of pension particularly in at least three consecutive years in the ten-year period before retirement as dividends do not constitute pensionable earnings. For details of efficient pension provision see 9.22;

(*b*) dividends do not attract NICs and therefore a certain level of remuneration is required to secure certain earnings related social security benefits;

(*c*) a dividend payment may increase the value of minority shareholdings for tax purposes. This is because the valuation of a minority shareholding may be determined by the expectation of dividend income. Share valuations for controlling shareholders are unlikely to be affected (see 13.16–13.17);

(*d*) as shareholders receive dividends in proportion to their holdings, the amount of dividends received by each shareholder may not provide a fair reward for the working shareholders and may prove too generous for the non-working or 'passive' shareholders. A 'dividend waiver' may be the answer here, provided it does not create any 'settlement' problems (see 8.16–8.22). Use of a separate class of shares for the non-working shareholders might also be considered (see 3.9).

Some conclusions

2.16 Where the company is paying tax at the small companies rate, it is still beneficial to pay surplus profits out as dividends, particularly if there is a long delay before the higher rate tax has to be paid. If there is no NIC liability or the NIC liability can be avoided (see 6.4), it will be cheaper to pay a bonus. Similarly, where directors need to boost their pension provision, their remuneration should be maximised.

If the company is paying tax at the full or higher marginal rate of corporation tax, the overall tax liability is lower if surplus profits are paid out as additional remuneration. If the company's profits are likely to fall in the marginal rate band, a bonus could be paid to reduce the profits to the small companies rate level (thus taking relief for the remuneration at the marginal rate) and the remainder can be paid as a dividend.

Family companies should therefore consider a sensible combination of bonuses and dividends, the precise mix depending on the particular circumstances of each company and shareholder.

Remuneration paid to other members of the family

2.17 As a general rule, tax will be saved if income can be paid to other members of the proprietor's family in order to use their annual personal allowances and benefit from their lower marginal tax rates.

Transferring income to the spouse

2.18 Under independent taxation, each spouse has their own personal allowance together with their personal lower and basic rate bands.

A married couple's allowance is also available which can be shared or given to either spouse. It is sensible to ensure that both spouses have sufficient income to use these reliefs and lower tax rates.

The income tax benefits of giving a salary to the spouse are often reduced by the NIC cost. In 1995/96, if the spouse earns £58 or more per week, (a rate of more than £3,016 per annum), employees' NIC is payable at 2% on the first £58 per week and 10% on any excess amount. Employer's NIC of 3% is also due, which increases on a sliding scale up to 10.2% when weekly earnings reach £205 (a rate of £10,660 per annum). No further employee's NIC is due once annual earnings reach the upper earnings limit of £22,880. The optimum amount to be paid to the spouse must be carefully considered.

Unless the spouse works for the company on a full-time basis, the Inland Revenue will require the amount to be substantiated in relation to the duties performed (*Copeman v William Flood & Sons Ltd (1940) 24 TC 53*). If the spouse is a director, then the duties and responsibilities of being a director will help in justifying a certain level of remuneration which can be paid to the spouse.

If the Inspector disallows all or part of the remuneration, a Schedule E tax liability can be avoided by the spouse formally waiving the remuneration and paying back the relevant amount to the company (ICAEW Tax Faculty Guidance Note TAX 11/93).

If the spouse is a shareholder, the Inspector may treat any non-waived 'disallowed' amount as a distribution, which should not increase the tax liability although an ACT liability would arise in the company. However, the Contributions Agency will still retain any NIC liability.

It is generally beneficial to bring the spouse in as a director or employee and pay him/her a salary, provided the following conditions are met:

(*a*)   the salary is taxable at a lower rate of tax (than that suffered by the proprietor on his/her income);

(*b*)   this income tax saving is not exceeded by the additional NIC liability;

(*c*)   the company is able to obtain a tax deduction for the salary.

The payment of remuneration to the spouse can also be used to fund a pension in his/her own right.

Where the spouse does little work for the company, the company is unlikely to obtain a material corporation tax deduction. In these cases, it is generally better to structure the shareholdings so that the spouse receives dividend income instead. Some caution needs to be exercised here as the Inland Revenue are showing increased interest in applying the 'settlement' legislation to counter transfers of dividend income to a spouse, particularly where non-voting shares are used (see 8.21).

Example 3

Salary or dividend for spouse

Mr Astle is deciding whether to pay £10,000 to his wife as a salary or dividend for the year to 31 March 1996. She has no other income.

Mrs Astle performs secretarial and administrative duties for the company which should be sufficient to justify corporation tax relief for the salary. Mrs Astle holds 20% of the shares in Astle Ltd, which pays corporation tax at 25%.

	£	*Salary* £	*Dividend* £
Available Profits		10,000	10,000
Less Employer's NIC (7% on £9,346)		(654)	
		9,346	
Employees NIC (2% × £3,016) + (10% × £6,330)		(693)	
Corporation tax at 25%			(2,500)
		8,653	7,500
Less Income tax thereon			
on *Salary*			
Salary	9,346		
PA	(3,525)		
Taxable	5,821		
First £3,200 at 20%	640		
Next £2,821 at 25%	655		
	1,295		
On *Dividend*			
Cash	7,500		
Tax credit (20/80)	1,875		
	9,375		
Less PA	(3,525)		
Taxable	5,850		
First £3,200 at 20%	640		
Next £2,650 at 20%	530		
	1,170		
Tax credit	(1,875)		
Refund	(705)		705
		7,358	8,205

Employing the children

2.19   The proprietor's children may also work for the company at weekends or in their school/college holidays (provided this is permitted by the appropriate by-laws). The wages received by the children can be paid tax free up to their personal allowance, with any excess being liable at the lower rate of 20% or basic rate of 25%, as appropriate.

Once again, the Inland Revenue will seek to establish the commercial justification for the payment in relation to the work done by the children. Payments made to the proprietor's children which constitute 'disguised pocket money' will be disallowed (see *Lyon v Dollar [1981] STC 333*).

Charging rent on personally owned assets used by the company

2.20   A number of family company proprietors leave the trading property outside the company to mitigate the effect of the potential double tax charge and to create wealth outside the company, free from the claims of its creditors (subject to personal guarantees) etc.

In such cases, the proprietor can extract funds from the company by charging the company a market rent for the use of the property. The rent paid by the company would be deductible against its profits and the rent received would be taxable in the proprietor's hands. The tax effect is therefore similar to the payment of remuneration, except that no PAYE or NIC is payable.

If the proprietor has borrowed money to purchase the property, he would normally charge rent to secure immediate tax relief for the interest. [*FA 1995, s 42*] and [*ICTA 1988, s 21(3)*]. The rental charge would restrict the availability of retirement relief on a subsequent 'associated disposal' of the property but it is often more important to secure interest relief. In some cases, the shareholder or director does not charge a rent but arranges for the company to pay the interest on his behalf. As the company is settling his pecuniary liability, the interest paid would be treated as part of his Schedule E remuneration. The amount would therefore be deductible against the company's profits (see SP4/85).

If the company does not pay rent or loan interest, the director would not obtain any income tax relief for his interest, but there would be no restriction in the 'associated disposal' retirement relief.

Selling an asset to the company for value

2.21   As mentioned in 2.20, the controlling shareholder may personally own the company's trading premises. The property would not be exposed to the company's creditors on a winding up, although in many cases, banks will secure a fixed charge on the property. Consequently, as far as the commercial risk is concerned, it makes little difference whether the property is owned by the company or shareholder.

If the proprietor requires funds, he should consider selling the property to the company. This will give rise to a disposal for CGT purposes, based on the market value of the property (irrespective of the actual amount received). However, given current property values, the gain may not be significant, particularly by reference to the March 1982 value.

An immediate chargeable gain can be avoided by selling the property to the company at its original base cost (March 1982 value, if appropriate). Although the disposal will still be computed by reference to market value, the 'unrealised element' of the gain can be held over under the Business Asset Gift Relief provisions in *TCGA 1992, s 165*. This relief is not affected by previous rent charges. By concession, it is not necessary to agree the market value of the gifted asset with the Inland Revenue. The 'transferor' proprietor and the company must request this treatment in writing (SP8/92). Where the proprietor sells the asset at its original base cost, the company will effectively acquire it at that amount plus the accrued indexation allowance up to the date of the transfer.

Where the asset is sold to the company at its original base cost or a lower amount, this will be the acquisition cost on the company's balance sheet. However, it is possible to bolster the company's balance sheet by subsequently revaluing the asset. The uplift in valuation would be credited to a revaluation surplus account within shareholders' funds.

Charging interest on loans to the company

2.22   Where the shareholder-director has made a loan to the company or has a credit balance on his current account, there is nothing to stop him charging the company with interest on the loan. Interest paid by the company would be tax deductible. (If the loan exceeds one year, the interest would be deducted as a charge on income and the company must deduct basic rate tax at source from the interest.) The recipient shareholder-director will be taxed on the interest received (with credit being given for any basic rate tax withheld). The interest does not constitute earnings and therefore no NIC is payable.

Loans from the company

2.23   Although in practice loans and overdrawn current accounts often arise in family companies, they are technically in breach of the Companies Act. However, for private companies, loans to directors do not attract any criminal sanctions but there is a civil remedy whereby the company can require the borrower to return the amount loaned. Consequently, this remedy is unlikely to be used in practice.

A number of tax consequences will arise where loans are made to a director-shareholder. First, *ICTA 1988, s 419* will apply to any loan made to a participator (i.e. shareholder or loan creditor) of a close company. The charge can also apply where a loan is made to an associate of the shareholder, such as a spouse, parent, grandparent, child, grandchild, brother or sister. [*ICTA 1988, s 417(1)(3)*].

The aim of this legislation is to levy tax on what would otherwise be an easy method of extracting cash from the close company on a tax-free basis. *Section 419* of *ICTA 1988* requires the company to account for 'notional ACT' on the amount advanced — the term 'notional ACT' is used because the company cannot deduct this ACT against its mainstream tax liability. For loans made after 31 March 1994 this will be 20/80ths (or 1/4) of the cash advanced or lent. This tax therefore represents a stand alone charge which is deposited with the Inland Revenue. If the loan or overdrawn account is repaid in whole or in part, the appropriate portion of the tax assessed is then refunded on a claim being made. [*ICTA 1988, s 419(4)*].

It is not all gloom, however, as there are a number of points which can serve to alleviate the *s 419* tax charge:

(*a*)   loans up to £15,000 in total are exempt where the borrower works full time for the company and does not own more than 5% of the ordinary share capital. [*ICTA 1988, s 420(2)*];

(*b*)   indirect loans involving the supply of goods on credit by the close company are exempt which are in the normal course of trade (unless the credit given is over six months). [*ICTA 1988, s 420(1)*];

(*c*)   the tax charge does not apply where the company is a lending institution which makes the loan or advance in the ordinary course of its business. [*ICTA 1988, s 419(1)*].

It is important to note that under the Pay and File regime which applies for all accounting periods ending after 30 September 1993, the tax is payable 14 days after the end of the accounting period in which the loan is made (without the issue of any assessment by the Inland Revenue). In practice, this will mean that interest on tax will arise on any overdrawn director-shareholder's current account or loans, unless it can be cleared by the balance sheet date. In many cases, an overdrawn loan account may only be established later when the accounts are finalised or following audit adjustments. Where the director's account is subsequently cleared by a bonus, this will only be effective in clearing the account from the date the bonus is voted or determined (see 2.13). Shareholder-directors should therefore try to ensure that drawings made from their current accounts do not create an overdrawn position at the year end. There are proposals to defer the due date for the *s 419* tax to 9 months after the end of the accounting period (in line with the due date for the payment of the corporation tax). If enacted, this will reduce the interest exposure in the above cases as interest would only run if the *s 419* tax was not paid on the 9-month due date (see IR Press Release 25 July 1995).

The company must also notify its chargeability to the *s 419* tax within 12 months after the end of its accounting period. Failure to notify the

Revenue within the 12-month period may lead to penalties up to the amount of the tax. [*TMA 1970, ss 10(2), 109*]. As a matter of good housekeeping, it would be sensible to report the *s 419* tax at the same time as the Pay and File return form CT200 is made.

It is clearly stated in the ICAEW Tax Faculty Guidance Note TAX 11/93 that it is rarely appropriate to set off a debit balance in one account against a credit balance in another director's accounts, with disclosure only of the net figure. It is recommended that a company should draw a cheque to pay off the whole or part of the credit balance with another cheque being paid into the company to clear the debit balance. This will therefore evidence the date the loan is repaid, which should of course be done before the end of the relevant tax accounting period.

A shareholder-director will also suffer a Schedule E charge under the beneficial loan provisions (if he does not pay a commercial rate of interest on the loan). These provisions are fully explained at 6.11.

Example 4

Section 419 tax and interest on overdrawn director's loan

Ms Sadler, a shareholder in a close company, overdrew her director's loan account by £20,000 in March 1995. This amount was still outstanding at the end of the company's accounting period on 30 June 1995, although it was entirely cleared by the payment of a bonus on 31 August 1995.

The company's accounts, corporation tax computations and return form CT200 was submitted to the Revenue in May 1996, with a covering letter reporting the overdrawn loan account and the chargeability to *s 419* tax of £5,000 (20/80 × £20,000).

The Inland Revenue will not seek to collect the *s 419* tax as the liability has been cleared by the repayment of the loan on 31 August 1995. However, interest will be charged on the 'outstanding' £5,000 from 14 July 1995 to 31 August 1995.

Ms Sadler would also be subject to a Schedule E charge on the benefit of the interest-free loan.

Waiver of loans

2.24   An income tax charge arises if the company releases or simply writes off a loan to a shareholder (or associate). [*ICTA 1988, s 421*]. Effectively, the amount relieved is treated as though it were a 'dividend' received by the director and will only be chargeable to any higher rate tax liability on the grossed up amount (this charge takes priority on any

Schedule E tax charge on the waiver under *ICTA 1988, s 160(2)*, although the Schedule E charge will apply if the loan is made to a director who is not a shareholder or associate of a shareholder.

The disadvantage here is that the company gets no credit for the *s 419* tax (notional ACT) originally paid over. It is therefore preferable to clear the loan by voting a dividend/bonus of an equivalent amount to release the *s 419* tax.

Benefits-in-kind to participators

2.25 When a company makes a distribution, it must pay over ACT to the Revenue. Where a close company is involved, benefits-in-kind to a shareholder (or associate) not taxed under Schedule E under *ICTA 1988, ss 155–168* are also treated as a distribution with a resultant ACT liability. [*ICTA 1988, s 418*]. The value of the distribution is taken to be the same as would apply if a Schedule E tax charge did arise. This extended meaning of 'distribution' effectively covers non-working shareholders who receive benefits in kind. It does not include pensions or lump sums payable on death or retirement.

PLANNING CHECKLIST — STRATEGIES FOR EXTRACTING FUNDS FROM THE COMPANY
Company • Extraction of funds must be determined by company's cash flow and working capital position. • Shareholders can loan funds back to the company to restore liquidity. • Dividends must be timed to secure prompt recovery of ACT. Relief for bonuses can be effectively back-dated by making provision in the accounts under the 9-month rule.
Working shareholders • Require a sensible mix of remuneration/bonuses and dividends. • Shareholders in their late 40s and 50s will require high levels of remuneration (in at least three consecutive years) to maximise pension.
Other employees • Employees look for good remuneration package, with tax efficient benefits (although there is now an increasing preference for cash). • Should have an incentive-based bonus scheme, possibly using PRP.
Non-working shareholders • Dividends are more tax efficient as company is unlikely to obtain relief for 'remuneration'.

Chapter 3

Shareholding and Corporate Structures

Shares v debt

3.1 This chapter reviews the issues involved in deciding how a family company's shareholding should be split and the way in which its trading activities may be structured.

The proprietor(s) can inject funds into the company in two ways:

(*a*) by a subscription for shares, and/or;

(*b*) by lending money to the company.

It is far easier to obtain repayment of funds injected on loan account. Cash paid for shares can only be returned on a winding up, a company purchase of its own shares or under a Court approved capital reduction scheme. The company may of course issue redeemable preference shares provided that it is authorised to do so by its Articles and the company already has non-redeemable shares in existence.

The relevant tax/commercial considerations involved in choosing the mix between shares and debt are considered in Chapter 10, 'Raising Funds'.

Structuring the shareholdings

Formation of company

3.2 The shareholding structure of the company is best decided on its formation. Typically, the shares will be subscribed for at par when the company has little value. Subsequent changes can of course be made to the shareholding structure but, if the company has been profitable, its shares will have increased in value. Although transfers between shareholdings in a family company can often be made without incurring an immediate inheritance tax or capital gains tax liability, there may be risks. For example, if an individual shareholder dies within 7 years of gifting shares, an inheritance tax liability may arise (see 16.8). Similarly, the ability to hold-over the capital gain may be restricted if the company has some investment assets (see 12.12).

Inheritance tax issues

3.3   In a typical family company, the proprietor will often hold the majority of the issued share capital. The 100% inheritance tax ('IHT') exemption on private company shareholdings (in excess of 25%), introduced in the *Finance (No 2) Act 1992*, means that retention of the shares will often be a sensible policy, as the shares will be exempt from inheritance tax on death and will benefit from a tax-free uplift in value for CGT purposes (see 16.13).

However, there is a risk that the 100% inheritance tax exemption for non-controlling holdings may not survive a change of Government. Inheritance tax should not be the only consideration here. If the proprietor's children play an active part in the business, it may be necessary to give them some shares to motivate them. This proportion of value will therefore appreciate outside the proprietor's estate. Nevertheless, the proprietor will usually require a substantial holding to satisfy his personal financial needs (through dividends) and to provide him with adequate control, although effective control need not be relinquished if an appropriate trust is used. These issues are considered further in Chapter 16, 'Passing On the Family Company'.

Factors which may influence shareholding structure

Level of control required

3.4   The proprietor should consider whether it is necessary to own all the shares. From a capital tax viewpoint, he may consider that this is the best course, given the complete exemption from inheritance tax on death coupled with a tax-free uplift in the share values for CGT.

The proprietor can, in fact, obtain absolute control by holding at least 75% of the voting rights, since he would then be able to pass special resolutions, sell the company, vary its constitution and put it into liquidation. For effective day to day control, such as the appointment and removal of directors, determination of remuneration and dividend policy, it is only necessary to hold more than 50% of the shares.

The proprietor may be prepared to share effective control with his spouse and family trusts, of which he and his spouse would be trustees (see 16.33).

Likelihood of a future sale

3.5   If the proprietor's objective is to build up the company for a future sale or indeed flotation, then he should ensure that he has sufficient shares to achieve the desired share of the future sale proceeds.

Need to give the spouse income

3.6   Where the proprietor's spouse has little income of his/her own, it will often be beneficial for the spouse to hold some shares to obtain an appropriate level of dividend. This is best done by issuing the appropriate number of shares to the spouse on formation of the company. If the proprietor is reluctant to relinquish voting control, he might consider issuing a separate class of non-voting preference shares to the spouse on formation. However, where non-voting shares are used, the Inland Revenue may seek to counteract the perceived diversion of income under the settlement provisions (see 8.21). The protection of *ICTA 1988, s 660A(6)* might not be available if the non-voting shares are considered to carry 'wholly or substantially a right to income'.

A subsequent transfer of shares might be challenged by the Inland Revenue on the grounds that the proprietor has transferred a right to income which should be taxed on him but this type of argument should be resisted, particularly in the case of ordinary shares which carry a 'bundle of rights' and not merely a right to income.

Retirement relief

3.7   The proprietor need merely own at least 5% of the shares to qualify for retirement relief, *TCGA 1992, 6 Sch 1(2)* although he must also work for the company on a full-time basis in a technical or managerial capacity.

Inheritance tax planning

3.8   In order to secure 100% exemption from inheritance tax on death (or any other chargeable transfer) the proprietor must hold *more than* 25% of the voting rights. For these purposes, 'related property' as defined in the inheritance tax legislation can be taken into account which would enable the 25% plus interest to include shares held by a spouse and shares of a trust in which the proprietor holds an interest in possession (see 16.15).

The proprietor may well take the view that his shareholding (and his wife's) should be maximised to obtain the benefit of the 100% IHT exemption and CGT free step-up in base cost on death.

Employee share schemes

3.9   The proprietor may want to provide shares for his key managers or employees to foster a true sense of ownership and involvement in the company. The proportion of shares issued to employees is usually nominal to avoid disturbing the balance of power. The principal aim is to give employees shareholder status. The detailed considerations are set out in Chapter 6 'Benefits and Expenses'.

Close company legislation

3.10   The vast majority of typical family companies will be 'close companies' for tax purposes. Put simply, a company will be close if it is under the control of five or fewer shareholders *or* any number of shareholders who are also directors of the company, i.e., controlled by director-shareholders. [*ICTA 1988, s 414(1)*].

For these purposes, any shares held by any associate of an individual shareholder must be attributed to that shareholder. This would mean that any shares held by relatives of a shareholder, such as his parents, spouse, children (both minor and adult), brothers and sisters would be treated as held by him. One or more people would be taken as having control if they have or are entitled to have more than 50% of the issued share capital, voting power, or company's assets on a winding up.

3.11   Given this wide definition, particularly the attribution of relative's shareholdings, a family company will find it difficult, if not impractical, to structure its shareholdings so as to fall outside the close company definition. However, the consequences of being a close company are not as serious as they once were.

The Inland Revenue no longer have the right to insist on a certain level of close company profits being distributed with each shareholder being taxed on the amount of income apportioned to him. Apportionment was abolished for accounting periods beginning after 31 March 1989. [*ICTA 1988, s 423* repealed by *FA 1989, s 103(1)* and *17 Sch Pt V*].

3.12   Currently, the three main tax disadvantages of being a close company are:

(*a*)   the 'notional ACT' charge which arises under *ICTA 1988, s 419* when any loan or advance is made to a shareholder of the company (see 2.23);

(*b*)   where the company incurs any expense or provides any benefit to a non-working shareholder or 'associate', this will be treated as a distribution (i.e., the same as a dividend), upon which the recipient will be taxed [*ICTA 1988, s 418*], as shown in 6.27;

(*c*)   if the company is a close investment holding company it will be subject to corporation tax at the full rate, regardless of the level of its profits (see 4.19). [*ICTA 1988, s 13(1)(b)*].

Associated companies

Corporation tax rates and the associated company

3.13   If a company's profits fall below the lower limit, it is entitled to the lower small companies rate of tax. The full or main rate of corporation tax applies where profits exceed the upper limit. The corporation tax rates and limits for the financial year 1995 (i.e. 12 months ended 31 March 1996) are given below:

Full rate	33%
Small companies rate	25%
Lower limit	£300,000
Upper limit	£1,500,000

Marginal relief will apply where a company's taxable profits fall between the lower and upper limit. The company's profits are taxed at the main rate and the small companies' marginal relief is deducted, the formula for FY 1995 being:

$$(\text{Upper limit} - \text{Profits}) \times \frac{\text{Basic profits}}{\text{Profits}} \times 1/50$$

where

Profits   = Profits chargeable to corporation tax *plus* franked investment income (excluding dividends from subsidiaries)

Basic profits = Profits chargeable to corporation tax

A useful short-cut method of computation is to look at the effective marginal rate on the profits exceeding the lower limit, which is found as follows:

	Profits £	Tax £
33% × upper limit profits of	1,500,000	495,000
25% × lower limit profits of	300,000	75,000
Therefore tax on marginal band of	1,200,000	420,000

The marginal rate is therefore normally 35%, ($\frac{420,000}{1,200,000} \times 100\%$).

(This will vary if the company receives franked investment income (excluding dividends from subsidiaries).) Close Investment Holding companies cannot claim the benefit of the small companies lower rate of marginal relief. [*ICTA 1988, s 13(1)(b)*].

3.14   The small companies rate of marginal relief must be claimed — on the corporation tax return form CT200. The claim must include the number of 'associated companies' which the company had during the accounting period or confirmation that there were none (SP1/1991).

3.15   Where the proprietor (and/or members of his family) have interests in other companies, it is necessary to bear in mind the 'associated company' rule which applies for corporation tax purposes. This rule is designed to prevent a company from splitting its business between several companies to secure the maximum benefit from the small companies rate of corporation tax.

3.16   If the company is associated with another company or companies, then both the upper and lower corporation tax rate limits must be apportioned equally between them. [*ICTA 1988, s 13(3)*]. It is not possible to transfer any unused relief between the associated companies. Where a family business carries on a number of separate activities, this rule can be an important factor in determining the appropriate operating structure. If the company can regularly benefit from the small companies rate of corporation tax, then considerable amounts of tax can be saved over a number of years. For this reason it is often best to keep the number of associated companies to a minimum, although commercial requirements (such as the protection of limited liability) may dictate that certain trades or activities should run through a separate company (see 3.23).

A regular review should be taken to determine whether virtually inactive companies are unnecessarily reducing the availability of the small companies limit.

Example 1

Apportioning limits for tax rate calculations

Allen Ltd has taxable profits of £263,000 for the year ended 31 March 1996. During the period, Mr Allen also held controlling interests in five other trading companies.

The relevant upper and lower limits for the company would be:

Lower limit $\dfrac{£300,000}{6} = £50,000$

Upper limit $\dfrac{£1,500,000}{6} = £250,000$

Allen Ltd's taxable profits exceed the upper limit of £250,000 and therefore the liability will be at the full rate, i.e.

$£263,000 \times 33\% = £86,790$

As the limits are apportioned equally between the associated companies, this rule is particularly disadvantageous where the taxable profits arise unevenly between them.

3.17   Shareholding and Corporate Structures

3.17   Where there is a change in the lower limit between financial years and an accounting period straddles 31 March, the relevant part of each financial year is treated as a separate accounting period for the purpose of this calculation. [*FA 1994, s 86(3)*].

The lower limit was amended for the financial year 1994 (being increased from £250,000 to £300,000). Therefore, unless accounts are prepared to 31 March 1995, each part of the accounting period is treated as a discrete period for calculating the number of 'active' associated companies (see 3.19, as indicated in Example 2 below).

Example 2

Counting associated companies by financial year

Knowles Ltd made up its accounts to 31 December each year.

As of 1 January 1994, it was associated with three other companies. One of these companies ceased to trade on 31 March 1994 and then became dormant.

Knowles Ltd had taxable profits of £90,000 for the year ended 31 December 1994.

Knowles Ltd's tax liability for 1994 would be computed as follows:

	FY 1993 90 Days £	FY 1994 275 Days £
Time apportioned profits	22,192	67,808
Time apportioned lower limit	61,644	226,027
Number of Associates + 1	4	3
Divided by number of Associates + 1	15,411	75,342
FY 1993		
CT at 33% × £22,192	7,323	
Less Small companies taper relief		
1/50 × (£77,055 − £22,192)	(1,097)	
	6,226	
FY 1994		
CT at 25% × £67,808	16,952	
	23,178	

Upper and lower limits — periods less than 12 months

3.18   The upper and lower limits are proportionally reduced where under *ICTA 1988, s 13(6)* the corporation tax accounting period

('CTAP') is less than 12 months. Two apportionments will therefore be required where the company has associated companies and has a CTAP of less than 12 months.

What is an associated company?

3.19 Broadly speaking, associated companies are those under common control. A company is associated with another company if one of them has control of the other or if both are under the control of the same person or persons. [*ICTA 1988, s 416(1)*].

A person is considered to control a company if he exercises or is able to exercise control over the relevant company's affairs. This would be the case if the individual holds more than 50% of the share capital, voting power, distributable income or net assets on a notional winding up. Any future entitlement to shares, e.g. options, is deemed to be held currently for this purpose. [*ICTA 1988, s 416(2)(4)*]. In determining whether companies are under the control of the same person or persons for these purposes, the Revenue seek to determine whether the companies are under the control of the 'same irreducible group of persons'. An 'irreducible group of persons' means a group of persons that has control of the company but would not have control if any one of them were excluded (see *Taxation*, 2 September 1993, page 537).

This definition would catch companies which are controlled by the same individual or group of individuals, as well as by a parent company. For these purposes, associated companies which are not resident in the UK for tax purposes will also be included.

Dormant associated companies which have not carried on any trade or business at any time during the relevant accounting period are disregarded. The apparent rationale for this is that such companies would not be able to benefit from their share of the lower limit.

Example 3

Control by the irreducible group

The shareholdings of Stoke Ltd and Hammers Ltd are summarised as follows:

	Stoke Ltd	Hammers Ltd
	%	%
Mr Hurst	60	40
Mr Peters	20	30
Others	20	30

Mr Hurst and Mr Peters together control both Stoke Ltd and Hammers Ltd.

However, Mr Hurst can control Stoke Ltd on his own. Mr Hurst is therefore 'the irreducible group'. As he does not control Hammers Ltd on his own, the two companies will not be treated as associated.

Concession for non-trading holding companies

3.20   The Inland Revenue operate a concession for groups whereby a non-trading holding company does not have to be 'counted' as an associated company, provided it has:

(*a*)   no assets (other than shares in its subsidiaries);

(*b*)   no income (other than dividend is received from its subsidiaries, which have been passed on to its shareholders);

(*c*)   not claimed loss or group relief for any expenses (SP5/94).

Concession for relative's shareholdings

3.21   Strictly speaking, shares held by an individual's close relatives are attributed to him to determine whether he exercises control, according to the close company definition. This means shares held by an individual's spouse, parents, grandparents, children, grandchildren and brothers and sisters are treated as part of his holding.

However, the Inland Revenue operate a very important concession whereby they will not seek to attribute to a person the rights and powers of his relatives for this purpose, except those of his wife and minor children, provided there is no substantial commercial interdependence between the relevant companies (ESC C9). This concession removes what might otherwise be an impractical burden of obtaining detailed information about companies controlled by relatives.

Although general practice has been to treat any significant inter-company trading or service charge etc. as falling within this rule, it is possible to restrict the meaning of 'commercial interdependence' to a two-way situation. It has been argued successfully before the Inland Revenue that interdependence means that each company must be dependent on the other. The concession should not apply where dependence is only one way, as in Example 4 below.

Example 4

The meaning of substantial commercial interdependence

Robert and Jack Charlton are brothers. Robert Charlton owns all the shares in Bobby Limited and Jack owns all the shares in Jackie Ltd.

```
      Robert                                    Jack
     Charlton                                 Charlton
        |                                        |
        |                                        |
      100%                                     100%
        |                                        |
 ┌──────────────┐                         ┌──────────────┐
 │              │   - - - - - - - - - →   │              │
 │  BOBBY LTD   │                         │  JACKIE LTD  │
 │              │   Trade purchases       │              │
 └──────────────┘                         └──────────────┘
```

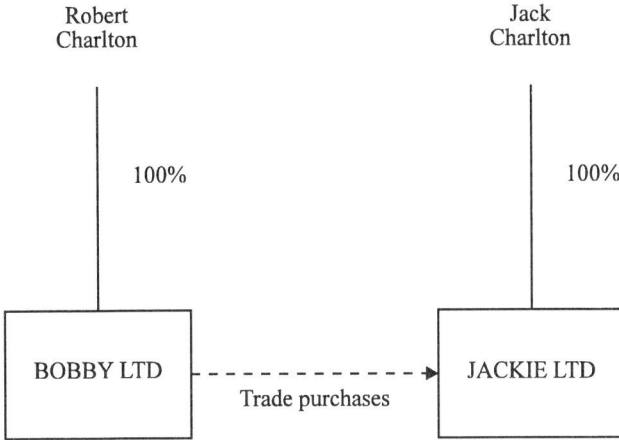

Jackie Ltd purchases most of its trade materials from Bobby Ltd. The sales made to Jackie Ltd were only about 5% of Bobby Ltd's turnover. Jackie Ltd is therefore dependent on Bobby Ltd for its trade but there is no trading *interdependence* (which implies an element of reciprocity).

An Inspector has agreed in at least one similar case that companies in such circumstances were not 'associated' with each other (see *Taxline*, Issue 2, Item 22).

Choosing an appropriate corporate structure

3.22   Where various members of the family carry on a number of trades or ventures, which will often be the case for medium or large sized businesses, it is necessary to choose the most appropriate and efficient operating structure from both the tax and commercial point of view.

The choice usually lies between the following types of arrangement.

(a) Divisionalised company

This would entail all or substantially all of the various trading activities being carried on through a single company, perhaps as separate operating divisions or branches.

29

(b) Parallel companies

In a parallel company structure, each business is run through a separate company, with the shareholding in each company being structured to reflect the management responsibility in each business.

(c) Corporate group structure

This would involve the grouping of companies with the various trades or activities being run through a number of operating subsidiaries.

The three main structures are illustrated in Example 5 below. The structures can of course be combined so that it is possible to have a single divisionalised company, but with certain risk ventures being kept in a separate parallel company. Chapter 12 discusses the main tax implications of reorganising the trading activities.

Example 5

Illustration of different operating structures

John and Paul Barnes have decided to incorporate their existing transport and haulage businesses. John manages the warehousing operation and Paul manages the haulage side of the business.

The main types of operating structure are illustrated below:

(a)   Divisionalised structure

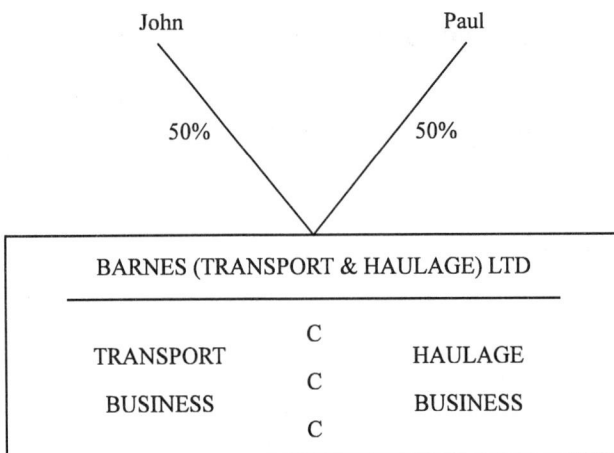

John   Paul

50%   50%

BARNES (TRANSPORT & HAULAGE) LTD

TRANSPORT   C   HAULAGE

                   C

BUSINESS   BUSINESS

                   C

(Carried on both businesses)

(*b*)   Parallel company structure

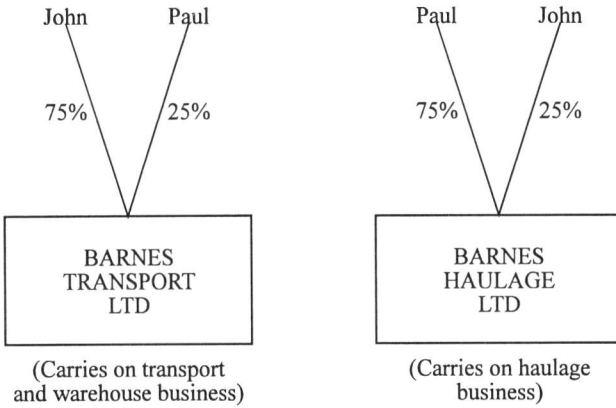

John   Paul   Paul   John

75%   25%   75%   25%

| BARNES TRANSPORT LTD | BARNES HAULAGE LTD |

(Carries on transport and warehouse business)   (Carries on haulage business)

(*c*)   Corporate group structure

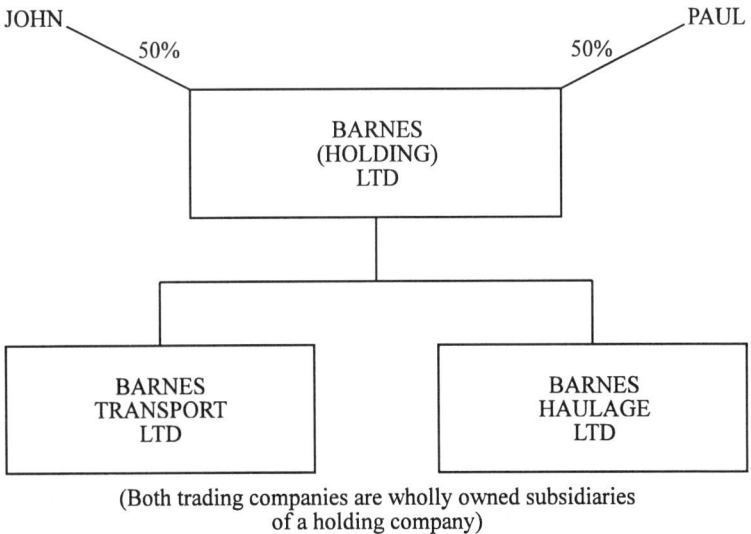

JOHN   PAUL

50%   50%

| BARNES (HOLDING) LTD |

| BARNES TRANSPORT LTD | | BARNES HAULAGE LTD |

(Both trading companies are wholly owned subsidiaries of a holding company)

Tax and commercial factors affecting choice of structure

3.23   The selection of a suitable structure depends upon the relative importance of the number of commercial, tax and legal factors.

3.23 Shareholding and Corporate Structures

The commercial consideration of limited liability may outweigh all other considerations, particularly in relation to certain types of trading activity, which are vulnerable to large claims and liabilities. This would point to the use of separate parallel companies or a group structure. However, from the tax viewpoint, a single company carrying on all the trades is probably ideal. Although certain tax reliefs are available to a group of companies, the tax legislation falls short of treating the group as if it were a single entity and various restrictions and anti-avoidance rules increase compliance costs and present a number of potential pitfalls. The detailed tax rules available to groups are considered further in 3.25.

The main tax and commercial considerations are summarised in the checklist overleaf.

Operating structure checklist

	Single company (divisionalised structure)	Parallel companies	Corporate group
Commercial liability	Risks and liabilities of any one trade may prejudice the viability of the other trades.	Limited liability for each company (therefore collapse of one company does not bring others down).	Limited liability for each company — parent company is not legally obliged to support an insolvent subsidiary, although may need to do so to avoid adverse commercial publicity.
Audit and administration	Single audit fee for one company. Minimum audit fees, secretarial and legal compliance costs.	Each company requires audit duplication of administrative costs etc.	Each company requires audit duplication of administrative costs.
	Detailed results of each trade can be hidden within one set of 'combined' accounts, which prevents competitors and potential predators obtaining detailed information about each trade.		Need to prepare consolidated accounts.

33

	Single company (divisionalised structure)	Parallel companies	Corporate group
	Brings pressure to harmonise employment terms and conditions etc. for employees and managers of all divisions, which may create problems. For example the key members of a management team may perceive the status of a divisional manager to be below that of a company director.		Shares normally held in holding company. Some shares may be given to managers in each subsidiary, although some care is required to avoid charge under the dependent subsidiary legislation (see 6.43).
Shareholder control	No direct relationship between shareholdings and management responsibility for each business.	Shareholdings can reflect management responsibility of each business, giving greater control and reward for efforts.	

	Single company (divisionalised structure)	Parallel companies	Corporate group
Sale of company/trade	Proceeds are received directly by shareholders and subject to CGT, therefore no element of double taxation. Sale of a division will generally involve a taxable asset sale, and therefore proceeds will be 'locked' in company and will involve a further tax charge on extraction by the shareholders.	Proceeds received directly by shareholders (as for single company). Each business can be sold separately through a company.	Proceeds will be received net of corporation tax by the holding company. A further tax charge will arise if net proceeds are required by the ultimate shareholders.
Tax implications			
— Small companies rate	Small companies rate will be available without any need to equalise profits between two or more associates.	If 'common control' can be avoided, this enables the benefits of the small companies rate to be maximised, particularly if there are relatives involved and there is no substantial inter-company trading (see 3.21). If companies are associated and profits are distributed unevenly, the overall tax liability may be higher as some companies may be taxed at full marginal rate.	May involve some loss of small companies rate, although profits may be equalised by group relief.

	Single company (divisionalised structure)	Parallel companies	Corporate group
— Tax reliefs	Very efficient for tax purposes — maximise available reliefs and provides full matching of payments, receipts and gains. In particular, losses of any trade can be relieved by offset against current year's total profits, and — offset against total profits of three preceding years — carried forward against profits of the same trade Chargeable gains will also be offset against allowable capital losses.	Within each company, the position is the same as a single company. However, trading losses and capital losses cannot be relieved by transfer between the companies.	Trading losses can be surrendered between each member of a 75% group on a current year basis. Various other reliefs are available (see 3.25). Although no group relief is given for capital losses, relief can be obtained by routing all disposals of chargeable assets through a designated company (subject to the pre-entry loss rules which broadly prevent the use of pre-acquisition capital losses generated by acquired group companies).

Divisionalisation — use of undisclosed agency companies

3.24   Where an existing group wishes to divisionalise, this can be done simply by transferring the various trading activities up to the holding company. Normally, the transfer of each trade and the related assets can be made on a tax neutral basis under *ICTA 1988, s 343* and *TCGA 1992, s 171*. The transferor (subsidiary) companies would then be dormant and may be wound up or dissolved. However, if the group wishes to protect the valuable trading names of its subsidiaries, it is normal for the 'divisionalised' company to enter into undisclosed agency agreements with the dormant subsidiaries under which the subsidiaries would continue to trade as undisclosed agents of the divisionalised company. The trading results would be reflected in the divisionalised company as principal, although the 'outside world' would still believe that it is dealing with the subsidiaries, e.g. sales invoices would be raised in the name of the dormant subsidiary company.

Tax treatment of corporate groups

3.25   Most groups of family companies will have wholly owned UK subsidiaries and will therefore enjoy all the main tax reliefs available to groups. However, the legislation and case law continue to demonstrate that the combined effect of the group rules does not put the group in the same position as a single company.

Furthermore, if outside minority interests are to be introduced in one or more subsidiaries, care must be taken to ensure that the shareholding structure does not unnecessarily prejudice important tax benefits. The minimum shareholding qualification necessary varies according to the type of relief.

Checklist of main reliefs for groups

	Required group structure	Main reliefs
1.	A 51% + group	ACT can be surrendered by a parent company to any subsidiary (but not vice versa). [*ICTA 1988, s 240*].
		Dividends can be paid by a subsidiary to the parent without accounting for ACT under a group income election. The election can be set aside in respect of any dividend payment by an appropriate entry on the CT61 return form. [*ICTA 1988, s 247(1)(3)*].
		Interest and other annual payments between group companies can be paid gross without deducting basic rate tax. [*ICTA 1988, s 247(4)*].

Required group structure	**Main reliefs**
2. A 75% + group	Current year tax losses generated by one group member can be surrendered to another by way of group relief. [*ICTA 1988, ss 402–412*].

Consortium relief may be available for a pro-rata share of current losses. [*ICTA 1988, ss 402–412*].

Chargeable assets can be transferred between group companies with the deferral of the relevant tax until the asset is sold outside the group, or the transferee company leaves the group within six years. [*TCGA 1992, s 171* and *s 179*].

Tax refunds can be surrendered to other group members (under the Pay and File regime) to minimise the group's net interest on unpaid tax. [*FA 1989, s 102*].

All group companies are effectively regarded as a single entity for the purposes of roll-over relief. This enables a capital gain realised by one group company to be rolled-over against qualifying assets purchased by another outside the group. [*TCGA 1992, s 175*].

Trades can be transferred between the group companies without the adverse tax consequences of a cessation; 'capital allowance' assets would be transferred at their tax written down values and unused trading losses are carried across into the transferee company (subject only to the restrictions applying where the transferor company is technically insolvent). [*ICTA 1988, s 343*].

Dutiable assets (such as land, goodwill and debtors) can be transferred between group companies without any stamp duty liability, provided the transfer is not part of arrangements for the transferee company to leave the group or consideration for the transfer is being provided directly or non-directly by a third party. [*FA 1930, s 42* as amended by *FA 1995, s 149; FA 1967, s 27*].

PLANNING CHECKLIST — SHAREHOLDING AND CORPORATE STRUCTURES

Company
- Keep number of companies to a minimum consistent with commercial objectives.
- Activities which carry a high level of commercial risk should be kept in separate company.

Working shareholders
- Effective control of the company can be obtained by owning more than 50% of the voting shares.
- May want to maximise own/spouse's shareholding to obtain most benefit from 100% IHT exemption.
- Need to maintain full time working status (and at least 5% of the shares) to secure retirement relief.
- Separate companies enable ownership to be more directly related to management of different businesses.

Other employees
- Employee share incentives increase identification with company and offer possibility of a large capital profit on future sale.
- Employees should avoid taking shares in subsidiary companies due to the 'growth in value' income tax charge for dependent subsidiaries (unless it can definitely be avoided).

Non-working shareholders
- Need to own more than 25% of the voting shares to obtain 100% IHT relief.

Chapter 4

Trading Company v Investment Company

Tax status of company

4.1　It is important to determine whether a company is a trading company or an investment company for tax purposes. The computation of the taxable profits for each type of company is computed in a different way. Furthermore, certain capital gains and inheritance tax reliefs may be enjoyed by shareholders of a trading company but not by shareholders of an investment company. Both of these aspects will be covered in this chapter.

The definition of an investment company or trading company is applied in relation to each accounting period. It is therefore possible for a company to be an investment company in one accounting period and be a trading company in the next period. However, it is not possible for a company to be both a trading company and investment company for the *same* accounting period. In the vast majority of cases, a company will clearly be a trading company or an investment company. It is possible for a company to fit within neither category and the Inland Revenue have sometimes advanced this type of argument — such companies will find it difficult to claim relief for their expenses. For example, in *Tintern Close Residents Society Ltd v Winter* (HMIT) and other similar appeals (SC 3115/94) [1995] STI 574 the Special Commissioner decided that a residents society which owned and managed common property (including gardens, roads, footpaths and garages) was not an investment company. The company's management expenses claim was therefore refused.

Where family businesses are operated through a holding/subsidiary company structure, the holding company may qualify as an investment company even though it does little more than hold shares in its trading subsidiaries. However, the various tax reliefs given to the shareholders of trading companies are extended to situations where the shareholder's own shares in a holding company of a trading group. Of course, where a holding company carries on a substantial trading activity in its own right, for example supplying management and administrative support services to its trading subsidiaries for a management charge, it will often be treated as a trading company for tax purposes.

Trading companies

4.2   Broadly, for tax purposes a trading company is one which exists wholly or mainly for the purpose of carrying on a trade. In many cases, it will be clear that the company exists for trading purposes. In marginal cases, it may be possible to demonstrate that the company is a trading company by applying the 'wholly or mainly' test to the company's turnover, net profits, net assets and management time. Ideally, more than two should 'wholly or mainly' relate to the trading activities. The Revenue usually regard the expression 'wholly or mainly' as meaning more than 50%.

Corporation tax computation

Pro-forma computation

4.3   A detailed pro-forma corporation tax computation for a typical trading company is set out below, together with accompanying notes. For corporation tax purposes, the assessable profits represent the amount of income and gains arising in the accounting period. [*ICTA 1988, ss 6* and *8*]. (The pro-forma is comprehensive so all items will not necessarily occur in the same period, e.g. if the company claims relief for a current year Schedule D Case I loss, there will not be a Schedule D Case I trading profit, unless the company is carrying on another trade.)

PRO-FORMA TRADING CO. LTD

CORPORATION TAX COMPUTATION BASED ON THE
ACCOUNTING PERIOD ENDED

	£	£	Notes
Schedule D Case I trading profit (after deducting capital allowances) (see 4.5–4.8)		X	
Less Schedule D Case I trading losses brought forward under *ICTA 1988, s 393(1)* (see 4.12)	(X)	X	(*a*)
Schedule A rental income (net of allowable expenses)		X	(*b*)
Schedule D Case III bank interest received (gross)		X	
Interest received on loan stock		X	
Building society interest (gross)		X	
Schedule D Case V dividends received from overseas companies		X	(*c*)/(*d*)
Other income		X	
Chargeable gains (less allowable losses)		X	(*e*)
		X	
Less Current year Schedule D Case I trading loss offset under *ICTA 1988, s 393A(1)(a)* (see 4.10)		(X)	(*f*)

	£	£	Notes
Less Charges on income paid (gross)			(g)
Interest paid on loan stock	(X)		
Patent Royalties	(X)		
Gift Aid and covenanted donations	(X)	(X)	
		X	
Less Group relief		(X)	(h)
		X	
Less Schedule D Case I trading losses carried back			
under *ICTA 1988, s 393A(1)(b)* (see 4.11)		(X)	(i)
PROFITS CHARGEABLE TO CORPORATION TAX		X	

Pro-forma computation of corporation tax liability

	£
Corporation tax on 'profits' @ X%	X
Less Small companies marginal relief (see 3.13)	(X)
	X
Less Double tax relief	(X)
	X
Less Advance corporation tax (see Chapter 8)	(X)
	X
Less Income tax on excess of unfranked investment income over charges paid	(X)
MAINSTREAM CORPORATION TAX LIABILITY	X

Notes

(*a*)   Unused Schedule D Case I trading losses brought forward from the previous period are only offset against Schedule D Case I trading profits of the *same* trade. Such losses are vulnerable to forfeiture if a major change in the conduct of the company's trade occurs within three years of a change in ownership. [*ICTA 1988, s 768*].

(*b*)   The 'old' Schedule A expense and loss relief rules still apply for corporation tax. [*ICTA 1988, s 25*].

(*c*)   Dividends from UK companies are not chargeable to corporation tax. [*ICTA 1988, s 208*].

(*d*)   Dividends from overseas companies are grossed up for any withholding taxes and (where the company holds more than 10% of the voting rights of the overseas company) the underlying tax — which is the tax payable out of the profits from which the dividend was paid. [*ICTA 1988, ss 795(1)* and *799*]. Double tax relief can be claimed for these amounts up to a maximum limit, representing the UK corporation tax on the grossed-up dividend. [*ICTA 1988, ss 788* and *790*].

(*e*)   Chargeable gains are computed in the normal way. Roll-over relief may be available for gains arising on most types of fixed assets used in the trade.

(*f*)   A current year Schedule D Case I loss is deducted against profits before deducting charges on income. [*ICTA 1988, s 338(1)*].

(*g*)   Charges on income includes loan interest or other annual payments such as royalties and gift-aid donations, but no item which is deductible in computing profit elsewhere may be treated as a charge on income, such as interest paid to a UK bank. Charges on income are deducted in the period in which they are paid.

(*h*)   Losses claimed from other group companies are deducted in priority to Schedule D Case I trading losses carried back from a subsequent period. [*ICTA 1988, s 407(1)(a)*].

(*i*)   If Schedule D Case I losses are carried back under *ICTA 1988, s 393A(1)(b)* they are set off *after* deducting trading charges on income only. In such cases, non-trading charges (such as gift aid or covenanted donations) are the last item to be deducted and may therefore become unrelieved.

Calculating the Schedule D Case I profit

4.4   The principal source of income for a trading company would be its trading profits. The starting point for computing the assessable profit for Schedule D Case I purposes will be the accounting profit, which will have been prepared on generally accepted commercial and accounting principles.

The company's profit and loss account will invariably include non-trading and capital items and various adjustments must be made in order to arrive at the assessable Schedule D Case I profit. Certain types of expenditure charged in the accounts are not deductible for tax purposes. For example, depreciation on fixed assets must be added back to the profits and replaced by capital allowances, which is the statutory tax relief for capital expenditure. Furthermore, income which is assessed under a different Schedule or Case must be excluded from the accounting profit and dealt with under the rules for that appropriate Schedule or Case. Similarly, income which is exempt from tax must be included.

A Schedule D Case I loss will arise where the allowable expenses and capital allowances exceed the trading receipts.

A pro-forma computation for the adjustment of profits for Schedule D Case I purposes is given overleaf.

4.5   Trading Company v Investment Company

Pro-forma adjustment of profits

	£	£
Net profit on ordinary activities before taxation per accounts		X
Add Depreciation	X	
Loss on disposal of fixed assets	X	
Capital expenditure (e.g. alterations, improvements) charged to repairs etc.	X	
Interest on overdue tax	X	
Entertaining	X	
Charges on income	X	
Legal and professional charges (e.g. relating to disposals/purchases of property)	X	
Donations	X	
Increase in general provisions	X	
Pension contributions charged to profit and loss account	X	
Remuneration accrued but not paid within nine months of end of CTAP	X	
		X
Less Profit on sale of fixed assets/investments	(X)	
Other capital profits/gains	(X)	
Dividends received from UK companies (FII)	(X)	
Income from overseas companies	(X)	
Bank deposit interest	(X)	
Building Society interest	(X)	
Net rental income taxed under Schedule A/D VI	(X)	
Other investment income	(X)	
Decrease in general provisions	(X)	
Pension contributions paid in CTAP	(X)	
Pension scheme refund	(X)	
Non-taxable income	(X)	
Accrued remuneration paid more than nine months after end of previous CTAP	(X)	
Capital allowances (net of balancing charges)		
— Plant and machinery	(X)	
— Industrial buildings	(X)	
— Other	(X)	
		(X)
Schedule D Case I profit/(loss)		X

4.5   It is well-known that a trading company can only obtain relief against its trading profits for those expenses which have been incurred wholly and exclusively for the purposes of its trade. [*ICTA 1988, s 74*]. The strict application of this principle in practice may cause certain types of expenditure to be disallowable if the Revenue can prove that the expenditure was incurred partly for another (non-trading) purpose. If this is the case, the Inspector will usually be able to disallow the whole of the expense on the grounds that it was incurred for a dual purpose (both trading and non-trading) and therefore the whole amount would fall to be disallowed. In practice, the Inland Revenue may often be prepared to apportion the expenditure and give relief for the trading element.

Capital allowances

4.6   Capital expenditure incurred by a trading company cannot be deducted against its Schedule D Case I profit. Expenditure charged to fixed assets in the accounts will invariably be treated as capital expenditure. The periodic write-off of fixed asset expenditure through depreciation charges will be disallowed. Certain capital expenditure may also be charged directly against profits and, for tax purposes, this must also be disallowed.

Provided the capital expenditure falls into one of the defined categories, tax relief will be given through the capital allowances system.

The main types of capital allowances and the current rates obtainable for each class of expenditure is set out below.

Table — Main rates of capital allowances

	Writing down allowance	Basis
Plant and machinery	25%	(reducing balance)
Industrial buildings and hotels	4%	for new buildings (straight line)
Patent rights	25%	(reducing balance)
Know-how	25%	(reducing balance)
Agricultural works and buildings	4%	(straight line)

Enterprise zone buildings and scientific research expenditure qualifies for a 100% initial allowance.

4.7   Generally, capital allowances are less generous than they were before 31 March 1986 when most initial and first year allowances were abolished. Although first year and initial allowances were re-introduced on a temporary basis (for expenditure incurred within the 12 months ending 31 October 1993), the rate of allowances are not as generous as they once were. In practice, companies will be keen to establish in borderline cases that expenditure should be classed as a revenue deduction, in order to receive a 100% write-off against profits.

4.8   Case law and Inland Revenue Practice have established that, in certain circumstances, structural and other items included in buildings qualify as 'plant' for capital allowance purposes. However, the Inland Revenue have attempted to restrict any further extension in this area by introducing a statutory code in the *Finance Act 1994* (mainly due to a number of cases brought by certain large supermarket chains to the Commissioners). Broadly, expenditure incurred after 29 November 1993 on buildings (including any assets forming part of a building), structures and on land alterations *will not* qualify as plant unless it falls into one of the various categories laid down in *CAA 1990, AA1* and *AA2 Schs* (which represent an attempt to codify existing case law and practice).

Relief for trading losses

4.9   The basic reliefs available for Schedule D Case I trading losses are summarised below; their order of offset is shown in the pro-forma computation in 4.3.

Current year offset against total profits

4.10   Schedule D Case I losses arising in a corporation tax accounting period can be offset against the company's other profits (calculated before relieving charges on income) of the same period. Relief is only available if the trade is operated on a commercial basis with the view to making a profit. A claim (which may be on the face of the computation) must be made within two years after the end of the loss-making accounting period, although the Inland Revenue can extend this period. [*ICTA 1988, s 393A(1)(a)*].

Three-year carry back against total profits

4.11   Where the current year trading losses cannot be fully deducted against the profits of the current period, any remaining loss can be carried back against the company's total profits (after deducting trading charges on income but before non-trading charges on income) of the corporation tax accounting periods for the three preceding years. [*ICTA 1988, s 393A(1)(b)*]. The losses are carried back against later periods in priority to earlier ones. The trading losses can only be offset if the company was carrying on the same trade in which the loss arose in the previous accounting period.

The relief is subject to the same two year time limit and 'commercial basis' test as the current year offset in 4.10. The detailed operation of the relief is illustrated in Example 1 below.

Example 1

Carry back of trading losses

Armfield Limited's agreed tax computations for the three years to 31 December 1993 were as follows:

	1991 £'000	1992 £'000	1993 £'000
Schedule D Case I profit	110	85	30
Less Charges on income			
— Interest on loan from venture capitalist	(10)	(15)	(20)
— Gift Aid donation	–	(5)	(5)
	100	65	5
Corporation tax at 25%	25.00	16.25	1.25
Less ACT on dividend	(4.00)	(4.00)	–
	21.00	12.25	1.25

In the year ended 31 December 1994, the company made a trading loss and its tax computation shows:

	1994 £'000
Schedule D Case I loss	(170)
Charges on income	
— Interest on loan	(20)
— Gift Aid donation	(5)

Relief for the Schedule D Case I loss can be claimed under the three-year carry back rule, as follows:

	1991 £'000	1992 £'000	1993 £'000
Schedule D Case I profit	110	85	30
Less Trading charges on income (loan interest)	(10)	(15)	(20)
	100	70	10
Less Loss relief	(90)	(70)	(10)
	10	-	-
Corporation tax at 25%	2.50	–	–
Less Revised ACT offset	(2.50)	–	–
	–	–	–

Notes

(*a*) The unrelieved trading charges of £20,000 in 1994 must be carried forward. The non-trading charge (Gift Aid donation of £5,000) cannot be relieved and is lost.

(*b*)   The unrelieved non-trade charges in 1992 and 1993 have been lost.

(*c*)   The loss carry back claim displaces the previous ACT offsets.

> 1991 — The unrelieved amount of £1,500 (i.e. £4,000 less the revised offset of £2,500) cannot be carried back under the six year rule as the two year limit for the claim has expired. The surplus ACT of £1,500 must be carried forward to 1992.

> 1992 — The surplus ACT of £4,000 must be carried forward as a competent carry back claim cannot be made. Surplus ACT of £5,500 (£4,000 plus the £1,500 brought forward from 1991) is therefore carried forward to 1992.

> 1993 — The surplus ACT brought forward of £5,500 is treated as surplus ACT arising in the year. Provided a claim is made before the end of 1995, the surplus ACT can be carried back (against 1990, 1989, 1988 and 1987 if there are sufficient profits to absorb the ACT).

Carry forward against future trading profits

4.12   Unused Schedule D Case I trading losses can be carried forward for offset against the first available Schedule D Case I profits of the same trade. [*ICTA 1988, s 393(1)*]. It follows that if the trading activity ceases, any excess losses are effectively forfeited.

The current year loss offset may give rise to unrelieved trading charges on income. Where the excess charges were incurred wholly and exclusively for trading purposes, they can be carried forward as part of the Schedule D Case I loss for offset against future profits of the same trade. [*ICTA 1988, s 393(9)*].

Relief for losses against surplus franked investment income (FII)

4.13   Dividends received by a company from other UK companies are not subject to corporation tax. The dividend received plus the related tax credit is known as franked investment income or FII. The tax credit is available to reduce the ACT which a company is liable to pay on its own dividends.

Where a company's FII exceeds its franked payments (i.e., dividends paid plus the related ACT) it will have surplus FII available to carry forward. A company can recover the tax credits comprised in its surplus FII when it pays a subsequent dividend or makes a claim under *ICTA 1988, s 242.*

By making a claim under *ICTA 1988, s 242*, a company can offset a trading loss against its surplus FII. The claim effectively treats the surplus FII as though it were a taxable profit. The offset of the Schedule D Case I loss gives rise to a repayment of the tax credit comprised in the surplus FII. However, the loss is effectively reinstated when the company pays the subsequent dividend. The ACT on the dividend is not offset against the mainstream liability but is regarded as a repayment of the tax credit, thus enabling the loss to be reinstated. This is therefore a form of cashflow relief, enabling the benefit of the tax credit to be realised sooner.

Group relief

4.14　Schedule D Case I trading losses (as well as certain other items of relief) can be surrendered by a member of the group in whole or in part to another group member for offset against the claimant's current total profits. For this purpose, all group companies must be part of a 75% UK corporate group. Group relief can only be offset against the total profits of a corresponding accounting period of the claimant company.

Investment companies

What is an investment company?

4.15　An investment company is defined as 'any company whose business consists wholly or mainly in the making of investments and the principal part of whose income is derived therefrom'. [*ICTA 1988, s 130*]. Both of these tests must therefore be satisfied. The practical interpretation of each test is examined in 4.16 and 4.17 below.

The company's business must consist wholly or mainly in the making of investments

4.16　This means that the company's main activity must be to hold investments for the receipt of income in the form of interest, dividend and rents. In the Irish case of *Casey v Monteagle Estate Co. [1962] IR 406*, the Judge said that 'what has to be looked to is the nature of the operations or functions of the company. The search is not for the company making investments but for the company whose main business is the making of investments. That, to my knowledge, involves the purpose as well as their nature'. Consequently, the principal objectives of the company, as stated in its Memorandum of Association, would be an influential factor in determining the company's status. An investment company would be expected to demonstrate that the making of investments was the company's main object or at least one of them. It is also helpful to ensure that the director's report attached to the statutory accounts states that the company's principal activity is that of an investment company, perhaps describing the nature of its activity. In *Tintern Close Residents Society Ltd v Winter* (HMIT) and other similar appeals (SC 3115/94) [1995] STI 574, the Special Commissioner held that a residents' society company which owned and managed common property was not an investment company. The holding of investments must constitute a business which entailed making a financial return. The society did not make any money from holding the land (with the exception of the small ground rent). It received residents' contributions for the maintenance of the property and this was its main purpose and activity.

Although there is no definition of what 'wholly or mainly' means for this purpose, it probably means at least more than 50% although it is interesting to note that the Inland Revenue have interpreted this phrase as meaning 70% or more in the context of SP1/1988 (now obsolete).

An investment dealing company, whose object is to make a profit from buying and selling investments would be treated as carrying on an investment dealing trade. The receipt of any investment income from its investments would be incidental to its main activity.

It is unlikely that a company in liquidation will be treated as an investment company. Only rarely will a liquidator carry on a business existing wholly or mainly in the making of investments. The liquidator's main objective is to realise the company's assets to the best advantage.

The principal part of the company's income must derive from investments

4.17   For these purposes, income would include dividends etc. from UK companies even though they would not form part of the company's taxable profit. It is necessary to demonstrate that more than half of the company's income is derived from investments.

In the *Tintern Close Residents Society Ltd* case (see above), the principal part of the society's income consisted of membership subscriptions and did not derive from its investments. The company's claim for investment company status also failed this test.

In *FPH Finance Trust Limited v CIR (1944) 26 TC 131*, it was held that this test should be applied over a representative period rather than the accounting period under review. An investment company does not have to make or turn over its investments each year (*CIR v Tyre Investment Trust Limited (1924) 12 TC 646*). However, it would be important to demonstrate that some definite activity had taken place, such as the holding of directors' meetings to consider alternative investments, or the obtaining of independent investment advice. The simple placing of funds on deposit in a bank account is unlikely to constitute a business or investment activity.

Investment company — pro-forma tax computation

4.18 An investment company's tax computation brings together the assessable income and gains from all sources and then deducts from its total profits its management expenses and charges on income etc.

A pro-forma corporation tax computation for an investment company is provided below, together with accompanying notes.

PRO-FORMA INVESTMENT CO. LTD

CORPORATION TAX COMPUTATION BASED ON THE ACCOUNTING PERIOD ENDED

	£	£	Notes
Schedule A rental income			
Rents receivable	X		(a)
Less Allowable letting expenses	(X)		
Capital allowances on let property	(X)		(b)
		(X)	
		X	
Schedule D Case III bank interest received		X	
Schedule D Case III royalties received		X	
Unfranked investment income		X	
		X	
Less Relief for capital losses on disposals of shares in unquoted trading companies		(X)	(c)
		X	
Income		X	
Chargeable gains		X	
Total profits		X	
Less Capital allowances re. investment business		(X)	(d)
Management expenses			
Excess management expenses b/fwd	X		(e)-(g)
Amount incurred for period	X		
	X		
Offset against profits	(X)	(X)	
Excess management expenses c/fwd	X		(f)
		X	
Less Charges on income		(X)	(h)
		X	
Less Group relief		(X)	
PROFITS CHARGEABLE TO CORPORATION TAX		X	

Notes

(a) Where a company receives rental income, such as in the case of a property investment company, the Schedule A or D Case VI income will be calculated in accordance with the normal rules. The company must split its expenses between those incurred in managing its investment properties and those of managing the company itself. This may also necessitate an apportionment of expenditure such as directors' remuneration. The property management expenses are deducted against Schedule A income. The expenses of managing the company are deductible as management expenses (see note (*e*) below).

(*b*)   Plant and machinery which is used for the management of let properties must be deducted first against the company's Schedule A rental income. Any excess allowances can be added to the company's management expense claim. [*CAA 1990, s 28(2)*]. Industrial buildings allowances may be claimed if the lessee is using the building for a qualifying industrial purpose.

(*c*)   Where an investment company realises a capital loss on a disposal of (or negligible value claim made in respect of) an unquoted trading company's shares, it may elect to offset that loss against its income of the same period or the previous period.

A number of conditions must be satisfied to obtain relief. Relief can only be claimed if the investment company originally subscribed for the shares (i.e., it is not available for 'second-hand' shareholdings). The shares must be in an unquoted company which was either trading at the date of the disposal or has ceased to trade within three years of the disposal date (and has not since become an investment company or engaged in certain excluded activities, such as dealing in shares, land or commodities). Furthermore, the investee company must not be an 'associated company'. [*ICTA 1988, s 573* and *s 576(4)*].

(*d*)   Capital allowances can be claimed on plant and machinery etc. purchased for the purpose of a company's investments business in the same way as a trading company. This would include, for example, the purchase of office furniture, office equipment, computers, motor cars etc. [*CAA 1990, s 28(1)*]. If the capital allowances exceed the company's income for a period, the excess is added to the company's management expenses for general offset against its total profits. Any unrelieved capital allowances are treated in the same way as excess management expenses.

(*e*)   An investment company can obtain relief for its management expenses against its total profits. Generally, such expenses are those incurred in managing the investments and would therefore include normal office running costs, and reasonable directors' remuneration.

The scope of expenses allowed by the definition is often unclear. An investment company will not necessarily obtain relief for every expense. In practice, difficulties often arise in obtaining relief for director's remuneration (see note (*g*) below) and expenses relating to the changing of investments. For example, brokerage and stamp duties on purchase or sale investments are considered to be part of the cost of purchasing or selling an investment and would therefore not be allowed as a management expense (*Capital & National Trust Limited v Golder (1949) 31 TC 269*).

(*f*)   If the investment company's management expenses exceed its profit (i.e., effectively the company has a loss), the surplus management expenses are carried forward to the next accounting period. They will then be treated as management expenses of the next period (and offset against total profits). [*ICTA 1988, s 75(3)*]. Excess management expenses can be carried forward indefinitely, unless the company ceases to be an investment company, for example by commencing a significant trading activity or where there is a major change in the conduct of the company's business etc. within three years either side of a change in ownership occurring on or after 29 November 1994. [*ICTA 1988, s 768B*].

(*g*)   Directors' remuneration. Inspectors often seek to limit the deduction to the amount they consider reasonable, having regard to the duties performed. (In contrast, directors of trading companies generally have no difficulty in voting themselves significant levels of remuneration.)

In the case of an investment company, the Revenue would argue that only a modest amount relates to the cost of managing the company's investments and the company itself. Where there are likely to be difficulties in obtaining relief for directors' remuneration, the use of dividends should be considered as a means of extracting funds from a company (see 2.7–2.11). If the Inspector disallows excess remuneration, it is possible to eliminate the Schedule E liability by formally waiving the remuneration and reimbursing the amounts to the company (see 2.18).

In the case of a property investment company a higher level of remuneration can be justified on the basis that it relates to the management of the properties, which would require a greater degree of management time. In practice, directors' remuneration of between 7.5% and 15% of a company's rental income might be allowed, although a higher amount could be substantiated where the directors are personally involved in collecting rent, supervising maintenance and improvements and negotiating rent reviews etc., but this would be relieved as a Schedule A expense rather than a management expense (see note *a* above).

The '9-month rule' for accrued remuneration also applies to director's remuneration deductible as a management expense (see 5.8). This restriction on the level of allowable remuneration an investment company can pay also means that the directors can only make modest provision for pensions.

(*h*)   Interest costs cannot be treated as a management expense as they are a cost of financing the company. Interest paid to a UK bank and other forms of annual interest can be deducted as a charge on income. However, other forms of short-term interest (i.e., interest on a loan stated to be for less than 12 months) cannot strictly be deducted as a charge on income or management expense.

Close investment holding companies (CIHCs)

4.19   A CIHC is a special category of company which cannot obtain the benefit of the small companies rate of corporation tax or small companies marginal relief.

4.20   First of all, the company must be a *close* company, which broadly means that it is controlled by five or fewer shareholders *or* by shareholders (of any number) who are directors of the company. [*ICTA 1988, s 414(2)*].

4.21   Secondly, *ICTA 1988, s 13A(2)(3)* applies a negative definition in that a company will *not* be treated as a CIHC if throughout its corporation tax accounting period it exists wholly or mainly for any one of the purposes listed below:

— carrying on a trade or trades on a commercial basis. (This will include land dealing and share dealing companies);

— making investments in land, such as the letting of property to non-connected persons (A company would therefore be a CIHC if it let property to a person connected with the company);

— the holding of shares in or making loans to companies which are not CIHCs;

— companies whose business is mainly managing subsidiaries (which are not themselves CIHCs).

4.22   Where a trading company is wound up, it is unlikely to satisfy one of the above qualifying purposes. However, there is a let-out in that it will not be treated as a CIHC in the accounting period following the start of the winding up provided it was not a CIHC for the last period. [*ICTA 1988, s 13A(4)*]. If the company ceases to trade before the start of the winding up, the Revenue consider that it will become a CIHC immediately before it goes into liquidation and the relief in *s 13A(4)* will not apply (*Inland Revenue Tax Bulletin*, Issue 3). If there is sufficient tax at stake and it is practicable, the company should trade up to the date it is wound up.

Summary of tax treatment — Trading company v investment company

	TRADING COMPANY	INVESTMENT COMPANY
Small companies rate available (if profits below relevant limit)	Yes.	Yes, but not if company is a Close Investment Holding Company.
Relief for expenses	Trading expenses deductible against trading profits, provided incurred wholly and exclusively for the purposes of the trade.	Management expenses (basically all costs of running the company) are deducted against total profits (including capital gains). (There is no statutory 'wholly and exclusively' restriction, but in practice the Inland Revenue tend to apply one.)
Relief for directors' remuneration	Usually no problem in practice for proprietoral directors (although subject to the 'wholly and exclusively' test).	Level of deduction frequently challenged — remuneration generally limited to a (much lower) justifiable figure.
Relief for interest costs	All UK bank interest and other interest on loans taken out for less than one year is deductible as a trading expense on an 'accruals' basis. Other types of annual interest are deducted as a charge on income when paid.	All UK bank interest and interest on loans taken out for more than one year is deductible when paid as a charge on income. Strictly, there is no relief for short term interest paid to a non-UK bank.
Relief for capital expenditure	Relief given under the capital allowances system.	Relief given under capital allowances system (on same basis as trading company).
Relief for losses	Trading losses can be carried back against total profits for 3 previous years and/or carried forward against future *trading* profits of the same trade.	Excess management expenses (effectively an investment company's 'loss') can be carried forward against total profits (but not carried back).

	TRADING COMPANY	INVESTMENT COMPANY
Roll-over relief	Available on certain categories of asset (such as property, fixed plant and goodwill), used for trading purposes.	Not available for investment property.
Income deduction for capital losses on unquoted shares	No relief.	Can elect to offset loss against income subject to certain conditions.
Availability of shareholder reliefs, e.g. retirement relief, hold over relief for gifts of business assets, capital treatment for purchase of own shares, IHT Business Property relief	Relief available (but in most cases reliefs are restricted where company holds investment property).	No relief, unless company qualifies as a holding company of a trading group.
Interest relief on loan to buy shares	Yes.	Yes, unless company is a Close Investment Holding Company.

Chapter 5

Remuneration Strategies

The picture

5.1   Many family companies do not follow any particular remuneration strategy and simply leave matters to market forces. Whilst a rigid set of rules may well be inappropriate, nevertheless proper planning can be to everyone's advantage.

For working shareholders the level of remuneration will be determined by several factors:

(*a*)   dividend strategy as a means of avoiding national insurance contributions (see Chapter 2, paragraph 2.7);

(*b*)   the required level for funding a pension scheme (see Chapter 9);

(*c*)   the possible commercial need to retain a specific level of profits.

It is unlikely that non-working shareholders will concur to profits being voted as remuneration but will be keen to see the adoption of a properly formulated strategy. General personnel are likely to seek an appropriate level of basic remuneration topped-up by modest fringe benefits and with the prospect of performance-related bonuses being paid.

Taxation of earnings

Basic position

5.2   The Schedule E charge to income tax under Cases I and II is made on the full amount of earnings received during the year of assessment. For Cases I and II earnings are treated as received on the earliest of:

(*a*)   actual payment made of emoluments, or made on account of emoluments; or

(*b*)   entitlement to payment of emoluments, or to payment on account of emoluments.

These timing rules do not necessarily apply to benefits in kind (see Chapter 6).

5.3   Remuneration Strategies

The basic rules may sound reasonably straightforward, but not surprisingly there are further provisions where directors are concerned. For them, (*a*) and (*b*) above apply but so also do the following determine when emoluments are received:

(*c*)   the time at which the sums are credited to the company's accounts or records (any restrictions on the right to draw them are ignored);

(*d*)   the end of a period of account where emoluments are determined before the end of that period;

(*e*)   determination of emoluments for a period of account if the emoluments are determined after the end thereof. [*ICTA 1988, s 202B*].

A director resigning during the year of assessment does not avoid these special rules for that year. [*ICTA 1988, s 202B(3)*].

Meaning of 'director'

5.3   For this purpose, a 'director' means:

(*a*)   in relation to a company whose affairs are managed by a board of directors or similar body, a member of that board or similar body;

(*b*)   in relation to a company whose affairs are managed by a single director or similar person, that director or person, and;

(*c*)   in relation to a company whose affairs are managed by the members themselves, a member of the company. [*ICTA 1988, s 202B(5)*].

Furthermore, a director includes any person in accordance with whose directions or instructions the company's directors are accustomed to act. Someone giving advice in a professional capacity is ignored. [*ICTA 1988, s 202B(6)*].

Further details for directors

5.4   In looking at the additional aspects for directors in (*c*), (*d*) and (*e*) of 5.2 above, further comment is necessary.

In the case of agreed payments under (*c*) the Inland Revenue will treat payments as being paid when the director's emoluments are credited to the accounts and a legal restriction prohibits him from drawing on them until a later date or some later event occurs. However remuneration that enjoys no right of payment unless a pre-determined condition occurs is not treated as paid until the right to payment becomes unequivocal.

When accounts are prepared in readiness for an AGM they will invariably include an entry for directors remuneration. This will not normally constitute pay, except in the case of controlling shareholders, until the amount has been formally agreed by the Board from which date it will be necessary to operate PAYE. Such a payment falls within (*e*). However, if the remuneration has been formally agreed and is not credited to an account in the director's name but to another account or record of the company it will still be deemed to be pay for Schedule E purposes.

If the shareholders approve the remuneration by formal agreement earlier than the AGM a receipt may be deemed to arise *Re Duomatic (1969) 1 All ER 161* (see 2.13).

For all deemed payments PAYE should be calculated and accounted for as for actual payments.

If the amount of remuneration is determined before the end of the period to which it relates, but by the end of the period some or all of it has not actually been paid, or become due to be paid, or been credited, then payment of the unpaid amount is not regarded as having taken place until the end of the period (this comes within (*d*) above).

Where the level of remuneration is profit-related, payment thereof is made when all the relevant profit information is known so the amount can be calculated, and not when the actual formula is agreed.

The PAYE system and the family company

Basic position

5.5   The time of payment of emoluments for PAYE purposes is specifically defined in *ICTA 1988, s 203A*, and indeed the wording is the same as in *s 202B* already mentioned in 5.2 above.

Inland Revenue approach

5.6   With a family company the Inland Revenue are often particularly keen to check that PAYE is being applied to sums received by directors.

Interest is chargeable from 14 days after the end of the tax year on unpaid PAYE. [*Income Tax (Employments) Regulations 1993, Reg 51 (SI 1993 No 744)*]. However, it has not yet been announced when interest will be charged on the late remittance of the monthly PAYE due during the tax year.

5.7   *Remuneration Strategies*

Another weapon already available and which the Inland Revenue often use is a *Regulation 49* determination. This is also under *SI 1993 No 744* and can be used where the Inspector of Taxes considers tax is due under PAYE and has not been remitted to the Collector. In the context of a family company it is often used by reference to directors' remuneration voted in the accounts. The problem with a *Regulation 49* determination is that it carries interest which runs from 19 April following the year of assessment to which it relates. [*Regulation 50*].

Payment in assets

5.7   PAYE has to be accounted for on the provision of a tradeable asset to an employee, which at one time was a popular means of paying bonuses. Such an asset is one which is capable of being realised on a recognised investment exchange, or the London Bullion Market, or on any market specified in PAYE regulations; and also any other asset where trading arrangements exist. [*ICTA 1988, s 203F*].

PAYE also has to be accounted for on the provision of a non-cash voucher capable of being exchanged for goods coming within the tradeable assets definition above, and on credit-tokens to obtain money or such goods. Finally, PAYE has to be accounted for on the provision of a cash voucher. [*ICTA 1988, ss 203F(4), 203G–203I*].

Where the employee does not reimburse the employer for the PAYE accounted for under any of the above provisions, within 30 days of receipt of the item concerned, he is treated as receiving income assessable under Schedule E on the amount of the receipt and PAYE (see Example 1).

Example 1

Payment in assets

Mr Reaney receives a bonus of £5,000 paid by way of gold bullion on 10 March 1996.

PAYE due, say, £2,000 (40%), and this is paid to the Collector of Taxes by 19 April 1996.

If Mr Reaney does not pay £2,000 to his employer by 8 April 1996 (30 days from 10 March), he is taxed on £7,000 in the 1995/96 Schedule E assessment with a credit of £2,000 tax.

Corporation tax relief for the company

5.8   The remuneration for directors and other employees is ordinarily deductible for the period of account to which it relates, subject to the overriding rule that the amount is commercially justifiable. Where however the remuneration is not paid within nine months from the end of the period, the deduction is given in the later period of payment under *FA 1989, s 43* and *s 44*.

The date of payment for this purpose is the same as the date of receipt for Schedule E purposes (*s 43(12)* and *s 44(11)*), but the deductibility rule also applies where emoluments are provided in the year end accounts and 'paid' within the nine months following the year end.

If the company submits its accounts and tax computations before nine months after the end of the period of account, any unpaid remuneration should not be claimed. An adjustment to the tax computations is then made if the remuneration is actually paid within the nine-month period, provided a claim is made under *s 43(5)* or *s 44(5)* within two years from the end of the period of account concerned. See also paragraph 2.13 for discussion of this topic.

National insurance contributions

5.9   Contributions are payable by reference to the gross earnings for an earnings period.

There are special rules to cater for directors which in practice have particular relevance to a family company. They have an annual earnings period even if they are paid at regular or irregular monthly or weekly intervals. This is so as to avoid a director receiving a large sum of remuneration as a single payment and then having his own NIC being limited to the upper earnings sum for that particular month.

For a director first appointed during a tax year, there is a pro-rata earnings period. No change is made to the annual earnings period when a director resigns. [*Social Security Contributions Regulations 1979, Reg 6A*].

Example 2

NIC Director appointed during the fiscal year

Ms Pegg is appointed a director of Perry Limited when there are 20 weeks left in the tax year 1995/96. With a lower earnings limit of £58 per week and an upper earnings limit of £440 per week, Ms Pegg's pro-rata limits are:

20 × £58   =   £1,160

and

20 × £440   =   £8,800

The NIC position for 1995/96 is then:

total earnings	*Ms Pegg*		*Perry Ltd*
	on first £1,160	*on remainder*	
less than £1,160	nil		nil
£1,160 to £2,099.99	2%	10%	3%
£2,100 to £2,999.99	2%	10%	5%
£3,000 to £4,099.99	2%	10%	7%
£4,100 to £8,800	2%	10%	10.2%
over £8,800	no additional liability		10.2%

Some companies pay selected personnel by way of a transfer of assets. This can be attractive for the family company as some assets do not attract national insurance contributions. However, the number of assets within that attractive category diminishes on a regular basis and at the time of writing there is little left. The whole question of NIC on benefits is considered fully in Chapter 6, section 6.4.

Profit-related pay

Introduction

5.10   A registered PRP scheme can provide tax-free pay up to a limit of the lower of 20% of total pay, or £4,000. [*ICTA 1988, s 171*]. Pay for this purpose is as defined in the Employer's Guide to PAYE (booklet P7, para P1). It therefore includes round sum allowances; payment of telephone bills; travel costs from home to office etc., even where there may be a *ICTA 1988, s 198* claim applicable to cover all or part of the payment. The total pay is then reduced by superannuation contributions and payroll giving to charity.

The maximum tax saving per employee is £1,600 per annum (£4,000 @ 40%), but for the family company the maximum saving per employee is £2,204 or £1,969 as shown below.

Example 3

PRP — Tax savings

Mullery Limited compares paying a bonus with payment via a PRP scheme, with the employees concerned being 40% taxpayers.

	£4,000 net paid as normal earnings	£4,000 PRP
	£	£
gross	6,667	4,000
PAYE @ 40%	2,667	NIL
net	4,000	4,000
Mullery's NIC on gross (10.2%)	680	408
total tax and NIC	3,347	408
corporation tax relief @ 25% on:	7,347	4,408
=	1,837	1,102
corporation tax relief @ 33% on:	7,347	4,408
=	2,425	1,455
cost to company – 25% rate	5,510	3,306
– 33% rate	4,922	2,953

PRP saving = £2,204 (25% rate)
£1,969 (33% rate)

A family company is likely to consider using PRP as a bonus, but in the right circumstances it could be used as part of current pay (possibly with a salary sacrifice) or to cover a pay increase. There is no doubt that a properly structured PRP scheme is a valuable and comparatively new part of a family company's remuneration strategy.

Registration

5.11   An application for registration must be made in the prescribed form in accordance with *s 175* to The Profit-Related Pay Office, Inland Revenue, St Mungo's Road, Cumbernauld, Glasgow G67 1YZ. A check-list is included in booklet PRP2, and model rules are included in the booklet 'Setting up a Scheme' (September 1991).

If the application for registration is made over three months before the start of the profit period, the Revenue notifies its decision before the profit period starts. Later applications may well be dealt with in time (following IRPR 17 September 1987 and Revenue practice).

Within 30 days of receiving the application, the Revenue must issue a notice of registration, refuse registration, or request further information. [*ICTA 1988, s 176*]. The Revenue do not approve a PRP scheme; they merely consider whether any errors have been made on the application for registration and whether the basic information given on the distributable pool is within the statutory limits.

The scheme must specify the following:

(*a*)   scheme employer;

(*b*)   employment unit;

(*c*)   category of participating employees;

(*d*)   profit periods;

(*e*)   method of determining the distributable PRP pool;

(*f*)   method of frequency of payment of PRP;

(*g*)   method of determining profits;

(*h*)   length of scheme.

[*ICTA 1988, Sch 8*].

The registration application must be accompanied by an independent accountants report confirming the statutory requirements of the scheme have been met and that the employer's records will contain the relevant information for future auditing. [*ICTA 1988, s 175(2)*].

Scheme employer and employment unit

5.12   The scheme employer is the person paying the emoluments. A scheme can cover employees of group members, with different companies paying the scheme employees. In that case the parent company can apply to register the scheme and is then the **scheme employer**. A group is the parent and its 51% subsidiaries. [*ICTA 1988, s 173(3)*]. Apart from this, employees in a scheme must be paid by the same person.

The choice of employment unit is very flexible and can be any of:

(*a*)   group of companies;

(*b*)   independent company;

(*c*)   subsidiary company;

(*d*)   division within a company, provided separate approved accounts are produced;

(*e*)   whole or part of a business carried on by a sole trade or partnership, provided separate approved accounts are produced.

Participating employees

5.13   Not surprisingly, there are restrictions on working shareholders joining a PRP scheme. The restriction by reference to shareholdings is however more generous than might be expected as it covers an employee who alone or with associates controls at least 25% of the ordinary share capital in the company which employs him within the employment unit. [*ICTA 1988, 8 Sch 7*]. Working shareholders with under 25% of the shares are therefore eligible.

The scheme rules can (but do not have to) debar those not employed for three years or for a lesser time. [*ICTA 1988, 8 Sch 8*]. The scheme must cover at least 80% of the employees in the employment unit at the start of each profit period, ignoring those excluded above. The exclusion of a maximum of 20% could be by reference to rank or any other measure.

Part-time employees working less than 20 hours a week can be debarred but for PRP schemes approved from 1 May 1995 they have to come within the 20% exclusion.

Distributable PRP pool — Method A [ICTA 1988, 8 Sch 13]

5.14   This is a fixed percentage of the profits of the employment unit in the profit period. The percentage used is up to the employer, but once fixed it cannot change under the same scheme. It can be fixed in whatever way the employer may decide on registration.

An upper percentage limit (UPL) on the size of the distributable pool may be set of at least 160%. A base year is then required if the upper limit is to apply straight away. Often, it applies from the second profit period so that the first profit period provides the base. In later years, the comparison is with the preceding profit period.

Example 4

PRP pool — Method A

UPL for a PRP scheme introduced by Nish Limited

upper percentage limit	=	170%
percentage applying to profits	=	10%
Nish profits in year 1	=	£100,000
Nish profits in year 2	=	£185,000

The increase in Nish Limited's profits to £185,000 represents 185% of the year 1 profits.

The year 2 distributable pool is therefore restricted to:

£100,000 × 170% × 10%	=	£17,000

A lower profits limit can be set, to ensure there is no distributable pool unless the profits in the profit period reach a specified level. This level must not be more than the profits in the base year, which is any period of 12 months ending at some time within the two years up to the date the PRP scheme starts. There are three alternative ways of expressing this restriction in the PRP scheme rules:

(a) *base year profits known when PRP application made* (say £100,000) 'There will be no distributable pool for a profit period if profits are £X (insert any amount up to £100,000) or less';

(b) *base year profits not known* 'There will be no distributable pool for a profit period unless the profits for the period exceed X% (insert any % up to 100%) of the profits in the base year';

(c) *base year profits not known* 'There will be no distributable pool for a profit period unless profits in the period reach the lower of £X (insert any amount) or the profits in the base year'. If base year profits turn out to be less than the monetary sum in (a), the lower limit is then of course the base year profits for that particular profit period. Any sum, however determined, can be used provided it is not more than the base year profits.

Salary sacrifice PRP schemes cannot be used in an artificial manner unless the scheme was registered before 30 November 1993. For later schemes where a UPL exists, there must be a provision which ensures that the basic UPL of 160% or above is increased by a further percentage whenever the taxable pay of participants is less in the current profit period than in the previous period or base year. This reduction in taxable pay is expressed as a percentage of the earlier profits and that percentage is added to the basic UPL. This increased percentage is then the UPL for the profit period concerned, and stops PRP being used to virtually guarantee that it will meet any salary sacrificed.

Distributable PRP pool — Method B [ICTA 1988, 8 Sch 14]

5.15 This is a percentage of a sum of money which fluctuates in line with annual profits. There are three elements involved:

(a) the profits for the current period;

(b) the profits for the previous period (or for the previous 12 months when looking at the first PRP profit period);

(c) the distributable pool for the previous period (or the notional pool when looking at the first PRP profit period).

Yearly rises or falls in profits will of course affect the distributable pool, but this can be restricted by applying a fraction of not more than 1/2 to the percentage difference or change in profits from one year to the next. If a fraction is used in this way it must always be applied, but it does not have to be introduced immediately the PRP scheme starts.

The notional pool used in the first PRP profit period can be fixed however the employer wishes, but the application to register must either state the notional pool or how it is to be calculated. This flexibility can allow substantial PRP to be paid out by reference to the number of employees. It could for example be fine-tuned to equate to the tax-free maximum of £4,000 each which may be particularly attractive to a family company; or provide tax-free PRP in place of part of normal pay or commissions.

Example 5

PRP pool — Method B

Method B PRP scheme introduced by Summerbee Wingers Limited

year 1 profits	–	£100,000
previous year profits	–	£90,000
year 2 profits	–	£120,000
notional pool (say)	–	£9,000

year 1 distributable pool

$$\text{notional pool} \times \frac{\text{year 1 profits}}{\text{previous year profits}}$$

$$= £9,000 \times \frac{£100,000}{£90,000}$$

$$= \underline{£10,000}$$

year 2 distributable pool

$$\text{year 1 pool} \times \frac{\text{year 2 profits}}{\text{year 1 profits}}$$

$$= £10,000 \times \frac{£120,000}{£100,000}$$

$$= £12,000$$

Taking the same facts, but with the notional pool deliberately fixed at £27,000, this would serve to increase all the distributable pools in the Summerbee Wingers Ltd PRP scheme:

year 1 distributable pool

$$= £27,000 \times \frac{£100,000}{£90,000}$$

$$= £30,000$$

year 2 distributable pool

$$£30,000 \times \frac{£120,000}{£100,000}$$

$$= \underline{£36,000}$$

An upper limit can be set on the amount of profits used in calculating the Method B distributable pool, by fixing a percentage of at least 160%.

Example 6

PRP — Method B upper limit

Method B PRP scheme introduced by Stamford Tambling Limited

upper percentage limit	=	180%
year 3 profits	=	£300,000
year 2 profits	=	£150,000
year 2 pool	=	£10,000

year 3 distributable pool   year 3 profits (as a percentage)

year 2 profits

$$= \frac{£300,000}{£150,000} \times 100$$

$$= 200\%$$

the upper % limit therefore applies and the pool becomes:

£10,000 × 180% = £18,000

A lower profits limit can be set to ensure there is no distributable pool unless the profits reach a specified level. This cannot be more than the profits in the 12 month period up to the date the PRP scheme starts.

There is clearly a good deal of flexibility which can be catered for via the use of a fraction; an upper profits limit; and a lower profits limit. Complete flexibility, however, is available by carefully determining the notional pool.

If there is a loss for any profit period under Method B, the scheme's registration has to be cancelled. This would not apply under Method A, where there would simply be no distributable pool in that period.

Payment of PRP

5.16   The whole of the distributable PRP pool must be distributed to eligible employees in the employment unit. The method and frequency of payment must be stipulated, with interim payments allowed.

Employees can receive the same amount of PRP, or it can vary to reflect levels of pay, length of service or other similar non-discretionary factors. This is subject to the proviso that distorted or disproportionate results must not arise. On levels of pay, this could be within specified bands or exact levels. Pay for this purpose can be all or only some of the elements of pay as defined in paragraph P1 of the Employer's Guide to PAYE. The length of service factor is clear, but it is also possible to include hours worked or actual attendance over the profit period.

Determining profits

5.17   The profit of the employment unit is the post-tax profit on ordinary activities as defined in *Companies Act 1985, 5 Sch*. Adjustments can (but do not have to) apply in respect of any or all of the following under *8 Sch 19*:

(*a*)   interest etc. receivable and payable;

(*b*)   goodwill;

(*c*)   tax (but not interest or penalties) on profit or loss on ordinary activities;

(*d*)   R & D costs;

(*e*)   PRP payable under the scheme;

(*f*)   exceptional items and tax thereon.

Of the above items, normally excluded from profits are goodwill, R & D costs (where they could be substantial) and PRP payable under the scheme.

The 'exceptional items' referred to above apply to profit periods beginning on or after 1 May 1995. These items are:

(i)   profits/losses on sale or termination of an operation;

(ii)   costs of a fundamental reorganisation/restructuring having a material effect on the nature and focus of the employment unit's operations;

(iii)   profits/losses on disposal of fixed assets.

Remuneration of non-eligible employees having at least a 25% interest (with associates) is disregarded in the profit calculation. [*8 Sch 19(4)*]. Remuneration for this purpose includes non-cash benefits, pension contributions etc. [*8 Sch 19(4)(a)*].

If a PRP scheme employer wishes, the employer's NIC can be excluded in calculating the profits on which the distributable PRP pool is calculated p.a. and this is normally the case.

The accounting policy and profit determination method specified by the scheme must be used consistently, unless not affecting the results by over 5%.

Example 7

Typical PRP scheme for a family company in the service industry using Method A — as outlined to participants

PHELAN LIMITED
PRP SUMMARY FOR THE YEAR TO 31 MARCH 1996

1. Provided the pre-tax profits of Phelan Ltd reach a specified percentage of revenue, a proportion of the profits will be distributed to staff via the PRP scheme. The rules state that provided profits are at least the lower of 15% of revenue or the profits of the year to 31/03/95, the distribution will be 8% of profits. However, the rules refer to PRP profit which is not the same as Phelan's operating profit calculated on a standard accounting basis. Operating profit is lower than PRP profit, so the PRP distribution is higher than 8% of operating profit, e.g.:

	£'000	
Revenue	4,600	100%
Phelan Ltd profit	598	13%
PRP adjustments	138	
PRP profit	736	16%

PRP pool 8% × 736 = 58.88

PRP pool as a percentage of Phelan Ltd profits $= \dfrac{58.88}{598} = 9.84\%$

2. The pool will be distributed as a proportion of the salaries of qualifying staff, e.g.:

Salaries	£1.472 million
Pool	£58.88K
Pool as a percentage of salary	= 4%

3. Qualifying staff are staff who:
    — will have been employed during the whole of the year ending 31/03/96
    — *and* will be employed at the date of distribution
    — *and* will not have served or been served with a notice of termination on or before that date

4. Qualifying staff with two years' service or more at 31/03/96 will have 100% of salary count for PRP purposes. Qualifying staff with more than one but less than two years' service at 31/03/96 will have 50% of salary count for PRP purposes.

5. The PRP distribution will be made on completion of the audit for the year ending 31/03/96. It is anticipated that the distribution will be made in July 1996.

General points on PRP

5.18   The employer must submit to the Revenue an annual return on PRP 20 plus an independent accountant's report and certificate confirming the scheme terms have been complied with. The time limit is seven months after the end of the profit period for a plc; ten months for any other business. An extension of up to three months can be allowed where the business is carried on overseas. The PRPO mainly monitors the operation of a registered PRP scheme via information obtained at PAYE inspections.

Method B of determining the PRP pool gives scope for maximum flexibility by careful selection of the notional pool. That pool normally affects the distributable pool for all future profit periods, but any problems this could create may be avoided by setting the scheme to last for only one or two profit periods. Alternatively, the scheme could be cancelled with a replacement scheme registered, a new PRP scheme introduced for registration or PRP dropped altogether. A replacement scheme can last for two profit periods and the distributable pool must be a fixed percentage of profits.

The anticipated level of PRP can be indicated by an employer and indeed it makes sense to do so. If, however, a guarantee is given that if PRP falls below a particular level then the employee will receive a taxable cash bonus to make up the difference, the Inland Revenue consider this will result in non-registration or cancellation of the PRP scheme on the grounds that the scheme is not one which provides for the payment of emoluments calculated by reference to profits as is required under *ICTA 1988, s 169(1)*.

Other bonus schemes

5.19   Cash bonuses, liable to income tax in the normal way, are of course simple and can be paid on a discretionary bonus. They naturally provide maximum flexibility and may be particularly appropriate in a family company where a small workforce often gives rise to a few people being of particular importance to the current and future profitability of the business.

A shareholder stops working for the company

5.20   Where an employee retires, is made redundant, or otherwise has his employment terminated, there can be scope for receiving the first £30,000 of any pay-off without being liable to income tax thereon. This is under *ICTA 1988, s 148*, but this only applies where the payment would not otherwise be taxable under the basic Schedule E rules.

71

Where the director/employee is also a shareholder he often will want to sell his shares on ceasing to work (indeed he may be forced to sell them in certain circumstances). In that case, where his holding is of a size that exerts influence it is not surprising that the Inland Revenue often attempts to argue that a lump-sum payment on leaving the employment does not enjoy the *s 148* treatment. Instead, they seek to treat it as a distribution by the company or as part of the sale proceeds for the shares.

Great care must be taken in these circumstances, and there are several points to take into account:

(*a*)   statutory redundancy pay is exempt from income tax under *ICTA 1988, s 579E(1)*. It is however taken into account in exempting the first £30,000 of any overall redundancy package. [*ICTA 1988, s 580(3)*]. The exemption for a statutory redundancy payment applies where it is within the *Employment Protection (Consolidation) Act 1978*. This includes the definition of a relevant redundancy payment for this purpose, and if the actual payment is in excess of that there can be a tax charge;

(*b*)   for non-statutory redundancy payments, the tax treatment is the same as for statutory payments provided there is a genuine redundancy in accordance with Statement of Practice SP1/94. Basically, this situation arises where the Inland Revenue are satisfied that the payment falls within the definition of a redundancy payment under the 1978 Act referred to above and that a genuine redundancy arises. The payment must not represent a terminal bonus for carrying out additional duties. Applications can be made to the Inspector for advance clearance to pay lump sum redundancy payments of up to £50,000 free of tax;

(*c*)   it may be possible to show that the payment to the director represents compensation for loss of office. If so, the amount of compensation should be determined properly, and take into account:

   (i)   the gross future remuneration lost to the director because of the breach of contract;

   (ii)   a discount to reflect the difference in timing between the date the compensation is paid and the date(s) on which the remuneration would actually have been paid under the terms of the contract;

   (iii)   a reduction to reflect the prospect of the director obtaining employment from which he will derive earnings which in whole or in part replace the earnings which he would have received under the contract;

(iv) a reduction by reference to unemployment benefit receivable;

(v) a reduction to take account of the fact that, whilst the whole of the remuneration payable under the contract would have been taxable in the hands of the director, only the excess of the compensation payment over £30,000 is actually taxable;

(*d*) in practice, where a working shareholder ceases to work for the company the most likely scope for his receiving a tax-free payment is to make it of an ex-gratia nature. This is not taxable up to £30,000, provided it is not made by reference to past services;

(*e*) for ex-gratia payments on retirement or death, the Statement of Practice SP13/91 applies. Here, the Inland Revenue's view is that ex-gratia payments on retirement or death are receipts from an unapproved retirement benefit scheme [*ICTA 1988, s 596A*] and so do not enjoy the £30,000 exemption. The SFO Memorandum 111 (October 1991) also covers the position and makes it clear that where an employee is made redundant, then the fact that he is able to take early retirement and immediately get benefits from an approved pension scheme does not result in the ex-gratia redundancy payment being taxable. Instead, the first £30,000 would be exempt. The Revenue have currently been fairly aggressive with regard to termination payments and often seek to deny the £30,000 exemption on the basis that the amount represents a taxable payment in lieu of notice or payment for a restrictive covenant given by the employee which is taxable under *ICTA 1988, s 313*. Each case will have to be argued on its merits and it is particularly helpful if the underlying documentation is worded to show that the payment is 'in satisfaction of the employer's obligations to the departing employee' (see also ICAEW Taxline Issue 95/9, page 3);

(*f*) if the director is to sell his shares in the company, the case of *Snook (James) & Co Ltd v Blasdale (1952) 33 TC 244* is important. Basically it shows how not to do things. It involved an agreement to sell shares, with a provision to pay compensation for loss of office being included in the agreement. To have any possibility of success, the payment must not be linked to the sale of the shares in any way whatsoever, otherwise the payment could be taxed as a distribution or as part of the proceeds of sale of the shares.

PLANNING CHECKLIST — REMUNERATION STRATEGIES
company • Consider commercial desirability of retaining a level of profits. • Surplus profits could be distributed as a bonus to selected personnel, or in the form of pension scheme contributions or other benefits. • Remuneration should be paid within nine months from the end of the accounting period. • Introduce PRP as a bonus device, with possibly also a discretionary bonus system but not linked to the PRP or guaranteed in any way.
working shareholders • Dividend strategy may determine level of profits available for distribution as remuneration. • Consider required level for pension funding.
other employees • Look for basic remuneration plus performance-related bonus.
non-working shareholders • Consider whether any excess remuneration is commercially justifiable or desirable.

Chapter 6

Benefits and Expenses

Strategy for working shareholders

6.1   Most working shareholders will want the company to meet the cost of all expenses which could be said to have a business connection — no matter how nebulous that connection may be. They will also want the company to provide them with as many fringe benefits as is possible, provided their personal income tax liability is not of such a magnitude that it would be cheaper for them to purchase the item in question.

That is a reasonable enough view on expenses. Although the employee is able to claim tax relief under *ICTA 1988, s 198* for those expenses which are wholly, exclusively and necessarily incurred in the performance of the duties of the employment this is notoriously restrictive terminology. From a strategic point of view it is generally sensible to arrange that the company meets all expenses (directly or by reimbursement) which would not have been incurred but for the existence of the employment in question.

The position on fringe benefits can be different. Leaving aside the company car which is covered separately in Chapter 7, there can be advantages in a whole host of goods and services and additional shares being provided by the company for the employee. There will be an income tax charge on the employee to cover the private element of the fringe benefit, but this is often less than the real value to him of having the benefit. This is especially the case when one considers that a higher-rate taxpaying employee who wants to purchase goods costing say £900 would need to use £1,500 of gross salary, whereas he would be charged to income tax on £900 (tax = £360) if the company provided the item. Care needs to be taken with this philosophy, however, as there could be no end to the private goods which the employer provides. Instead one should restrict consideration of the employer buying the goods to those which do have an employment aspect and which the working shareholder would purchase himself if his company did not do so.

Tax relief for the company

6.2   The corporation tax deductibility of the benefit must always be considered. This is something which the Inland Revenue sometimes question.

If the provision of a benefit constitutes revenue expenditure there should be no problem in obtaining corporation tax relief, on the grounds that it is simply part of the cost of obtaining the employee's services within a remuneration package and the expense is wholly and exclusively incurred for the purposes of the business. If capital expenditure is involved, however, the position can be difficult. For the employer to obtain capital allowances on the expenditure it has to be on the provision of machinery or plant wholly and exclusively for the purposes of the trade. [*CAA 1990, s 24*]. Taking the example of a boat, it is likely that only restricted capital allowances would be claimable to reflect the business aspect. This could typically cover the use as a marketing and advertising tool, where appropriate, but not where business entertainment is involved in view of the debarring provisions of *ICTA 1988, s 577(1)(c)*, which states that such use is not treated as use for the purposes of the trade. Restricted tax allowance for the employer (and possibly no allowance at all) would not avoid an income tax charge on the employee and overall an exotic company purchase may not be sensible.

Strategy for other employees

6.3   Turning to the employee who is not a shareholder, the strategy should be different. Fringe benefits should be provided as an incentive device, with particular emphasis on those where the income tax charge on the employee is less than the real value to him. A structured remuneration package could be introduced using the cafeteria system whereby the employer determines his fixed gross annual cost and the executive can then choose the components within limits. This is illustrated in this chapter with a comprehensive example after discussing separately various forms of fringe benefits which are worthwhile considering by a family company.

National insurance contributions

6.4   Commonsense would suggest that NIC's would be charged on fringe benefits on the same amount as the Schedule E income tax charge. If only life was so simple! Perhaps some day we will see something like a Class 1B NIC charge on the Schedule E assessable amount (as we have for cars and fuel under Class 1A), but at present we have to live with an unsatisfactory state of affairs where determining the NIC position on fringe benefits and expenses can often be difficult and uncertain.

The legislation does not have much to say. In *Regulation 19(1)(d)* of *SI 1979 No 591* we are told that a person's earnings for NIC purposes does not include 'any payment in kind or by way of the provision of board or lodging or of services or other facilities'. This has resulted in many NIC avoidance schemes being marketed. There is now regulation 19(5) which says that certain assets, mainly securities and shares (other than in the employing company), payments in gold or other traded commodities (including via vouchers) and life assurance contracts are not excluded from NIC. Indeed most of the esoteric NIC avoidance devices have now been stopped, and any that remain or are discovered are likely to be stamped upon quickly and decisively.

What can be said is that where the company meets the personal liability of an employee, this is a payment liable to NIC. Where however the liability is that of the employer then no NIC charge arises even where the employee does benefit. The company meeting the employee's home telephone charge will therefore ordinarily give rise to an NIC charge, but not if the subscriber to the telephone line is changed to the company. The Contributions Agency of the DSS has its own ideas on what are and are not liable to NIC and they are detailed in the employer's manual NI 269 by reference to many common payments and benefits. Not everybody accepts the legality of the views expressed, but on the other hand in some circumstances the stated NIC position is more favourable than might be imagined.

Use of assets

6.5   For the use of an asset (other than a car or living accommodation) an employee is charged to income tax annually on 20% of the market value of the assets when first provided, or on the rental paid for the asset if that gives a greater tax charge. [*ICTA 1988, s 154(1)* and *s 156(6)(b)*]. A fast-depreciating asset could be provided and the tax charge on the employee could be kept to a minimum in relation to the value enjoyed by him. There could also be a separate income tax charge on any expenses incurred by the employer in providing the asset.

If ownership of the asset is transferred to the employee an income tax charge then arises of the market value when first provided by the company *less* the amounts already charged for the use of the asset. [*ICTA 1988, s 156(4)*]. However, this can possibly be avoided in several ways.

(*a*)   For clothing, donating it to a charity shop.

(*b*)   Transferring by sale at market value rather than by gift. There is then no tax charge on the transfer (i.e. on the original cost less the annual charges for use of the asset) as it only applies when a benefit arises from the transfer [*ICTA 1988, s 154*] and as he is paying the market value can it be said that he is getting a benefit under the basic provisions?

(*c*)   The employee continuing to pay rent equivalent to the annual value so that no charge to income tax arises on the use of the asset.

6.5 Benefits and Expenses

The fast-depreciating assets could be furniture or consumer durables for the employee's home, but the advantage to the company would be less than for business clothing which help promote its image. Furthermore, non-working shareholders are unlikely to be willing to sanction furniture or consumer durables as part of a remuneration package. The company may well be able to make special arrangements so that it purchases the clothing at a discount.

Example 1

Assets provided to an employee

Clothing costing £1,000 is bought by Parker Limited and made available for an employee's use. The value after one year is £300 when the clothing is given to the employee. Income tax charges are on:

		£	£
Year 1 — 20% of £1,000	=		200
Year 2 — £1,000 *less* £200	=		800
			1,000

Possible ways of avoiding the complete tax charge are:

(*a*)   Donate to charity shop:

Year 1 — 20% of £1,000	=	200	
Year 2 —	=	nil	
			200

(*b*)   Transfer by sale at market value:

Year 1 — 20% of £1,000	=	200	
Year 2 —	=	nil	
			200

(*c*)   Employee pays rent:

Year 1 — 20% of £1,000	=	200	
Less made good by employee		200	
			nil
Year 2 — 20% of £1,000	=	200	
Less made good by employee		200	nil

Corporate clothing

6.6   Nowadays the Inland Revenue tend to accept that no income tax charge should arise on an employee wearing what could be called a 'uniform'. This can be extended to more attractive corporate clothing, including a suit, provided there is a prominent company name or logo sewn to the garment. The employer's policy should be consistent, so that, say, all employees meeting customers/clients or on view to them are able to wear the corporate clothing.

Within a family company, corporate identity through clothing certainly has its place.

Living accommodation

Representative occupation

6.7   There is no income tax charge where the accommodation is provided for the employee in certain circumstances (known as 'representative occupation'). This in most cases is of no use to the working shareholders as explained below. The exemption applies:

(*a*)   where it is necessary for the proper performance of the employee's duties that he should reside in the accommodation; or

(*b*)   where the accommodation is provided for the better performance of the duties of his employment, and his is one of the kinds of employment in the case of which it is customary for employers to provide living accommodation for employees; or

(*c*)   where, there being a special threat to his security, special security arrangements are in force and he resides in the accommodation as part of those arrangements. [*ICTA 1988, s 145*].

The exemptions in (*a*) or (*b*) do not apply to a director unless he owns under 5% of the shares and is either a full-time working director, the company is non-profit making so that it does not carry on a trade and its functions do not consist wholly or mainly in holding investments or other property, or the company is established for charitable purposes only. [*ICTA 1988, s 145(5)*]. For other employees, they could face difficulty in obtaining exemption following the case of *Vertigan v Brady [1988] STC 91*. The exemption in (*a*) above was held to be directed to a necessity based on the relationship between the proper performance of the taxpayer's duties and the accommodation provided, and not on the personal demands of the employee. The exemption in (*b*), generally thought to cover the 'flat over the shop' situation for a shop manager, was held to require identification of three constituent factors in identifying where the employment was 'one of the kinds of employment in the case of which it is customary for employers to provide living accommodation'. These factors are (1) the statistical evidence as to how common the practice was; (2) for how long the practice has continued; and (3) whether it had achieved acceptance generally by the relevant employers.

Beneficial occupation

6.8   Where representative occupation is not involved, there is an income tax charge on beneficial occupation. This is by reference to the value to the employee of the accommodation provided for any period. This is defined in *ICTA 1988, s 145(2)*, as the rent which would have been payable for the period if the premises had been let to him at an annual rent equal to their annual value, which in turn is defined in *ICTA 1988, s 837* as the rent which might reasonably be expected to be obtained on a letting from year to year if the tenant undertook to pay all his usual rates and taxes, and if the landlord undertook to bear the costs of the repairs and insurance, and the other expenses, if any, necessary for maintaining the subject of the valuation in a state to command that rent. This is basically the gross rateable value for the old rating assessments in the UK and would be less than the market rent ordinarily obtainable. If the premises are rented by the person at whose cost the accommodation is provided, normally the employer, rather than owned by him, the tax charge is on the rent payable if, as is likely to be the case, this is greater than the annual value.

In Scotland, the 1985 rating revaluations are reduced for tax purposes under ESC A56. With the introduction of the Council Tax throughout the UK, new rules are anticipated for the income tax charge on living accommodation. In the meantime, where there has been no material change of circumstances the existing property valuation continues to be used as the basis of the income tax charge. For new properties not within the old rating system, and those where there has been a material change of circumstances, employers should give an estimate of what the gross rateable value would have been under the old rating system. The relevant tax office then discusses this with the District Valuer (IRPR 19/4/90).

The tax charge increases where the property costs over £75,000. [*ICTA 1988, s 146*]. The charge is in addition to the *s 145* charge on the gross rateable value, and is 8% p.a. for 1995/96 on the excess of the cost (plus improvements) over £75,000. This rate is the same as the official interest rate for beneficial loans applying at the beginning of the year of assessment concerned. If the property is first occupied by the employee after 30 March 1983, and the provider of the accommodation acquired his interest more than six years beforehand, the 1995/96 tax charge is 8% p.a. on the excess over £75,000 of the market value when first occupied and not of the original cost. This extra tax charge means that properties costing over (say) £100,000 are not a tax-efficient part of the remuneration package.

There is a separate tax charge under *s 154* on directors and those earning at least £8,500 p.a. in respect of ancillary benefits such as expenditure incurred or reimbursed by the employer on heating, lighting, cleaning, repairs, furnishings etc. If the accommodation itself is exempt as representative, this tax charge is restricted to 10% of the net emoluments. [*ICTA 1988, s 163*]. There is no tax charge on alterations and additions to the premises of a structural nature, or repairs which would be the lessor's obligation if the premises were let under a lease to which Section 11 of the Landlord and Tenant Act 1985 applied, provided such expenditure is borne by the employer and not by the employee who is then reimbursed. [*ICTA 1988, s 155(3)*].

Example 2

Beneficial occupation

Peacock Limited purchases a house for £185,000. An employee occupies the property throughout the tax year 1995/96 and pays rent of £200 per annum. The gross rateable value is £1,000. The employee meets the lighting and heating costs and other normal tenant's running expenses. The accommodation was furnished by Peacock Limited at a cost of £5,000.

Income tax on:			£
s 145	–	gross rateable value	1,000
		Less rent paid	200
			800
s 146	–	8% of (£185,000 – £75,000) =	8,800
			9,600
s 154	–	20% of cost of furnishings of £5,000	1,000
			£10,600

The income tax charge on this £10,600 deemed income should then be compared with the market rent otherwise payable by the employee. This might well vary between £6,000 and £12,000 per annum.

Tax planning points

6.9   If an employee uses living accommodation provided by his employer for say 30 days in a year of assessment, it is necessary to consider whether he is charged to tax on the annual value for the complete year. *ICTA 1988, s 145(1)*, refers to the accommodation provided in any period, and to restrict the tax charge to the actual period of occupation by the employee or member of his family or household it might be necessary to show that the accommodation was only physically occupied by him for that period not because of the employee's choice but because of conditions imposed by the provider. If the employer provides living accommodation by acquiring a right to 'time-share' a holiday home for a specific period this would restrict the tax charge on the employees by reference to the period for which the home is available for occupation.

With the gross rateable value being the measure of the tax charge where the property is owned by the provider of the accommodation, the tax charge on the employee is less than the rent he would be expected to pay in the open market. Tax-efficient arrangements include the employer acquiring the freehold or long leasehold of premises and repairing and fitting them up to the standard requirement for furnished lettings. The employee is then granted a lease (after the repair work has been carried out so that no tax charge is levied thereon) on the normal basis of the employer/lessor meeting the cost of exterior repairs, ground rent etc., and the employee/ tenant paying the rates, lighting and heating costs etc.

For overseas coastal property owned by the employer, the tax charge would normally be based on the market rent obtainable on a letting in the absence of any rateable value. The Inland Revenue has been known to accept using the rateable value of a similar size property in a coastal part of England as a convenience measure.

Where the provision of the living accommodation is exempt from the tax charge on the basis of representative occupation, maximum advantage can be taken of the limitation of the tax charge on ancillary benefits to 10% of net emoluments. The furnishings and fittings can be of the highest quality without any additional tax charge arising, provided they are held to be '*normal for domestic occupation*' as required by *ICTA 1988, s 163(2)(c)*.

Example 3

Representative occupation — fixtures and fittings

Pearce Limited purchases antique furniture, household appliances, television, hi-fi equipment etc. for £20,000 which are placed in representatively occupied accommodation. This would normally give an annual income tax charge on the employee on deemed emoluments of £4,000 (20% of £20,000). His net emoluments are, say:

	£	£
Salary, benefits and expenses		28,600
Less Allowable expenses	400	
Pension contributions	2,200	2,600
Net emoluments		26,000

The tax charge is therefore based on 10% of £26,000 = £2,600, instead of the £4,000 deemed emoluments ordinarily applying.

The employer should make sure that the employee does not obtain a protected tenancy. This can be avoided by:

(*a*) providing a service tenancy, linked to employment and enabling the company to terminate the tenancy on termination of the employment if it can be shown that the accommodation is provided for the better fulfilment (not necessary fulfilment) of the duties of the employment; or

(*b*) the company showing it requires the accommodation for another employee; or

(*c*) the tenancy being outside the scope of the protected tenancy legislation.

The provision of holiday accommodation by a family company is not only tax efficient, it can also have the following advantages:

(i) the prospect of capital growth as a purchased investment;

(ii) an incentive to employees if situated in a desirable part of the world, awarding a varying period of stay based on predetermined performance targets;

(iii) it can force working shareholders to take a necessary and meaningful break from their work positions, which they might otherwise avoid;

(iv) an attractive venue for working conventions for salesmen or senior executives;

(v) a useful venue for entertaining customers or business contacts.

The tax charge on the provision of a holiday in a company owned property can be illustrated in the following manner, taking the property as not costing over £75,000.

Example 4

Holiday accommodation

Property owned by Spink Villa Limited

	UK property	*Overseas property*
Gross rateable value	£520	not applicable
Market rent	£3,120	£8,320
Period of stay	2 weeks	2 weeks
Tax charge on:	2/52 × £520 = £20	2/52 × £8,320 = £320
Marginal tax rate	40%	40%
Income tax payable	£8	£128

The amount of the charge as a benefit for the provision of living accommodation is reduced by an expense claim under *ICTA 1988, s 198*, of such an amount as would have been deductible if the accommodation had been paid for by the employee out of his emoluments. Some guidance as to the scope for this reduction in the tax charge is provided by the Inland Revenue's booklet IR 480 (1994):

'21.14   If accommodation is provided for an employee e.g. in a flat or hotel, whilst he is on business duties away from his home and his normal place of work, the cost of this may be allowable as a deduction under the expenses rule. For example a company in Yorkshire may rent a London flat for an employee who has to make frequent business trips to London. The extent of any tax allowance will depend upon the circumstances. If the accommodation is no more than an alternative to hotel accommodation and is not available for private occupation the whole cost of renting and running the flat may be allowed as a deduction. On the other hand if the employee or his family also had the use of the flat as a private residence any allowance would be restricted.

21.15   If however, a London flat is provided for an employee whose job is in London and the flat is used by him as a pied à terre no allowance would be due. Equally if the flat is used by the employee or his family as their only or second home, no deduction for tax purposes would be due.'

Private health insurance

6.10   This is a valuable benefit to provide, from all viewpoints — the company, the working shareholder, the non-working shareholder, and other employees.

The employee is charged to income tax on the cost to the company but where the company has generally at least six employees within a group scheme, it will be able to obtain a gross discount of an amount far greater than the employee could as an individual. The employee is then charged to income tax on a lower amount than the cost to him would be if he took out the insurance cover himself. From the company's viewpoint, it is an attractive proposition to arrange for senior personnel to have access to private healthcare where the service is generally quicker than under the NHS.

For employees and directors over the age of 60, it can be more tax efficient for them to fund their own health insurance premiums (with income tax relief available) via extra salary to cover.

Beneficial loans

6.11   The granting of a loan to an employee at a reduced rate of interest for the purchase of a house is a traditional benefit offered by banks and insurance companies. There is no real reason why a family company should not offer the same benefit, but it may not be wise in view of the substantial funds likely to be needed and the level of control required over the use of the loan proceeds. Furthermore, loans to participators of a close company may give rise to a tax charge on the company under *ICTA 1988, s 419*. The *Companies Act 1985* generally prohibits loans to directors subject to certain minor exceptions. However there is a civil remedy for the breach of this prohibition which provides that the loan is voidable at the option of the company. [*CA 1985, s 341*]. Consequently the company could recover the loan by rescinding the transaction.

The granting of a house-purchase loan is tax efficient as only a small income tax charge arises in the hands of the employee for loans up to £30,000 used to purchase his main residence, but for loans on which the interest is not tax deductible an employee is charged to tax on the difference between the interest at the official rate (7.75% from 6 October 1995) and the interest actually charged. There is no tax charge on such loans where the total borrowings do not exceed £5,000. Alternative assistance by the family company in the purchase of a house by an employee may be available by making temporary deposits with building societies for preferential mortgage treatment.

Example 5

Beneficial loans to employees (1)

Venables Limited, sugar refiners, provides house purchase loans of £30,000 to employees to help them purchase their main residence. The interest rate charged is 1.75% per annum. Taking the official rate of interest as 7.75% throughout 1995/96, the income tax liability on the employees based on £30,000 × (7.75 – 1.75)% is as follows:

tax rate	liability
25%	£1,800 @ 10% = £180
40%	£1,800 @ 25% = £450

The above example is accurate in terms of stating the income tax liability, but technically there are two steps in the tax computation:

(*a*) charge the employee to tax on the interest foregone (i.e. interest at the official rate less the interest actually paid); and

(*b*) if a qualifying loan, give the employee tax relief on the interest forgone, the relief being at the fixed rate of 15% for 1995/96 where the loan is to purchase the employee's main residence.

Example 6

Beneficial loans to employees (2)

Facts as in previous example.

		£
25% taxpayer taxed on £1,800 @ 25%	=	450
Less relief on £1,800 @ 15%	=	270
tax liability		180
40% taxpayer taxed on £1,800 @ 40%	=	720
Less relief as above		270
tax liability		450

There is no tax charge on loans made to employees on commercial terms (albeit at less than the official rate) by employers who lend to the general public, provided the following requirements are met:

(i) the loans are made by an employer whose business includes the lending of money; and

(ii) loans are made to employees on the same terms and conditions as are available to the public; and

(iii) a substantial proportion of loans on those terms are made to public customers.

This is unlikely to apply to a family company. What may well be useful, however, is that cheap loans made to employees by an individual are exempt if the loans are made in the normal course of domestic, family or personal relationships. [*ICTA 1988, Sch 7(1)(5)*].

Insurance

6.12   Life cover for death in service, and sickness and disability insurance, often forms part of a pension scheme and, as such, is tax efficient. The attractiveness of permanent health insurance as part of a benefits programme lies in its ability to provide an income of 75% of salary on disability right up to the normal retirement date, thereby ensuring continued participation in the pension scheme instead of having to rely on benefit levels applicable at the enforced early retirement date.

The remuneration package

6.13   For senior employees who are not shareholders, or who only have an uninfluential minority holding, a structured remuneration package could be provided. This is generally easier to provide for a new employee, as otherwise there could be an element of salary sacrifice by the employee which may be effectively annulled by reference to the case of *Heaton v Bell [1969] TC 211*. As, however, there is no tax charge as an emolument in certain circumstances where there is an offer of cash or car (see Chapter 7), with care there should be no problem where an existing employee takes fringe benefits at the time of a salary review or on promotion.

A relevant package is illustrated below for 1995/96. Reference is made to pension contributions as part of the package. The subject of pension schemes is covered in Chapter 9.

Example 7

Remuneration package

Pallister Limited is to spend £40,000 per annum on a new executive who is offered the cafeteria system of choosing a remuneration package.

He decides upon:

	gross cost to Pallister Ltd £	gross benefit to employee £	taxable on employee £
salary cost	27,550 (*a*)	22,953 (*f*)	25,000
NIC contribution		2,047	
pension contribution	3,741	3,741	nil
2½ litre car	5,400 (*b*)	6,000	5,133 (*g*)
petrol	1,227 (*c*)	1,227	1,260 (*h*)
NIC Class 1A	652 (*j*)		
clothing	1,080 (*d*)	1,200	216 (*i*)
private health insurance	350 (*e*)	500	350
	40,000	37,668	31,959

Notes

(*a*)   salary £25,000 + employer's NIC 10.2%;

(*b*)   contract hire charge of £600 per month net of 10% company discount, *less* 25% business use (car list price £22,000);

(*c*)   75% private use = 10,000 miles @ 22 mpg @ £2.70 per gallon;

(*d*)   10% company discount;

(*e*)   30% company discount under a group scheme;

(*f*)   salary £25,000 *less* employee's NIC of maximum £2,047 (1995/96);

(*g*)   £22,000 @ 35% × 2/3 with 25% business use of 3,333 miles;

(*h*)   scale charge 1995/96;

(*i*)   20% of £1,080 (clothing *not* exempt as not corporate clothing);

(*j*)   NIC Class 1A £(5,133 + 1,260) × 10.2% = £652.

Relocation packages

The system

6.14   There is an income tax exemption for directors/employees of a maximum of £8,000 of qualifying removal expenses/benefits reasonably incurred/provided in connection with a change in the employee's residence. The expenses/benefits must be incurred/provided before the end of the tax year following that in which the job change takes place or a later time if reasonable.

The change in residence must be made wholly or mainly to allow the employee to reside within a reasonable daily travelling distance of his employment base. Furthermore, the change must result from:

(*a*)   the employee becoming employed by a new employer; or

(*b*)   the duties of an existing employment being changed; or

(*c*)   the place of performance of the duties of an existing employment being changed.

The old residence must not be within a reasonable daily travelling distance of the new work place, but it does not need to be disposed of for the tax exemption to apply. The requirement is to cease to use the old residence as the main residence and instead use the new residence as such.

The exemption deems the expenses/benefits not to be emoluments under Schedule E. They are therefore ignored for all purposes, including the form P11D. Control is largely via a PAYE audit.

The qualifying terms are considered below, taken from *ICTA 1988, 11A Sch* except where otherwise stated.

Selling interest in old home

6.15   This covers legal expenses on disposal; legal expenses on loan redemption; loan redemption penalty; estate agent/auctioneer fees; advertising; public utilities disconnection charges; security, maintenance and insurance costs when unoccupied and rent payable when unoccupied. [*ICTA 1988, 11A Sch 8*].

The interest disposed of by a member of the employee's family or household is included. The Revenue accepts this also covers the interest owned by a co-habitee.

Buying/renting new home

6.16   Legal expenses on acquisition; legal expenses on loan raised; loan procurement fee; survey fee; Land Registration fee; stamp duty; public utilities connection charges.

Again, the interest acquired by a member of the employee's family or household is included. [*ICTA 1988, 11A Sch 9*].

Abortive acquisition

6.17   This is as for buying/renting new home above, provided the interest in the residence fails to be acquired because of circumstances outside the employee's control, or because he reasonably declines to proceed. [*ICTA 1988, 11A Sch 10*].

Removal costs

6.18   Transporting domestic belongings; insurance cover; temporary storage; detaching/attaching/adapting domestic fittings from the old residence to the new residence.

Travel and subsistence

6.19   This covers a wide range of expenditure. Travel and subsistence (i.e. food, drink and temporary living accommodation) of employee and family/household on temporary visits to new area in connection with the residence change; employee's travel to/from old residence and new employment base; costs of temporary living accommodation for the employee (but not family/household); employee's travel to/from old residence and any temporary accommodation; travel of employee and family/household from old residence in connection with the change in residence; subsistence of a child under 19 being a member of employee's family/household, while remaining in living accommodation in the old area for education continuity after the change or in the new area for education continuity before the change; travel of the child between his living accommodation and the employee's new or old residence as appropriate.

Expenses under this head must not be incurred before the start of the tax year of job change. If the move is early in a tax year, this restriction is a problem. [*ICTA 1988, 11A Sch 12*].

Bridging loan expenses [ICTA 1988, s 191B]

6.20   Interest on a bridging loan where a period elapses between incurring expenditure on acquiring residence and receiving the proceeds of sale of the old residence. Loan limit is the market value of the old residence, and no account is taken of that part of the loan used to purchase the new residence or to redeem a loan on the old residence.

If the bridging loan is at a beneficial rate and is provided by the employer, this is excluded from relief under this head. However, if the rest of the relocation package does not exceed £8,000, the balance can be included in this way.

Replacement of goods not suitable for new residence

6.21   This covers the cost of replacement of domestic goods used at the old residence but unsuitable for use at the new residence, *less* any sale proceeds of the goods replaced. [*ICTA 1988, 11A Sch 14*].

Other aspects

6.22 A flat rate allowance may be paid rather than reimbursing specific expenditure, in which case the allowance can be paid gross provided the Inland Revenue is satisfied that it does no more than reimburse eligible costs. The allowance should be included on the form P11D, if not exempt under the specific relief.

The £8,000 limit is unlikely to be reasonable for many UK moves, and is certainly unreasonable for international relocations. Take this example which exceeds the £8,000 limit even where some eligible heads have nil entries:

Relocation package

	£
Expenses on sale (house sold for £100,000)	1,500
Expenses on purchase (house bought for £100,000)	2,000
Abortive acquisition costs	Nil
Removal costs	2,500
Temporary accommodation	3,500
Bridging loan expenses	Nil
Replacement of domestic goods	2,500
	£12,000

PAYE is not applied to the excess of eligible costs over £8,000. Instead the excess over £8,000 is included on the form P11D (see below).

The form P11D

Introduction

6.23 This innocent looking form is the return of expenses payments and benefits. It is an extremely important form, with the maximum penalty for fraudulently or negligently making an incorrect return being £3,000. [*TMA 1970, s 98(2)*]. For 1995/96 the deadline for submission is 6 June 1996. From 1996/97 onwards the form must be submitted by 6 July following the end of the relevant tax year failing which a penalty of up to £300 may arise plus a daily penalty thereafter of up to £60. [*TMA 1970, s 98(1)*].

Dispensations

6.24 Expenses payments and benefits covered by a dispensation given by the Inspector of Taxes do not have to be included on the form P11D. A dispensation can be given under *ICTA 1988, s 166*, and involves the employer explaining the arrangements for paying expenses and providing particular benefits. Provided the Inspector is satisfied that in all circumstances the item concerned would be fully covered by an expenses deduction, so that no income tax charge could arise, a dispensation would normally be granted.

It typically covers reasonable travel and subsistence expenses. With a family company the Inspector of Taxes might well look closely at the arrangements when a dispensation is claimed, and in particular the method of controlling reimbursements to working shareholders.

Completing the form

6.25   The Inland Revenue P11D Guide provides a good deal of information, from which it is clear that the form P11D requires greater care in its completion than a quick glance at the headings on the form might suggest. This is further confirmed by the copious references on the P11D Guide to various chapters of the Inland Revenue Booklet 480 which covers various benefits and expenses. The main problem section of the form P11D is that somewhat shyly headed 'other expenses and benefits'. This is a potential minefield, and basically covers everything which does not clearly come within any of the other items. A full analysis should be provided by the employer, rather than just stating a monetary sum in the box. Furthermore, from 1996/97 employers will have to calculate the cash equivalents of various benefits, such as company cars, beneficial loans, use of assets and living accommodation for entry on the P11D.

Allowable expenses

6.26   When an item appears on a form P11D it does not automatically mean that the employee concerned will suffer income tax on it. Technically what happens is that all items are brought into charge to income tax and some of them can then be covered by an expenses claim. Such a claim can only succeed if broadly the expenditure concerned comes within any one of the following restrictive heads:

(*a*)   travel in the performance of the duties of the employment. [*ICTA 1988, s 198(1)*];

(*b*)   fees and subscriptions to professional bodies or learned societies which are on the Inland Revenue approved list and whose activities are relevant to the employment. [*ICTA 1988, s 201*];

(*c*)   any other item of expenditure which is incurred wholly, exclusively and necessarily in the performance of the duties of the employment. [*ICTA 1988, s 198(1)*].

Transactions between the family company and its shareholders

6.27   Where the family company's business involves the provision of goods or services, and the company provides them to a director (or indeed to any employee) at a discounted price there can be an income tax charge. Where the same arrangement is made for a non-working shareholder there can be a distribution (based on the cash equivalent under Schedule E) made by the company under *ICTA 1988, s 418*.

The income tax charge is based on the cost to the company of providing the goods or service *less* so much as is paid by the director. [*ICTA 1988, s 156(1)* and *(2)*]. For goods this should mean that the director has no tax liability if he pays at least the wholesale price. For services there may be a negligible additional cost of providing them to a specific individual given that further expenditure may not be incurred. Indeed, following the case of *Pepper v Hart [1992] STC 898*, in-house benefits are taxed by reference to the marginal cost only. From an Inland Revenue Press Release dated 21 January 1993, the position can be summarised as follows for a family company and its directors or employees:

(*a*)   goods sold at a discount to a director or employee which results in him paying at least the wholesale price involve no or negligible net benefit;

(*b*)   if the family company is running a private school, teachers paying at least 15% of the normal school fees for their children have no tax charge;

(*c*)   professional services not requiring any additional personnel can be provided free of tax to directors or employees; this covers for example, legal or financial services provided by in-house personnel (any disbursements would involve a tax charge on the user, if he does not pay them);

(*d*)   if an asset is used both for business and private purposes, fixed costs relating thereto are not included in determining the tax charge where the private use is incidental to the business use as they are not *additional* costs (this does not apply to cars or vans where a fixed scale charge applies);

(*e*)   where a mobile telephone is provided for private use the fixed charge on £200 as the cash equivalent does not apply where the cost of private calls is reimbursed by the director or employee, and there is no requirement to also pay a proportion of standing charges.

A working shareholder buying a chargeable asset from the family company at an undervalue would suffer an income tax charge on the undervalue. [*ICTA 1988, s 156(1)* and *(3)*]. The company would have to substitute market value in calculating its chargeable gain on the disposal, and the shareholder would be treated as acquiring the asset at market value, if the transaction is between connected persons. This applies under *TCGA 1992, s 18*, where the shareholder has control of the company or the shareholder and connected persons have control of it. [*TCGA 1992, s 286(6)* and *(7)*].

Uses and strategy

6.28 An employee may view the ownership of shares as a benefit or as an incentive. There are several methods available for an employee to obtain shares in his employer company.

Quite apart from simply giving shares to an employee the employer may wish to make use of one of the share option scheme or profit sharing scheme plans.

If a plan is approved by the Inland Revenue it generally means that the tax consequences for the employee are just the same as for shares held in any other company, whereas under an unapproved scheme the tax charge can be greater because the shares are received by reason of the employment. Typically, under an approved scheme there is a capital gains tax (CGT) charge on sale of the shares. Under an unapproved scheme there is an income tax charge which can sometimes arise before the shares are actually sold.

There are a number of particular factors which must be considered within a family company, however, and these are now discussed.

6.29 The Inland Revenue approved plans are not available to an individual who owns more than a certain percentage of the voting rights, so in practice the plans are limited to small minority holdings of employees.

6.30 The existing shareholders (both working and non-working) may be loath to see a fragmented share ownership with several people owning very small holdings.

6.31 The employee being offered a small number of shares in a family company may not consider them to be of any real value, with future capital growth only being capable of realisation in the event of flotation on the Stock Market or a take-over. The lack of marketability in the meantime could however be partly alleviated by using an employee share ownership plan or by purchase of own shares.

6.32 Further share capital will have to be issued, thereby diluting the value of existing shareholdings, and this may be objected to by non-working shareholders who are less likely than working shareholders

94

to appreciate the overall benefits of allowing certain employees to acquire shares.

Executive share option schemes (ESOS)

6.33 Executive share option schemes were particularly attractive within a family company until the Chancellor of the Exchequer made his announcement on 17 July 1995. IRPR 17 July 1995. Before this date selected executives could be granted an option to purchase shares at a later date, but with the price fixed at the outset and usually being the market value at the date of the grant. The rules allowed any executive who together with his associates owned not more than 25% of the voting rights to be granted an option without incurring a charge to income tax. To claim CGT treatment on selling the shares and with no income tax liability on exercising the option, the options must have been capable of being exercised after three to ten years, but not more frequently than once every three years. [*ICTA 1988, s 185(3)*].

Transitional relief will apply for options granted under approved schemes before 17 July 1995 and for options granted on or after 17 July 1995 provided a written offer or invitation to apply for the options was made before that date and the options were granted within 30 days of that offer or invitation.

It is intended that the provisions for the approval of new executive share option schemes will be withdrawn with effect from Royal Assent to the *Finance Act 1996*.

The tax reliefs for the all-employee approved savings-related share option schemes and/or all-employee approved profit sharing schemes are unaffected by the changes to executive share option schemes.

Tax position

6.34 An income tax charge could also arise if the option price (often nil or just £1) plus the exercise price is less than the market value on the option date. This Schedule E charge is on the deficit and is assessed in the tax year of grant. Taking an option granted for £1 per share with the right to exercise at £5 per share but a market value on grant of £8 per share, an income tax charge arises on £2 per share. If £5 is regarded as 'manifestly less' than £8, the scheme would not in any event be approved. The option price can be at a discount of up to 15% on the market value without an income tax charge arising, but only if an approved SAYE share option or an approved profit-sharing scheme is also in existence. [*ICTA 1988, s 185(6)(A)*].

There is a maximum value of share options which could be held by an individual under approved schemes established by his employer or any associated companies at the time of the grant. This is the greater of

£100,000, or 4 × emoluments taxed under PAYE and excluding benefits, for the year of assessment or for the preceding year if greater. This figure is the limit of unexercised options at any time.

Approved savings related share option scheme

6.35   An approved savings related share option scheme or SAYE scheme as it is more familiarly known is an all-employee share scheme using Save As You Earn contracts issued by a building society or bank. A National Savings model is anticipated.

It involves the employee agreeing to pay a fixed regular monthly amount of between £10 and £250 for five years. The employee can withdraw his savings at any time and for any purpose. Although a SAYE share option scheme is likely to be of limited application to a private company, they can be used as a tax-efficient vehicle for saving. [*ICTA 1988, 9 Sch 24*].

Where the employee withdraws his savings on the fifth anniversary he receives a tax-free bonus equal to 15 monthly contributions. By delaying the withdrawal a further two years he gets a further tax-free bonus equal to 15 monthly contributions. The share options normally cannot be exercised before the chosen bonus date of five years or seven years. The option price can be discounted by 20% of the market price at the date of grant and overall there can be significant tax-free growth to the employee.

Example 8

SAYE share option scheme

Radford saves the maximum £250 per month via a SAYE share option scheme.

At the end of five years he would obtain a capital sum of £18,750 (savings made of £250 × 60 plus bonus £250 × 15) plus interest. At the end of seven years he would get £22,500 (£250 × 60 plus bonus £250 × 30).

The value of the shares remains the same throughout, and the 20% discount is therefore worth £4,687 after five years and £5,625 after seven years.

All employees who have been employed for a qualifying period of no more than five years must be eligible to participate but those with over 25% of the voting rights (with associates) are debarred. For schemes approved from 1 May 1995, part-time employees must be eligible to participate as well, with part-time directors being eligible if the scheme rules allow. [*ICTA 1988, 9 Sch*].

Unapproved share option scheme

6.36   With CGT at the same nominal rate as income tax, the tax advantages of approved share option schemes were not always significant. The added flexibility of an unapproved share option scheme as compared with approved ESOS's was, in fact, often preferred, subject to:

(*a*)   the framework of an approved scheme being felt to be useful;

(*b*)   CGT indexation allowance possibly being valuable for an approved scheme;

(*c*)   CGT being charged on sale of the shares under an approved scheme whereas income tax on an unapproved scheme is on exercising the option which may be at an earlier time.

There are some specific advantages of unapproved share option schemes and there is of course no longer any difference for executive share options granted after 17 July 1995:

(i)   an option can be granted at a lower price than the share price at that time, giving an immediate value to the option rights as a *golden hello* to a new executive or as *golden handcuffs* to a key existing executive; this benefit is not taxed provided the option is not capable of being exercised more than seven years after the grant date;

(ii)   the 100% deduction for overseas employment can apply if the option holder is so entitled at the time of exercise;

(iii)   they can be used for executives owning over 25% voting rights whereas they are debarred from any of the approved schemes.

Profit-sharing scheme

6.37   A profit-sharing scheme is an all-employee scheme. No options are involved — a trust is set up and shares are appropriated to employees each year up to a maximum value of the greater of £3,000 or 10% of earnings up to £80,000 (= £80,000 maximum each year). After five years there is no income tax charge on the profits on sale and CGT applies instead.

Within a family company, a profit-sharing scheme approved by the Inland Revenue can have a useful role to play. In particular it can provide a market in the shares for those with very small holdings, and the issue of shares by the company attracts corporation tax relief. As far as the employees are concerned, they can obtain what is effectively a deferred bonus of up to £8,000 per annum tax-free.

Employee share ownership plan (ESOP)

Overview

6.38   An ESOP can be used as a store to hold the shares which may be transferred to employees via option schemes or profit-sharing schemes. As such, a fixed number of shares can conveniently be allocated to an ESOP without the potential problems of diluting existing shareholdings every time new options are to be granted.

Basic structure

6.39   A company establishes an ESOP trust (sometimes known as an ESOT) which acquires new or existing shares. The acquisition is normally funded by external borrowing. The ESOP holds the shares for a number of years for distribution in due course to employees. The distribution is either direct or via an employee share scheme (although the latter might well in practice have to be of the unapproved variety). The ESOP repays its borrowings out of voluntary contributions made by the company. These contributions are automatically deductible by the company for corporation tax purposes if the following conditions are met to enable the ESOP to be a qualifying ESOP (N.B. there are very few qualifying ESOPs in existence, with the 'case law' version more popular — see 6.41):

(*a*)   all employees benefit on similar terms;

(*b*)   only employees can be beneficiaries of the ESOP trust;

(*c*)   shares are acquired promptly by the ESOP following receipt of funds;

(*d*)   the ESOP distributes shares to employees within seven years of acquisition;

(*e*)   a majority of the ESOP trustees are independent of the company and of any shareholder with a material interest.

However, annual company contributions to a non-qualifying ESOP will normally be tax deductible following the decisions in *Heather v P E Consulting Group Ltd [1972] 48 TC 293*; *Jeffs v Ringtons Ltd [1985] STC 809*; and *Bott (E) Ltd v Price [1987] STC 100*.

Benefits

6.40   The likely advantages of an ESOP within a family company include:

(*a*)   shares can be acquired at a low price for distribution to employees up to seven years later; that is an attractive proposition for flotation or management buy-out expectations;

(*b*)   new capital can be raised cheaply as corporation tax relief is usually claimable on company contributions which are used to repay external borrowings, (the principal as well as the interest);

(*c*)   it can be used as a warehouse for problem shareholdings such as those acquired from an outgoing shareholder;

(*d*)   an internal share market is created for unquoted companies, enabling employees to buy and sell shares;

(*e*)   it can form part of the defence in an unwelcome take-over attempt;

(*f*)   greater distributions to employees can be made than under an approved profit-sharing scheme.

Qualifying or case law

6.41   The 'case law' type of ESOP is likely to be preferred by a family company over a scheme qualifying under *FA 1989, s 67* and *Schedule 5*, in view of the conditions attached to the latter and the greater flexibility if an ESOP is properly constructed so as to obtain the corporation tax deductions under the case law referred to. Furthermore, a qualifying ESOP debars participation by an employee with over 5% of the voting rights (note the tighter restriction here, compared with the 25% holding applying to most types of employee share scheme).

One situation where a qualifying ESOP is attractive is where a shareholder provides the shares to go to an ESOP rather than new shares being issued. The shareholder's chargeable gain on sale to a qualifying ESOP can attract roll-over relief under *TCGA 1992, s 229*, against any chargeable assets purchased by the shareholder and provided certain conditions are met. One condition is that the ESOP holds at least 10% of the ordinary share capital. In fact, a 10% holding may well be just right within a family company.

Phantom share options

6.42   This is simply a plan whereby a cash bonus is paid if the share price increases by a specified amount, or where shares are issued by reference to pre-determined profit targets being met.

Within a family company such a plan is of limited use. Its share price is not going to be an appropriate measure of performance, as there is no market to trade the shares, and a cash bonus scheme linked to profits is more realistic.

Gifting shares

6.43 There may seem little point within a family company to involve share options or other means of deferred share ownership, and instead a simple issuing of shares to selected employees could be made. Income tax charges could arise in a variety of circumstances, however:

(*a*) the first income tax charge is on the issuing of shares to a director or employee as an emolument equivalent to the value of the shares. The case of *Weight v Salmon [1935] 19 TC 174* confirmed the charge under Schedule E of the benefit of shares issued at undervalue. No charge arises on a priority allocation when an offer of shares in the employee's company or group member was made to the public at a fixed price. [*FA 1988, s 68*]. If shares are transferred by an existing shareholder, a Schedule E charge will arise on the employee but the transferor shareholder will be deemed to transfer the shares at market value for capital gains purposes, although it will normally be possible for both parties to make a joint business asset hold-over relief election to avoid this problem (see 12.19–12.22 for further details);

(*b*) a Schedule E charge arises under *ICTA 1988, s 135*, on the gain made on the exercise of a right to acquire shares obtained as a director or employee other than under an approved share scheme;

(*c*) a charge under *ICTA 1988, s 135* can also arise where a right to acquire shares as a director or employee is obtained but the individual omits or undertakes to omit to exercise the right, or grants, or undertakes to grant, to another a right to acquire the shares or any interest therein; and he receives any benefit in money or money's worth in consideration;

(*d*) there can be income tax charge under *FA 1988, s 77* to *s 89*, on the growth in value over seven years or on the gain on an earlier sale, where the shares are acquired in pursuance of a right conferred or opportunity offered by reason of the employment. This essentially only applies where there is something 'special' about the shares concerned so that extra value could be added to them in a variety of specified circumstances or where shares are issued by a dependant subsidiary;

(*e*) if directors, or employees earning at least £8,500 per annum, acquire shares at an undervalue by reason of the employment, there is an income tax charge under *ICTA 1988, s 162(3)*, by treating the undervalue as a notional interest-free loan. The charge generally covers shares being issued at full value (thereby avoiding an automatic Schedule E charge under (*a*) above) but being only partly paid. The notional loan is charged to tax at the official rate (8% from 6 November 1994), but with the normal exemption of £5,000 of beneficial loans applying. [*ICTA 1988, s 161(1)* — see 6.9 for full details]. Also available is the normal exemption where the interest otherwise payable would be tax deductible. In the context of a family company, this exemption would apply where the shares are acquired at undervalue in a close trading company in which the person concerned either works for the greater part of his time in the actual management or conduct of the company (this of course is likely to be the case); or owns over 5% of the ordinary shares. [*ICTA 1988, s 360*];

Example 9

Shares issued by reason of employment

Ramsay, a director of Reeves Limited, has shares in the company worth £10 each issued to him for £1 each. He would be assessable under Schedule E on £9 per share.

If instead the shares were issued for the market price of £10 each but with a part call of £6 per share, he would be charged to income tax on a notional loan of £4 per share unless either owning over 5% of the ordinary shares or working for Reeves Limited for the greater part of his time in its management or conduct.

(*f*) another potential income tax charge arises where the company indemnifies a director or employee against a financial loss under stop-loss arrangements. A notional loan is then made for the purposes of the *ICTA 1988, s 162* charge (under *subsection 6*), of the excess of the proceeds of disposal over the market value. Again, the exemptions discussed in (*e*) above can apply.

Limitations on employee shareholdings

6.44   Investor protection committees endeavour to prevent dilution of shareholder's equity by publishing various guidelines. An unquoted company could ignore the guidelines. They do, however, provide a useful starting point for non-working shareholders' involvement in developing a strategy, albeit that an unquoted company would probably wish to have greater flexibility.

In general terms, limiting the issued share capital for all employee share schemes to a maximum of 10% is a sensible and simple strategy.

PLANNING CHECKLIST — BENEFITS AND EXPENSES

company
- Meet all expenses with a business element.
- Consider corporation tax deductibility.
- Do not provide unnecessary goods for private use of directors.
- Structure expenses and benefits so as to avoid payment of NIC.

working shareholders
- Maximise claim for income tax relief on business element.
- Arrange for company to meet all expenses and benefits which have a business element.

other employees
- Look to fringe benefits as an incentive, where income tax liability is less than the real value.

non-working shareholders
- Attempt to achieve a balance between commercial acceptability and tax advantages to the recipient of benefits.

company
- Consider limiting shares to 10% of ordinary share capital.
- Use an employee share option trust as a warehouse.

working shareholders
- Consider selling some shares to an employee share ownership trust.

other employees
- Look upon a share option scheme as a possible means of obtaining a lump sum on flotation or take-over, as a bonus which may or may not occur.

non-working shareholders
- Balance the advantages of an incentive device to employees with the dilution of shareholders' funds.

Chapter 7

The Company Car and Other Company Vehicles

The basic position

7.1   As from the tax year 1994/95, the measure of a taxable benefit of having a company car for private use was changed. Now, the taxable benefit is 35% of the list price (including extras) when first registered, subject to a capped list price of £80,000. This taxable benefit is reduced by one-third where annual business mileage is between 2,500 and 17,999 in the tax year concerned, and by a further one-third where the annual business mileage is at least 18,000.

There is also a reduction in the car benefit of one-third where the car is at least four years old at the end of the tax year. So for 1995/96, if the car is at least four years old at 5 April 1996 there is a reduction in the taxable benefit. If the car is over 15 years old and has a market value of over £15,000 (the value being taken at the end of the tax year concerned), then the market value is taken if that is greater than the original list price.

The list price is the sum of the following:

(*a*)   published price when first registered;

(*b*)   VAT (plus any other tax which may be charged on a car);

(*c*)   delivery charge;

(*d*)   the published price of optional extras provided at any time, unless these are less than £100 in total in which case they can be ignored.

Where a replacement accessory is provided, its list price is included in calculating the taxable benefit.

Car fuel

7.2   If fuel is provided for private use, there is a further charge to income tax on the following amounts for 1995/96:

engine size	petrol £	diesel £
to 1,400cc	670	605
1,401 to 2,000cc	850	605
over 2,000cc	1,260	780

The above taxable benefit for private fuel is not altered by reference to any particular level of business mileage.

How to reduce the tax charge on a company car

Car not always used

7.3   The taxable charge for the use of the car and for private fuel are reduced, on a time basis, when the car is incapable of being used at all for at least 30 consecutive days or it is not actually provided throughout the year of assessment. The employee could hand in his keys when he does not need the car for a period, and the company should prepare a memo stating the non-availability of the car until the keys are returned to him. Provided this period is of at least 30 consecutive days, there would be a pro-rata reduction in the tax charge. [*ICTA 1988, Sch 6(9)*].

The perk car

7.4   Where the business use is what is called 'insubstantial' which covers under 2,500 business miles in the tax year concerned, the basic tax charge is on 35% of the list price when first registered. If however the employee is taxed on more than one company car, it is only the car with the greatest business use which is taxed by reference to the business mileage band, and the fixed 35% charge would automatically apply to the other(s). [*ICTA 1988, Sch 6(4)*].

When to purchase

7.5   From the employee's tax viewpoint only, the company should consider buying a car to be registered just before the end of the tax year, so as to reduce the waiting period before the one-third reduction for the car being at least four years old comes into play. Taking an example of a car bought and registered on 1 April 1996, the fourth birthday falls in the tax year 1999/2000 and the reduction of one-third therefore applies from 6 April 1999 which is only just over three years after the car was purchased.

Employee contributing to the cost of the car or accessories

7.6   It could well be that a family company will have a policy on company cars which allows a group of employees to have the use of a car up to an allotted price level. If an employee then wishes to have a more expensive car, the family company may be happy to arrange this provided the employee meets the difference out of his own pocket. If this happens, there can be a reduction in the tax charge on the employee as where he contributes to the cost of the car or accessories when the car is first made available to him. The contribution up to a fixed level of £5,000 reduces the list price which of course determines the taxable benefit. This reduction applies to cars even made first available before the new system came in on 6 April 1994. [*ICTA 1988, Sch 6(7)*].

This may be regarded as giving a fair reflection of the capital contribution made by the employee, but of course he is only getting the benefit each year by reference to 35% of the capital sum contributed (or indeed less than 35% if it has the one-third reduction for business mileage of over 2,500 miles). The reduction in the taxable benefit will apply for every year he uses that particular company car for private purposes, but overall it may be better to arrange for the sum the employee is to contribute to be paid over a period rather than as a lump-sum, and then it could be expressed as a condition of the car being made available to him for his private use. In that way, the legislation allows the annual contribution to be deducted from the actual taxable benefit.

Taking a lower-rated car

7.7   Looking at the other extreme, an employee could choose to take a car below the price range allotted to him by the family company. In that case, the family company could make a payment of the difference to a pension plan for the employee's benefit. This is tax-neutral where the payment is structured as an additional voluntary contribution, with the payment being charged to tax on the employee but then covered by deduction of the same amount (subject to the overall limit for additional voluntary contributions which is 15% of the earnings).

Car for spouse

7.8   The taxable benefit arises even where the car is basically used not by the employee but by a member of his family or household. If this was not the case it would of course be easy to avoid the tax charge. It is possible nevertheless for the employee's spouse to be provided with a car with, in certain circumstances, no tax charge arising. This applies if the employee's spouse is separately employed by the company, as an employment where it is not unreasonable for her/him to be provided with a company car, and furthermore other employees in the same category also get a company car. The Inland Revenue extra-statutory concession A71 gives the full guidance. Naturally, if the spouse is earning at least £8,500 per annum including expenses, he/she would be taxed on the company car in his/her own right.

The car pool

7.9   Instead of having the exclusive use of a car, the employee could be entitled to use a car which forms part of a car pool. If this is the case there can be no charge to income tax in his hands, but for a car to form part of a car pool there are several conditions which have to be met. Firstly, the car must actually be used by more than one employee and not ordinarily be used by any one of them to the exclusion of the others. Secondly, any private use must be merely incidental to business use, and finally must not normally be kept overnight at or near the residence of the director or employee unless that person happens to live in the vicinity or premises occupied by the employer and where the car is garaged. [*ICTA 1988, s 159(2)*].

The Inland Revenue booklet 480 (1994) gives some useful explanations. In paragraph 15.4 it says that private use being 'merely incidental' to business use, which is one of the requirements for a car to be treated as part of a car pool, imposes a quality of test rather than a quantity of test. A given example is where an employee who is required to undertake a long business journey is allowed to take a pool car home the previous night in readiness for an early morning start. The journey from office to home is of course normally private use, but in this particular context it is subordinate to the lengthy business trip the following day and is undertaken to further the business trip. The Inland Revenue say in that case it would be regarded as merely incidental to the business use, unless it happened too often. They also give information in paragraph 15.5 by accepting that a car is treated as not normally kept overnight at or near the homes of employees if the number of occasions on which it is taken home by employees does not amount to more than 60% of the year. Where a car is garaged at employees' homes on a large number of occasions, but within the 60% limit, the Revenue suggest that the private use from home to work would *not* be merely incidental to business use. These are stringent conditions, and room for manoeuvre is limited. However, a prestige car kept at the forecourt of the company's premises could fit the bill and help promote the company's image.

Information given to the Inland Revenue

7.10   Employers have to complete a form P46 (car) each quarter at 5 July, 5 October, 5 January and 5 April giving details of changes in company cars. A list of employees has to be given showing those:

(*a*)   first provided with a car;

(*b*)   provided with a change of car;

(*c*)   provided with an additional car;

(*d*)   already provided with a car who start to earn £8,500 or more, or become a director;

(*e*)   no longer provided with a car.

For each car concerned, details have to be given of:

(i)   car make and model;

(ii)   engine size;

(iii)   petrol or diesel;

(iv)   list price of car and accessories;

(v)   capital contribution by employee;

(vi)   expected business mileage band.

Company car v own car

7.11   The best way to calculate whether or not a company car (plus fuel) is worthwhile for any tax year is to ascertain the cost per private mile in terms of the tax charge, and then compare that with the actual cost. Sometimes it is easy to see whether the employee is on to a winner by having a company car, but in other cases it will be necessary to study the AA or RAC tables of car costs.

Here are a few examples:

			Tax per private mile	
			miles	tax
(*a*)	list price	£10,000		
(*b*)	35% × 2/3 × £10,000	£2,333	2,000	37.55p
(*c*)	engine size	1,400cc	5,000	15.02p
(*d*)	petrol charge	£670	8,000	9.39p
(*e*)	add (*b*) and (*d*)	£3,003	10,000	7.51p
(*f*)	tax @ 25% on (*e*)	£751	12,000	6.26p

			Tax per private mile	
			miles	tax
(*a*)	list price	£20,000		
(*b*)	35% × 2/3 × £20,000	£4,667	2,000	118.55p
(*c*)	engine size	2,500cc	5,000	47.42p
(*d*)	petrol charge	£1,260	8,000	29.64p
(*e*)	add (*b*) and (*d*)	£5,927	10,000	23.71p
(*f*)	tax @ 40% on (*e*)	£2,371	12,000	19.76p

Looking at the above examples, it seems that 5,000 annual private miles is close to the magic minimum number for the company car to be a valuable benefit to the user (e.g. in the second example, the actual cost per private mile for a 2,500cc car costing £20,000 should be around 50p for 5,000 private miles). That may well be the mileage level for a number of cars although there is no substitute for working out the figures on an individual basis. In broad terms, given a band of annual business mileage, the minimum number of annual private miles for the company car to be worthwhile can be stated as under:

Annual business mileage	*Minimum required annual private mileage*
to 2,499	7,000
2,500 to 17,999	5,000
18,000 +	3,000

The company's position

The NIC charge

7.12 There is an extra burden on a company when it provides a car for private use by an employee. This is the Class 1A national insurance contribution at a flat rate of 10.2%, levied on the same amount as is taxable on the employees for income tax purposes for the private use of a car and for private fuel.

This Class 1A NIC is a substantial cost factor within a family company. It is based on the assumption that business mileage is less than 2,500 miles p.a. Records must be kept to substantiate higher business mileage, and proper procedures should be in place. This could be in the shape of a form completed by the employee to cover each business journey in the month concerned, with the mileage record excluding travel from home to business base and vice versa. The Contributions Agency has stated that in practice they will only require mileage evidence for those employees who normally cover close to the 2,500 miles borderline. For business mileage of at least 18,000 miles, sufficient information has to be kept to show that. Where business mileage is between 2,500 and 17,999 miles for the tax year, the records only need to show that business mileage did exceed 2,499 miles.

No NIC liability applies where:

(*a*) the employee earns less than £8,500 p.a.; or

(*b*) the car is not available for private use; or

(*c*) the employee fully reimburses the cost of private motoring.

Leasing v purchasing

7.13 The income tax charge on the employee is unaffected by the method the employer uses to provide the car. The VAT position is such, however, that for cars leased from 1 August 1995 the leasing charges will be less than before due to the ability of the leasing company to recover the VAT suffered when it purchased the car. The reduction might well make car leasing more attractive to a family company.

The employer can claim capital allowances when a car is acquired via:

• outright purchase;

• loan;

• hire purchase.

For expenditure incurred after 10 March 1992, the maximum 25% writing-down allowance per car is £3,000 per annum. This equates to a car costing £12,000. Where a car costs more than £12,000, the full cost will eventually attract tax relief but it will take longer with an allowance of only £3,000 per annum.

For leased cars, tax relief as revenue expenditure is claimable on the leasing costs when a car is acquired via:

• contract hire;

• finance leasing.

For finance leasing, the tax deductibility of rental payments follows IRSP 3/91 for leases effected after 11 April 1991. Where SSAP21 is applied for accounting purposes part of the capital repayment element is allowable as revenue expenditure to the extent of the properly computed depreciation charge to the profit and loss account. The finance charge is also deductible. This normally means that no adjustment is necessary for corporation tax purposes in respect of post-11 April 1991 leases, relief being given for the depreciation and finance charge. See *Gallagher v Jones (1993), Threlfall v Jones [1994] STC 537.*

The tax deductible leasing costs on contract hire and finance leasing are restricted where the retail price when new is over £12,000 for leases dated after 10 March 1992. The deductible costs are calculated using the fraction:

$$\frac{£12,000 + (50\% \text{ of: retail price} - £12,000)}{\text{retail price}}$$

[*CAA 1990, s 35(2)*].

It has been known for the Inland Revenue to accept the discounted price paid by the lessor for the car as a substitute for the list price in applying the fraction.

109

Example 1

Allowable hire costs

Morley Limited contract hire a car from 1 October 1995 with a retail price when new of £20,000. The annual lease cost is £7,000.

deductible lease cost:

$$£7,000 \times \frac{£12,000 + (50\% \text{ of: } £20,000 - £12,000)}{£20,000}$$

$$= £7,000 \times \frac{£12,000 + £4,000}{£20,000}$$

$$= £5,600$$

(tax relief on £1,400 p.a. is lost for ever)

The disallowable lease charges can be considerable:

retail price when new		disallowed
to	£12,000	NIL
	£16,000	1/8
	£18,000	1/6
	£20,000	1/5
	£24,000	1/4
	£30,000	3/10
	£36,000	1/3

For contract hire under a with maintenance contract, it should be arranged for the maintenance element to be the subject of a separate contract. In that way the cost of the maintenance element is segregated and fully tax deductible, whereas ordinarily it would be subject to the normal restriction as being part of the hire cost for the car.

Choice of company car or salary

7.14   Some employers offer an increase in salary for those employees who decide not to accept a company car for private use. If the salary increase is the same amount as the scale charge which would have arisen if they had taken a company car, the decision is tax-neutral. If the salary alternative is greater than the scale charge, there could be a Schedule E tax charge problem based on the decision in *Heaton v Bell [1969] 46 TC 211*. However, *ICTA 1988, s 157A* removes this problem from 1995/96 and prior to then the Revenue often did not take the point.

For VAT purposes there is no VAT charge on the employer where there is a reduction in an employee's salary in return for the provision of a company car. This follows the Tribunal decision in *Co-operative Insurance Society Ltd [1992] VATTR 44 (SI 1992 No 630)*. VAT is however chargeable where the employee makes a payment for the private use of a company car. However no VAT is payable where the company has reclaimed 50% of the VAT on the cost/lease charge of the car after 1 August 1995.

The alternatives to the company car

7.15   We have seen that for the nominal business user (i.e. business mileage 2,500 to 17,999) where annual private use is less than 5,000 miles the income tax charge is excessive. The alternative is for the employee to purchase a car, and one arrangement involves an interest-free loan to the employee to fund the purchase. The company then does not have to suffer any depreciation on the car, and could consider waiving part of the loan each year of an amount equal to the capital allowances claimable by the employee. The company then still meets all running costs, with the employee being taxed on the following where the cheap loan does not exceed £5,000 (if it did, there would be a tax charge on the interest foregone. [*ICTA 1988, s 161(1)(a)*].

private use running costs

+

loan waiver

−

business use capital allowances

=

tax charge on private use

In the right circumstances, an alternative arrangement could be for an employee to purchase a company owned car at market value after the company has suffered the heavy first year's depreciation.

Where the employee does own the car, a mileage allowance could be paid by the company for business use. This could be paid tax-free if it is under the Fixed Profit Car Scheme (FPCS) where the allowance must not exceed the amounts shown below for 1995/96:

engine size	to 4,000 miles	over 4,000 miles
to 1,000cc	27p	15p
1,001–1,500cc	34p	19p
1,501–2,000cc	43p	23p
over 2,000cc	60p	32p
'any car'	39p	21p

Where the same rate of mileage allowable is paid irrespective of the engine size, the average of the two middle bands is used (= 'any car' in above table).

Any excess allowable under the FPCS is taxable via the PAYE system and this simplifies matters all round. At the end of the tax year the employee can still make a *ICTA 1988, s 198* claim to ascertain the correct position if he or she so wishes.

The FPCS rates include a proportion of standing costs (depreciation, insurance, road tax) and all business use running costs (fuel, servicing, repairs). They do not include interest on a loan used to purchase a car. This qualifies for tax relief on the business use proportion and is claimable separately by the employee for up to three years.

The company could pay a fixed car allowance. This is subject to tax under PAYE (and NIC as well), with the employee claiming the business use element as allowable expenditure, such a claim usually permitting an estimated expense figure to be included in the employee's Notice of Coding.

The company van

7.16   Instead of having a car provided by his employer for private use, an employee may be given the use of a van.

From the tax year 1993/94, where a van is made available for the private use of an employee (or member of his family or household) there is a fixed tax charge on deemed income of £500. This is reduced to £350 where the van is at least four years old at the end of the tax year.

There is no extra tax charge on private fuel — the £500 or £350 scale charge applies in any event.

Unavailability of the van creates a pro-rata reduction in the tax charge as for cars, and a contribution to the private use of the van (as a condition of it being made available for private use) also reduces the tax charge as for cars.

112

Where a van is made available for the private use of more than one employee (called a *shared van*), either on the same day or on different days, a reduction in the tax charge can arise. The revised tax charge, if less than the normal amount, is calculated by adding together the charge for all shared vans of the employer and dividing that equally between the total number of employees using a shared van privately, irrespective of the comparative private uses of each employee. Where a van is made available to a single employee for over 30 days, it cannot be a shared van.

Example 2

Taxable benefits for a company van

Swan Limited own 12 company vans, used privately in varying degrees by 24 employees.

		£
New vans 1, 2, 3, 4, 5, 6	= 6 × £500	= 3,000
New van 7 used by a single employee for two months	= £500× 10/12 =	417
Vans 8, 9, 10, 11 registered in 1989	= 4 × £350	= 1,400
Van 12 registered in 1988 off the road for crash repairs for two months	= £350 × 10/12 =	292
		£5,109

$$\text{Benefit per employee} = \frac{£5,109}{24} = \frac{£213}{}$$

The employee exclusively using van 7 for two months would be charged to tax on £500 × 2/12 = £83. If he also had use of a shared van in the same tax year he would have an additional tax charge on £213, but no individual can be taxed on more than £500 or £350 per tax year.

An alternative tax charge on shared vans is available on a claim being made by an employee. This gives a tax charge on £5 per day of private use of a shared van, and is beneficial for limited private use. Sharing a van for part of a day is treated as sharing for a day. A typical situation for this shared van tax charge is where a group of employees work on a building site. The foreman keeps the van at home, collects the employees on the way to the site, and for the rest of the day the van is used to collect goods. The return journey in the van is to the employees' homes and then to the foreman's home. With, say, the foreman plus four other

113

workers this potentially gives a tax charge which could be regarded as excessive to the latter. Depending on the number of days where this arrangement exists, the alternative tax charge on £5 per day could be appropriate.

Claims for exemption as a van pool can be made, as for a car pool. A van is defined as a mechanically propelled road vehicle (other than a motor cycle) of a construction primarily suited for the conveyance of goods or burden, with a design weight of not more than 3,500 kilograms.

Within a family company there could be some personnel who are happy to have a company van for private purposes, with the disadvantages perhaps being more than matched by the significant reduction in the income tax charge.

PLANNING CHECKLIST — THE COMPANY CAR
company • If it is tax efficient for the car user, the company should be happy. • Purchase of a fast-depreciating car is unattractive. • Finance lease or contract hire can assist.
working shareholders • Generally, over 5,000 private miles per annum means go for the company car. • Choose a car which is good value, thereby getting the best out of the tax structure and not imposing a strain on the company.
other employees • Go for the company car unless private use is below 5,000 miles per annum.

Chapter 8

Dividend Strategies

Introduction

8.1   Family companies may need to pay dividends for a number of reasons. Where the company is subject to the small companies' tax rate, dividends may prove to be a tax efficient way of extracting profits for the working shareholders, as illustrated in 2.7 and 2.8. Dividends may also need to be paid to those shareholders who have invested in the company to provide a regular income. Where the company was acquired by means of a buy-out, venture capitalists may hold a significant part of the equity investment, often a preferential class of shares, upon which a dividend must be paid.

On the other hand, certain shareholders may have invested for capital growth and do not require dividends. In practice, any conflicting requirements of the shareholders can often be satisfied by the use of separate classes of shares, with different rights as to dividends, votes and return of capital.

Available profits

8.2   A company cannot legally pay a dividend unless it has sufficient distributable profits to cover the dividend. [*CA 1985, s 263*]. For these purposes, distributable profits represent the company's accumulated realised profits less its accumulated realised losses. It is not therefore necessary for a company to make a profit for the year in which the dividend is paid, but there has to be sufficient retained profits from prior years to cover it. Profits must be realised and it is not therefore possible to pay a dividend from an unrealised profit, such as a revaluation surplus. A dividend can either be paid in cash or *in specie*. An '*in specie*' dividend involves the transfer of an asset to the shareholder, which may involve a 'market value' disposal by the company for capital gains purposes.

If a company's dividend exceeds its distributable reserves, this will be an illegal distribution and the company can require the recipient to repay it.

Dividend taxation

8.3 Fundamental changes were made to the taxation of dividends in the *Finance Act 1993*. In calculating a shareholder's tax liability, the dividend income is treated as forming the top slice of income. Shareholders who receive other income will have the full amount of the lower rate band of 20% available to offset against this income.

8.4 The tax treatment of the dividend in the hands of the shareholder will depend on his tax position and is summarised below:

(*a*) shareholders who do not pay tax, e.g. a spouse who has no other income, gains or company pension funds etc. will be able to obtain a repayment of the tax credit of 20%;

(*b*) shareholders whose marginal rate of tax is 20% will be treated as having satisfied their liability in full and no further tax will be due;

(*c*) basic rate shareholders will have no further tax to pay. This is because the 20% tax credit underlying their dividend income will cover their lower rate tax liability on their dividend income;

(*d*) shareholders who pay tax at the higher rate (which would apply to many controlling shareholders) will be subject to higher rate tax of 40% on their dividend income. The higher rate liability on the dividend income will be reduced by the 20% tax credit. The Inland Revenue will therefore collect additional higher rate tax of 20% (see 2.14 for date of payment).

Example 1

Taxation of dividends

The shares in Goalies Limited are owned equally by Miss G Banks, Miss Shilton and Miss Woods. A cash dividend of £8,160 was paid in May 1995. The treatment of the dividend in the hands of the shareholder is set out below:

	£	Miss Banks £	Miss Shilton £	Miss Woods £
Salary		–	15,000	30,000
Dividend:				
Cash	2,720			
Tax credit (20/80)	680			
Gross		3,400	3,400	3,400
		3,400	18,400	33,400
Less Personal allowance		(3,525)	(3,525)	(3,525)
Taxable income		Nil	14,875	29,875

	£	Miss Banks £	Miss Shilton £	Miss Woods £
Tax liability				
Miss Banks		Nil		
Miss Shilton				
First	3,200 at 20%		640	
Next	8,275 at 25%		2,069	
Salary	11,475		2,709	
Dividend	3,400 at 20%		680	
	14,875			
Miss Banks				
First	3,200 at 20%			640
Next	21,100 at 25%			5,275
Next	2,175 at 40%			870
Salary	26,475			6,785
Dividend	3,400 at 40%			1,360
	29,875			
Total liability		Nil	3,389	8,145
Taxed under PAYE		–	(2,709)	(6,785)
Tax credit on dividend		(680)	(680)	(680)
Tax credit repaid		(680)		
Higher rate assessment on dividend			Nil	680*

* Proof £3,400 × (40% − 20%) = £680

Advance corporation tax

8.5   A company must account for advance corporation tax under the CT61 procedure whenever it pays a dividend, or makes any other form of distribution. A distribution may arise, for example, where assets are distributed by the company for less than full consideration or where a non-working shareholder obtains a benefit or has personal expenses paid by the company.

8.6   Advance corporation tax represents an advance payment on account of the company's corporation tax liability. When a dividend/distribution is made, the company must account for ACT to the Collector of Taxes within 14 days of the end of the CT61 return quarter/period in which the dividend is paid. The return quarters end on the last day of March, June, September and December. If the company's year end does not fall at a quarter end, there will be a short CT61 period up to the year end with any ACT falling due within 14 days. The balance of the company's corporation tax will be paid within 9 months

117

after the end of its accounting period. This has important implications for the timing of the dividend payments (see below).

8.7   After 6 April 1994, the rate of ACT is 20/80ths, which mirrors the tax credit carried with the dividend. The tax credit is used to discharge the shareholder's tax liability at 20% (see 8.4). (A transitional ACT rate of 22.5/77.5 applied in 1993/94, although the tax credit was still 20%.)

8.8   As indicated above, a company can offset ACT arising on dividends paid in the accounting period against its corporation tax liability for that period. However, the ACT which a company can offset against its corporation tax liability is restricted. [*ICTA 1988, s 239(1)(2)*].

Period	Maximum offset
6 April 1988 to 31 March 1993	25% × profits
1 April 1993 to 31 March 1994	22.5% × profits
1 April 1994 to 31 March 1995	20% × profits

If the company does not prepare its accounts to 31 March, the maximum offset is computed by time-apportioning the profits and then calculating the restriction for each financial year. Where the ACT offset is restricted, the balance which cannot be offset against the company's current liability is known as surplus ACT. Surplus ACT can be basically recovered by a company in three ways, which are explained in 8.9–8.11 below.

Example 2

Calculation of maximum ACT offset

Hurst Ltd paid a dividend of £360,000 in May 1994, upon which it paid ACT of £90,000. The company's taxable profits for the year ended 31 December 1995 were agreed at £200,000.

Hurst Ltd will therefore have surplus ACT of £48,750 arising in the year, calculated as follows:

	£	£
ACT arising in the year		90,000
Maximum offset:		
FY 1993 – 3/12 × £200,000 × 22.5%	11,250	
FY 1994 – 9/12 × £200,000 × 20%	30,000	
		(41,250)
Surplus ACT		48,750

Obtaining relief for surplus ACT

Carry back

8.9   As a general rule, companies should seek to recover any surplus ACT first by carrying the ACT back against its tax liabilities for accounting periods beginning in the preceding 6 years. The ACT is carried back against the later years first and the ACT offset is again subject to the relevant maximum restriction for each period. [*ICTA 1988, s 239(3)*]. The carry back of ACT will generate a repayment of tax for the earlier periods. Repayment interest on the surplus ACT is calculated from the 9-month due date of the period in which the surplus ACT arose, and not the earlier year(s) in which the ACT is offset. Where ACT is carried back against a pre-pay and file period, the '21-month' waiting period will invariably mean that no repayment supplement arises.

Surrender of ACT

8.10   If the company has 51% subsidiaries, it can also surrender its ACT to those subsidiaries. [*ICTA 1988, s 240*]. There is complete flexibility in the amount of ACT which may be surrendered. If the subsidiary cannot offset the surrendered ACT against its current year liability, it can be carried forward to be set against future tax liabilities (so long as the company remains a subsidiary).

Surrendered ACT can never be carried back by the subsidiary. If a subsidiary company does need to recover ACT from previous year's tax liabilities, it could pay a dividend (outside the group income election if one is in force) to create its own ACT which could then be carried back. (The tax credit comprised in the franked investment income will reduce the parent company's ACT liability.)

Carry forward

8.11   Surplus ACT can also be carried forward by the company for offset against its future tax liabilities. [*ICTA 1988, s 239(4)*]. This is generally considered as a relief of last resort as there will be an interest cost on the ACT paid until it is effectively recovered from the Inland Revenue by offset in a later accounting period.

Anti-avoidance rules

8.12   There are a number of anti-avoidance provisions which can restrict the ability to carry back or carry forward ACT. These provisions will apply where the company has been taken over and within a period of 3 years *either side* of the take-over, there is a major change in the nature or conduct of the company's trade or business. If the Revenue successfully apply these provisions, then any surplus ACT arising after a take-over cannot be carried back against any pre-acquisition tax liabilities. Similarly, any surplus ACT brought forward at the date of a take-over would be lost. [*ICTA 1988, s 245*].

Timing payments of dividends

8.13   For corporation tax purposes, dividends are treated as paid on the date when they become due and payable. [*ICTA 1988, s 834(1)*]. A final dividend is due and payable on the date it is declared and approved by shareholders at the annual general meeting, unless the resolution declaring it specifies some later date. The payment of an interim dividend could be rescinded by the directors at any time until it is actually paid out to the shareholders. Consequently, an interim dividend only becomes due when it is paid. (See *Hurll v IRC (1922) 8 TC 292* and *Potel v IRC (1970) 46 TC 658*).

8.14   The directors of the family company will normally have complete flexibility as to the timing and amount of dividend payments (assuming the company's Articles of Association follow article 70 in Table A or similar). The director-shareholders should therefore try to regulate the timing of dividends to ensure they make best use of their personal allowances, basic rate bands and other reliefs. For example, it would not be efficient to pay substantial dividends in one tax year, if the director-shareholders have little or no other income in an earlier and/or later year.

It is not possible to 'backdate' a dividend — any backdated dividend (if recognised at all) will be treated as being made on the actual date of payment for tax purposes.

8.15   As far as the company's cash flow is concerned, it will normally be beneficial for the company to pay the dividend just before its year end so the ACT relates to the year. This ensures that the ACT can be recovered against the company's tax liability in about nine months. If a dividend is paid as early as possible within a CT61 quarter/period, this will maximise the credit period between the dividend and the payment of ACT.

Dividend waivers

8.16   Dividend waivers are often used for planning purposes. Broadly, a dividend waiver involves a shareholder waiving his or her entitlement to the dividend before the right to the dividend has accrued. A dividend waiver can therefore be seen as a method of reducing the income the shareholder receives from the company.

A dividend waiver will be effective for income tax purposes (and for inheritance tax purposes (*IHTA 1984, s 15*)) if it is made before the right to the dividend has accrued. An interim dividend will not be counted as the shareholder's income provided the deed is executed before the relevant board resolution is passed. Similarly, a waiver of a final dividend must be made before the specified date of payment — in practice, it is normal to execute the deed before the company's annual general meeting (as a final dividend requires the shareholders' approval). A dividend waiver does not have to be made under seal.

8.17   A dividend waiver could also be used to divert income to one or more of the other shareholders. The Inland Revenue may challenge such dividend waivers on the basis that the waiver constitutes a 'settlement' for income tax purposes. *ICTA 1988, s 660G* defines a settlement as including 'any disposition, trust, covenant, agreement or arrangement' — this wide definition would clearly catch a dividend waiver.

Any income arising from a settlement will be deemed to be that of the settlor unless he or his spouse has no interest in the settled property. [*ICTA 1988, s 660A*]. Income paid to the unmarried child of the settlor is deemed to be the settlors, *ICTA 1988, s 660B*, and he will accordingly be assessed under Schedule D Case VI.

Case law demonstrates that an element of 'bounty' is necessary for the settlement provisions to apply (see, for example, *Bulmer v CIR (1966) 44 TC 1, CIR v Plummer (1979) STC 793*). The Inland Revenue's view appears to be that 'bounty' is present where a dividend waiver enables one or more of the shareholders to (legally) receive a larger dividend than would have been possible had no dividend waiver taken place.

It should therefore be possible to resist an Inland Revenue attack under the 'settlement' provisions if it can be demonstrated that the dividend declared per share multiplied by the number of shares in issue does not exceed the amount of the company's distributable reserves. The Inland Revenue would argue that 'bounty' had occurred where the dividend declared could not be satisfied out of the distributable profits unless a waiver was made — the waiver would enable the other shareholder to receive a greater dividend than would otherwise have been possible. Under the settlement legislation, this element would be deemed to be the income of the shareholder executing the waiver (i.e. the settlor) and therefore taxed in his or her hands.

Example 3

Effect of dividend waiver

Callaghan Ltd has an issued share capital of 100 £1 ordinary shares owned as to 20% by Mr Callaghan and 80% by The Callaghan Children's Trust.

8.18   Dividend Strategies

At 31 March 1995, it has distributable profits of £100,000.

If a dividend of £1,000 per share is declared and Mr Callaghan waives his entitlement before the right to the dividend accrues, there is no 'bounty'.

On the other hand, if the company declares a dividend of £1,250 per share in the knowledge that Mr Callaghan is going to waive his dividend, the Revenue would argue that 'bounty' had occurred and under the settlement provisions, Mr Callaghan would be taxed on the 'dividend' diverted.

The relevant figures are summarised below:

Dividend declared	*£1,000 per share*		*£1,250 per share*	
	£	£	£	£
Distributable profits		100,000		100,000
Less Dividend declared	100,000		125,000	
Amount waived (20%)	(20,000)		(25,000)	
Dividend paid		(80,000)		(100,000)
Retained profits		20,000		–

8.18   In practice, the Inland Revenue are only likely to take the 'settlement' point where the dividend waiver is considered to create a tax advantage. A dividend waiver diverting income from one 40% taxpayer to another would not be challenged, unless there were other circumstances involved. However, the Inland Revenue often attack dividend waivers which have been used to increase the dividends paid to the proprietor's spouse or children or the trustees of an accumulation and maintenance trust for his children.

8.19   If the company is a Close Investment Holding Company ('CIHC') (see 4.19–4.22), the Inland Revenue have a further weapon in *ICTA 1988, s 231(3A)* which enables the Inspector to deny a repayment of tax credits on dividends where, amongst other things, a dividend waiver has been made.

8.20   Outright gifts of income producing assets between husband and wife are protected from the settlement rules, unless:

(*a*)   the gift does not carry a right to the whole of that income; or

(*b*)   the property given is wholly or substantially a right to income. [*ICTA 1988, s 660A(6)*].

8.21   In relation to 'husband and wife' companies, the Inland Revenue have recently tried to use *ICTA 1988, s 660A* to nullify a dividend waiver by (say) a husband to his wife (the advantage being to provide the wife with dividend income against which her personal allowance and lower basic rate band could be used). If the Revenue succeeded (and much would depend upon the precise circumstances of each case), the dividend waiver would not be effective as it would still be deemed to be the income of the husband.

The Inland Revenue have also argued that the allotment of shares to a shareholder's wife may be regarded as an 'arrangement' so that the settlement provisions may apply. If the shares allotted to the wife are non-voting shares (e.g. preference shares), the Revenue would contend that the shares given are 'wholly or substantially a right to income', so that the protection previously in *ICTA 1988, s 660A(6)* (see above) is not available. However, in *Pearce v Young* (HMIT); *Scrutton v Young* (HMIT) (SC3113/94; SC 3114/94) *[1995] STI 968*, the Special Commissioner held that the alteration of a company's capital to enable non-voting participating preference shares (entitled to 30% of the company's net profit) to be issued to the wives of the two existing shareholders was not an 'arrangement' sufficient to constitute a settlement. Consequently, in what is likely to be a test case on this area, the Revenue have failed so far in their attempt to impute participating preference share dividends to existing shareholders under the settlement provisions.

8.22 To prevent a dividend waiver from being treated as a transfer of value for inheritance tax purposes, the shareholder must waive his right to the dividend (every time) by deed within the 12 months before it becomes payable. [*IHTA 1984, s 15*].

Use of jointly held shares for married couples

8.23 Shares can be held in joint names to 'share' dividend income between a husband and wife, even though the underlying beneficial interest in the shares may be 99% : 1%. This will be useful as a means of diverting income to a spouse who would otherwise have little income (and avoids arguments with the Revenue about dividend waivers (see 8.17–8.21)).

This technique makes use of the rule in *ICTA 1988, s 282A* (enacted on the start of independent taxation of married couples). Income from investments held in joint names, for example, dividends on jointly held shares are deemed to be split equally for income tax purposes under *ICTA 1988, s 282A*.

The couple can use this rule even if their beneficial interests in the jointly held asset are not the same, i.e., they do not have to beneficially own the asset on a 50:50 basis. However, where the couple wish to have the income allocated in accordance with their underlying (unequal) beneficial interest, a joint declaration can be made on Revenue Form

17. [*ICTA 1988, s 282B*]. The declaration must list the assets covered and the beneficial interest held in each asset. The declaration is only effective for income arising after the date the Form 17 is signed (provided it is submitted within 60 days of the declaration).

PLANNING CHECKLIST — DIVIDEND STRATEGIES
Company
• Dividend payments should be timed to minimise any delay in recovering the ACT.
• Companies may be able to carry back any surplus ACT; if not, consider alternative methods of extracting funds.
Working shareholders
• Dividends can be tax efficient if company pays tax at the small companies rate.
• Shareholder obtains longer credit period for payment of higher rate tax where dividends are paid early in tax year (but this must be consistent with company's ACT recovery position).
• Where dividends are used to extract 'bonuses' invite non-working shareholders to waive their dividend entitlement.
• Consider use of 'jointly held' shares in 'husband and wife' companies to avoid potential problems with dividend waivers.
Other employees
• Not affected by dividend strategies.
Non-working shareholders
• Often invited to waive their dividends by working shareholders, but they cannot be compelled to do so.
• Dividend waivers must be made in writing (by Deed) before the right to dividend vests.
• May be taxed on dividend waiver if made late.

Chapter 9

Pension Scheme Strategies

Choices and approach

9.1　Although the choice of pension scheme is supposedly between an occupational pension scheme and a personal pension scheme, within the former in particular there are a great number of options available and this chapter provides an overview of pensions strategies to be considered in a family company environment.

It is obviously a highly important area for a family company, yet there is little statutory legislation bearing in mind its importance. One has to rely very much on Pension Schemes Office practice which is generally found in PSO memoranda (previously SFO memoranda as the office used to be known as the Superannuation Funds Office). The reason for this is largely because of the powers given to the Inland Revenue to give discretionary approval to pension schemes under *ICTA 1988, s 591(1)*, viz:

'The Board may, if they think fit having regard to the facts of a particular case, and subject to such conditions, if any, as they think proper to attach to the approval, approve a retirement benefits scheme for the purposes of this Chapter notwithstanding that it does not satisfy one or more of the prescribed conditions.'

There is a caveat in *ICTA 1988, s 591(5)*, that 'the Board shall not approve a scheme by virtue of this section if to do so would be inconsistent with regulations made by the Board for the purposes of this section'.

The powers of the PSO are therefore immense, but so is the potential flexibility which can be available when considering the approach to introducing a pension scheme within a family company. These are the type of arrangements which could be appropriate within the framework of a family company:

(*a*)　occupational pension scheme for all employees;

(*b*)　occupational pension scheme for all employees *plus* top-up scheme for working shareholders and other senior executives;

(*c*)　self-administered scheme for working shareholders with personal pension schemes for other employees.

Occupational pension schemes (OPS)

9.2   The legislation is primarily in *ICTA 1988, ss 590–612*. This is the whole of Chapter 1 headed 'Retirement benefit schemes', to Part XIV of the Act.

Main features

9.3   The tax advantages of an OPS are:

(*a*)   company contributions attract corporation tax relief;

(*b*)   there is income tax relief at the member's highest rate on contributions made by him up to 15% of earnings (subject to an earnings cap — see 9.8);

(*c*)   the member has no income tax liability on contributions made by the employer on his behalf;

(*d*)   all contributions are accumulated in a tax-free fund;

(*e*)   at retirement the member may receive a tax-free lump sum of up to $1\frac{1}{2} \times$ salary;

(*f*)   life assurance cover on death in service may be obtained up to 4 × salary, and this is free of inheritance tax.

Final salary v money purchase

9.4   The traditional OPS provides benefits based on final salary. This can create difficulties, however, with the members not always knowing the value of their pension benefits at any given time before retirement. Funding in this way, by reference to future liabilities of the pension fund, can create problems of policing the funds. It can also result in substantial contributions being required by the employer when investment conditions are weak (and perhaps funds are not readily available then) and a contribution holiday being appropriate when investment conditions are strong. This lack of consistency has resulted in money purchase schemes becoming popular. Although benefits are limited to the normal Inland Revenue maxima, the value of the pension fund for each member is strictly by reference to the contributions made to it.

Pension benefits

9.5   Pension benefits may be provided by a final salary or a money purchase scheme. A final salary scheme bases the pension on a fixed percentage of salary either average or final for each year of service ranking for pension. A money purchase scheme purchases benefits with the accumulated contributions on the pensions account of an employee when he retires.

A pension of ²/₃ of final remuneration may be provided, generally based on ¹/₆₀ for each year of service. Such a pension can, however, be provided after 20 years' service for late entrants (after deducting retained benefits from previous schemes) based on a straight-line scale of ¹/₃₀ of final remuneration for each year of service. Members of pre-17 March 1987 schemes can get the maximum pension after only 10 years' service. [*ICTA 1988, s 590(3)*].

Pensions can be increased in line with inflation, but for funding purposes escalation of 8¹/₂% p.a. is the maximum.

On death after retirement, a widow's (or other dependant's) pension may be provided of ²/₃ of the pension that could have been provided to the member. [*ICTA 1988, s 590(3)(b)*]. In addition, if the member dies within five years of retirement the outstanding balance of the first five years' pension payments may be made as a lump-sum.

Lump-sum benefit

9.6   The maximum lump-sum depends on the number of years' service. The normal commutation is ³/₈₀ of final remuneration for each year of service, with a maximum of 150% of final remuneration after 40 years' service. This can be obtained after 20 years' service under discretionary approval. [*ICTA 1988, s 590(3)*].

For new schemes from 17 March 1987 or for new members of existing schemes, if the member's total pension benefits are boosted above the basic maximum (relating to ¹/₆₀ for each year of service), the lump-sum benefit can be increased commensurately.

Retirement date

9.7   The normal retirement date is in the age range 60 to 70 for men and 55 to 70 for women. A male employee can, however, retire at age 50 and receive a proportion of the actual pension otherwise receivable at normal pension age, based on the fraction

$$\frac{\text{actual service}}{\text{potential service to normal retirement date}}$$

A female employee may retire at age 45 if her normal retirement age is under 60 and she is already within ten years of it.

On retirement due to incapacity the pension benefits can be paid irrespective of age, and can be the benefits the employee would ordinarily have obtained on his normal retirement date (i.e. no proportionate scaling down). Indeed, anyone can retire on full pension at age 50 under schemes set up after 13 March 1989 (if the rules so allow) or where the member joins an old scheme after 31 May 1989.

Schemes involving retirement dates earlier than 50 (men) or 45 (women) have been approved.

Other restrictions and relaxations

9.8 The basic pension restrictions covered in 9.3 to 9.7 above are subject to changing legislation introduced in recent years. These are summarised below, by reference to the four possible categories of membership of an OPS:

(*a*) pre-16/03/87 member of an old scheme;

  (i) no monetary restrictions on lump-sum or pension benefits;

  (ii) benefit limits by reference to final remuneration and service;

  (iii) basically, the most valuable of categories;

(*b*) pre-01/06/89 members of pre-14/03/89 schemes;

  (i) lump-sum maximum based on final remuneration of £100,000 (= £150,000 maximum);

  (ii) no monetary restriction on pension benefits;

  (iii) benefit limits by reference to final remuneration and service;

(*c*) post-31/05/89 members of pre-14/03/89 schemes; and all members of post-13/03/89 schemes;

  (i) capped remuneration of £78,600 for 1995/96 tax year;

  (ii) maximum pension £52,400 per annum, with lump-sum maximum of £117,900 and reduced pension;

  (iii) earlier retirement age and faster accrual rates;

(*d*) pre-01/06/89 members of pre-14/03/89 schemes who elect to be treated as post-31/05/89 members; the position is as under (*c*) and can be advantageous for those with earnings under £78,600 per annum.

The capped remuneration limit is ordinarily adjusted annually by reference to the RPI increase over the 12 months to the previous December, and rounded up to the nearest multiple of over £600. However, this adjustment was not made in 1993/94 and the limits are:

tax year	limit
1989/90	£60,000
1990/91	£64,800
1991/92	£71,400
1992/93	£75,000
1993/94	£75,000
1994/95	£76,800
1995/96	£78,600

The earlier retirement possibility is from age 50, and the faster accrual rate allowed is the greater of $3/80$ for each year of service (up to $1\frac{1}{2}$ times final salary) for 40 years' service or $2\frac{1}{4}$ times the amount of pension. [*ICTA 1988, s 599*].

Final remuneration

9.9   This is the sum on which retirement benefits are based. It is calculated as:

(*a*)   remuneration for any one of the five years preceding the normal retirement date. For these purposes 'remuneration' means basic pay for the year in question, plus the average over a suitable period (usually three or more years) ending on the last day of the basic pay year of any fluctuating emoluments such as commission, bonuses or taxable benefits. Directors' fees may rank either as basic pay or as fluctuating emoluments according to the basis on which they are voted; or

(*b*)   the average of the total emoluments for any period of three or more consecutive years ending not earlier than ten years before the normal retirement date.

The calculation in (*b*) has to be used by a director who, either alone or together with his/her spouse and minor children, is or becomes the beneficial owner of shares which, when added to any shares held by the trustees of any settlement to which the director or his/her spouse had transferred assets, carry more than 20% of the voting rights in the company providing the pension or in a company which controls that company.

Remuneration can be 'dynamised' by reference to the retail price index increases up to the normal retirement date. This can give substantial extra benefits especially by reference to years when the RPI increase exceeds salary rises.

Company contributions

9.10   Ordinary annual contributions are tax deductible. For special contributions, paid to augment benefits or to provide benefits for past service, tax relief is available in the year of payment provided they do not exceed the greater of £25,000 or the employer's ordinary annual contributions. These alternatives relate to the total for all pension schemes of the employer. Where the payment does exceed the maxima, tax relief is spread as follows. [*ICTA 1988, s 592(6)*].

special contribution	years of spread
£25,000 to £50,000	2
£50,001 to £100,000	3
over £100,000	4

Certain special contributions are, however, tax deductible in the year of payment irrespective of the amount:

(*a*)   guaranteed payments on a year by year basis if investment income falls below a stated percentage or target;

(*b*)   special contributions payable by instalments over a period of five or more years, or paid annually on a specified basis where, although the amounts may be liable to fluctuate, substantial variations in successive years are not expected to occur;

(*c*)   special contributions which are certified as made solely to finance cost of living pension increases for existing pensioners, or any part which is so certified;

(*d*)   payments uniformly spread over at least three years in respect of a scheme tailored for an individual, provided the payments extend up to normal retirement date.

Example 1

Special contributions

Newton Limited has an OPS for an individual employee, which requires a contribution of £120,000. Company year end 31 December. It could pay contributions totalling £120,000 over a period of 1 year and 2 days and get tax relief in the year of payment, viz:

£40,000	31/12/94
£40,000	01/01/95
£40,000	01/01/96
£120,000	

Employee contributions

9.11   The contributions must not exceed 15% of the employee's remuneration. In order to help achieve a higher pension, it can be worthwhile increasing the employee's remuneration, with the increase then being used as a contribution. The employee then in net terms receives the same remuneration but his remuneration for determining his pension entitlement is the gross amount. The resultant increase in employer's NIC must not be ignored. [*ICTA 1988, s 592(8A)*].

Example 2

Employee contributions

Mr Nicholls earns £34,000 per annum. This gives him a projected pension of £22,666 (two-thirds of £34,000). If his salary is increased to £40,000 and he uses the increase of £6,000 as his maximum 15% contribution to the pension scheme, he will still enjoy the earnings of £34,000 but his projected pension will be £26,666 (two-thirds of £40,000). The additional cost to the company will be NIC of 10.2% of £6,000 = £612 p.a.

If normal contributions by the employee are less than 15% of his earnings, additional voluntary contributions (AVCs) by him can be most worthwhile as a means of increasing his pension entitlement with the additional contributions generally being made in the few years prior to retirement. Such contributions are tax deductible (subject to the 15% limit) and can be paid on a one-off basis if the pension scheme rules so allow.

Example 3

AVCs (1)

Mr Nish earned £38,000 in the year of retirement and £35,000 in the previous year. AVCs of 15% paid in both years, his tax rate being 40%.

contributions paid

— year 1	15% of £35,000	=	£5,250
— year 2	15% of £38,000	=	£5,700
			£10,950

interest credited to pension fund, based on 10% p.a. compound

— on £5,250 contribution	=	£1,102
— on £5,700 contribution	=	£570

increase in pension fund | | £12,622 |

net cost to employee

£10,950 @ 60%   =   £6,570

At a cost of £6,570 the pension fund is increased by £12,622. Net return = 92.12%.

The AVCs can go to the OPS, or they can be paid to a free-standing AVC plan for the individual employee and taken out by him. This free-standing plan is not however available to a director owning over 20% of the voting rights (inclusive of voting rights held by his spouse and minor children).

If total pension benefits exceed the Inland Revenue maxima because of AVCs (whether or not of the free-standing variety), that is acceptable but the excess must be returned to the employee less a tax charge.

Example 4

AVCs (2)

Ms Norman, a higher-rate taxpayer, retires with her AVC pension plan having a surplus of £1,000 by reference to her maximum benefits from the OPS and the AVC plans together.

	£
AVC fund surplus	1,000
Tax on scheme administrator (35%)	350
	650
Grossed up at basic rate	867
Tax on Ms Norman (40%)	347
Basic rate credit	217
Ms Norman to pay	130

Total tax = £350 + £130 = £480 = 48%

Executive pension plans

9.12   Funding limits for these plans were reduced from 1 September 1994, although there is a five year transitional period for schemes existing before then to get their funding levels in line with the new limits.

New schemes from 1 September 1994 have to comply with the new guidelines, and existing schemes can only top-up the benefits provided that by doing so they do not exceed the new limits.

The reason for the new reduced limits is that in the past, the contribution limits were what could only be regarded as extremely generous and they allowed large payments to be made into a pension scheme when a person was comparatively young. This often resulted in over-funding when young executives left the pension scheme early, and large contributions had already been made while they were employed. The new limits are based on lower actuarial assumptions and are meant to make sure that over-funding does not occur in the future.

The likely contributions as a percentage of salary at entry to an executive pension plan are as shown below on the following bases:

(*a*)   the age is that of entry to the scheme and to company service;

(*b*)   there are no retained benefits;

(*c*)   the normal retirement age is 60;

(*d*)   past service is taken into account of a sufficient amount to give maximum benefits;

(*e*)   earnings do not exceed the capped level;

(*f*)   annuity rates are based on payment monthly in advance with a five year guarantee and increasing in line with the retail price index.

age	married male – old funding	married male – new funding	married female – old funding	married female – new funding
25	106%	26%	106%	26%
30	112%	32%	112%	32%
35	121%	40%	120%	39%
40	124%	51%	124%	51%
45	144%	71%	143%	71%
50	177%	111%	176%	111%
55	270%	231%	269%	230%

Self-administered pension schemes

Overview

9.13   Working shareholders of a family company may well look upon a pension scheme as a tax saving vehicle during their working life, rather than as a means of providing income on retirement. Not surprisingly, the Inland Revenue is keen to remind everyone that a pension scheme is intended to provide benefits on retirement with the tax provisions providing appropriate encouragement.

9.14 *Pension Scheme Strategies*

As a tax saving vehicle, the family company would like to have a degree of control over the investments made by the pension fund (as opposed to leaving it to the pension scheme fund managers or insurance company concerned) and retain the use of the sums paid into the fund. Such a scenario is possible within limits — and these limits are likely to become more severe over the next few years given the perceived abuses and problems which can be created in the absence of any limits.

Certainly, there can be particular advantages to a self-administered pension scheme for a family company, and in particular one where membership is restricted to just a few executives (known as an SSAS for small schemes with less than 12 members). The share value will reduce for CGT and IHT purposes by transferring substantial funds to an SSAS, but with the funds still effectively being available to the company to a certain extent. Using an SSAS to the full, the contributions are likely to be greater than to an insured OPS. Consequently, non-working shareholders will need to be convinced of the overall advantages of an SSAS.

SSAS approval by the Inland Revenue

9.14   Schemes have to adhere to the following regulations from SFO memoranda 58 (February 1979) and 109 (August 1991). At the time of writing it is known that the way an SSAS is funded is under review by the Inland Revenue.

(i) Pensioner trustee

Appointment necessary, to ensure regulations are adhered to.

(ii) Borrowing

The trustees may not borrow an amount which is greater than the sum of three times the employer's ordinary annual subscription to the scheme plus three times the compulsory contributions paid by employees in the immediately preceding tax year plus 45% of the market value of investments held by the scheme. Temporary borrowings for a period of up to six months do not need to be notified to the PSO, if they are limited to the lesser of 10% of the fund of £50,000. Borrowing rolled over into a further term must be reported.

(iii) Investment

This is not allowed in:

(a)   personal chattels (i.e. antiques, works of art, rare books and stamps, jewellery, gem stones, oriental rugs, furniture, fine wines, coins, vintage cars, yachts, gold bullion and Krugerrands);

(*b*) residential property unless an unconnected employee lives there as part of the condition of employment (i.e. caretaker or an unrelated person lives in, for example, a flat integral with a shop held as a scheme asset);

(*c*) over 30% of an unlisted company.

There is a restriction applying to other pension schemes where the fund holds employer-related investments. This is defined in the *Social Security Act 1990* to include land occupied by the employer, and the restriction is not more than 5% of the market value of the scheme's resources. However, such a restriction does not apply to an SSAS provided each member is a trustee and agrees in writing before any employer-related investment is made. There is therefore scope for the SSAS to own a property which it lets to the employer company. The latter gets corporation tax relief on the rent paid and the SSAS receives it tax-free. Any capital growth on the property accrues tax-free within the SSAS.

(v) Loanbacks and shares in the principal company

Loans to members are banned, including loans to 'connected persons'. This includes a partnership where a member or relative has an interest. Loanbacks and investment in the employing company shares are limited to 25% of the fund for the first two years (less any transfers in) and 50% of the total fund assets thereafter. Loanbacks to the principal company have to be for business purposes, for a fixed term, at a commercial rate of interest (Clearing Bank Base Rate plus 3% for purposes of secured and unsecured loans) and be the subject of a written loan agreement. If the loan is for a term of less than 365 days the interest is paid gross. Otherwise, income tax must be deducted by the company and paid over to the Inland Revenue. The trustees then reclaim the tax deducted. The Inland Revenue usually frowns upon a series of 364-day loans as a means of avoiding tax.

(vi) Transactions with scheme members

This is debarred, except that an SSAS established by 4 August 1991 can sell assets held then to scheme members.

Hybrid schemes

9.15   These are schemes under which, say, 50% of the pension fund assets are invested via an insured scheme and 50% via a self-administered scheme. The life assurance company provides all the necessary administrative services, at a varying cost. Some companies make an initial charge, others make no direct charges at all but reduce the unit allocation on the insured part of the overall pension scheme.

These schemes have no minimum fund size requirement. They also offer a compromise solution to those companies who find a self-administered scheme attractive but who are wary of the administrative burden and of not being able to achieve substantial pension benefits.

Loanback schemes

9.16 Insurance companies also offer loanback schemes which have application where a self-administered scheme is not feasible due to lack of funds. An ordinary insured executive pension plan is effected and when funds build up to a specific level a loan of 25% can be obtained. A pensioner trustee will be required (provided by the insurance company, often at an annual charge) but not where the insurance company is lending from its own funds rather than via the pension fund.

Individual fund scheme

9.17 A third variation offered by some insurance companies involves an insured scheme where the trustees appoint their own investment manager who is acceptable to the life office. The funds must, however, be substantial before such a scheme can be implemented. Furthermore, although the investment manager has the responsibility of investing the pension fund assets according to the scheme members' wishes, nevertheless the investments must be acceptable and suitable for holding in the life offices' funds. The advantages are that there is no requirement for a pensioner trustee, as the fund is fully insured it can obtain exempt status without delay and by using a professional investment manager the members have a direct say in the investment of their fund but without the administrative burden.

Loans and pension mortgages to individual members of an OPS

9.18 Under an insured scheme, many insurance companies offer loans to individual members. Security is required and using the loan to purchase a private residence can be an attractive proposition.

In order to avoid any potential company law problem with loans to directors from a company's pension scheme the loan could either be made direct by a third party (e.g. a bank) who does not obtain any benefit from the director's company and who does not guarantee to lend money merely by virtue of the existence of the pension scheme; or made by the insurance company which has funds available for loans generally and which considers the loan application at its own discretion and entirely on its own merits.

The personal loans/mortgages available vary considerably but can be based on a maximum of $2\frac{1}{2} \times$ salary, or $15 \times$ the annual premium, or the equivalent of 80% to 100% of the member's anticipated tax-free lump-sum on retirement, or 35% of the anticipated value of the whole fund on retirement.

Withdrawal of tax approval to an SSAS

9.19   To counter the attractions of taking action to deliberately cause Inland Revenue approval to be withdrawn, thereby allowing the pension fund to be distributed to the scheme members before they reach retirement age, there is a special tax charge of 40% on the value of the fund at the time it loses its tax-exempt status.

Personal pension schemes (PPS)

9.20   Unlike the position with occupational pension schemes, here virtually the complete picture can be obtained from the legislation.

Main features

9.21   This is a scheme taken out by an employee and which goes with him from job to job or indeed from job to self-employment. The benefits are based on the level of contributions, not the level of final income on retirement. No employee can contribute to both a PPS and an OPS by reference to the same employment.

The tax advantages of a PPS are:

(*a*)   the member obtains income tax relief at his/her marginal rate on allowable contributions (basic rate tax relief is given at source to an employee);

(*b*)   if the employer pays any contributions they are not assessed on the member under Schedule E;

(*c*)   income within the scheme is exempt from income tax;

(*d*)   gains within the scheme are not chargeable gains;

(*e*)   on retirement a tax-free lump-sum can be obtained of up to 25% of the fund.

Tax relief on contributions

9.22   The maximum relief for 1995/96 is as under:

age at 6 April 1995	% of net relevant earnings	max on earnings cap of £78,600
under 36	17½%	£13,755
36 to 45	20%	£15,720

age at 6 April 1995	% of net relevant earnings	max on earnings cap of £78,600
46 to 50	25%	£19,650
51 to 55	30%	£23,580
56 to 60	35%	£27,510
61 and over	40%	£31,440

[*ICTA 1988, ss 640* and *640A*].

'Net relevant earnings' means for a family company employee the earnings for the year of assessment *less* allowable expenses. [*ICTA 1988, s 646*].

The income tax relief is claimable against the emoluments for the year of assessment in which the pension premium is paid. [*ICTA 1988, s 639(1)*]. Basic rate tax relief is obtained by deduction at source by an employee, with any higher rate relief being claimed separately from the Inland Revenue.

An election can be made to treat all or part of the premium as having been paid in the preceding tax year, the time limit being 5 July following the actual tax year of payment. If the net relevant earnings of the preceding year are nil, the relief can be claimed against the relevant earnings of the tax year before then (i.e. two tax years before the tax year of payment). This carry-back election treats the premiums as paid in the earlier year for all purposes. [*ICTA 1988, s 641*].

Where in any year of assessment the maximum PPS contribution on which tax relief could be claimed is not paid, the deficiency ('*unused relief*') can qualify for tax relief by it being paid in any of the next six years of assessment. The relief is given in the year of assessment in which the contribution is paid, but is only given in respect of unused relief to the extent that the maximum limit for the year of assessment in which it is paid has already been reached. Where a contribution is paid in respect of unused relief for any of the previous six years of assessment, it is allocated to an earlier year's unused relief rather than a later year. [*ICTA 1988, s 642*].

Example 5

Tax relief on contributions

Osgood was born on 31 January 1956. He has the following net relevant earnings (NRE) and PPS contribution record, thus enabling the unused relief potential to be calculated:

(a) *tax year*	(b) *NRE*	(c) *max relief (20%)*	(d) *contributions paid re (b)*	(e) *unused relief (c)–(d)*	(f) *latest date to pay (e)**
	£	£	£	£	
1990/91	10,000	2,000	1,200	800	5/4/97
1991/92	11,000	2,200	1,200	1,000	5/4/98
1992/93	12,500	2,500	nil	2,500	5/4/99
1993/94	14,000	2,800	800	2,000	5/4/2000
1994/95	18,000	3,600	3,000	600	5/4/2001
1995/96	20,000	4,000	3,000	1,000	5/4/2002

* add 1 year if carry-back election made

Employer contributions

9.23   If the family company has an OPS, an employee may be eligible to become a member. He can however decide to instead take out his own PPS. Whether or not that is the better option depends partly on the employer's policy on the matter. Will the employer contribute to the employee's PPS, or simply do nothing? If the employer does make an adjustment it is better for it to contribute directly to the PPS rather than increase the employee's salary, so as to save national insurance contributions which are not chargeable on the former.

Example 6

PPS — employer contribution

Osman Limited agrees to contribute £1,000 to an employee's PPS. It is willing to do this either directly to the PPS or indirectly by increasing the employee's salary to allow him to make the contribution. Osman Limited pays corporation tax at the rate of 25%.

contribution by Osman Limited

	£
gross	1,000
corporation tax relief	250
net cost	750

139

extra salary to employee

	£
gross	1,000
NIC (10.2%)	102
	1,102
corporation tax relief	276
net cost	826

The saving is £76 (or 7.6% of the contribution)

In the above example, the employee gets tax relief on his contribution of £1,000 which cancels his tax liability on the extra salary.

Fund investment

9.24 Schemes can be approved where members are able to choose the underlying investments. These are generally known as self-invested personal pension schemes (SIPPs). The guidelines are in SFO memo 101 (October 1989) and allow investment in:

(*a*) stocks and shares quoted on the UK Stock Exchange (including AIM);

(*b*) stocks and shares trade on a recognised overseas stock exchange;

(*c*) unit trusts;

(*d*) investments trusts;

(*e*) insurance company managed funds and unit linked funds;

(*f*) commercial property (if leased to a business connected with the member, it must be on commercial terms).

The minimum annual contribution to make a SIPP viable is likely to be around £3,000.

Other features

9.25 A PPS must allow the holder to transfer into another PPS if he so wishes. It must also ensure that any contributions paid in excess of the tax deductible limit are repaid.

The holder has the choice of insurance company paying the annuities. It can also choose the date of commencement of drawing the pension (or lump-sum with reduced pension) at any time from age 50 to age 75. Earlier commencement is possible if the holder is unable to work due to infirmity or if his occupation is one at which retirement earlier than at age 50 is customary.

Under *ICTA 1988, s 634A*, a PPS holder can defer the purchase of the annuity until age 75 at the latest, choosing the best time to buy but in the meantime taking income withdrawals. The maximum withdrawal is 100% of the annuity purchasable by reference to tables drawn up by the Government Actuaries and issued to all personal pension providers and there is a minimum withdrawal of 65%. Every three years, unless the annuity has been purchased, the figures have to be reviewed.

Mortgages are available via third parties such as building societies and banks up to a factor of the annual pension contributions (usually 15 ×) and with a minimum annual pension contribution being required. Such a facility is simply another source of finance (albeit of a greater amount than might be obtainable from traditional sources) with no benefit passing to the pension fund itself. To that extent, for a house purchase it should be compared to a mortgage on the capital repayment basis or to a mortgage linked with an endowment policy.

Unapproved pension schemes

Funded scheme

9.26 Such a scheme can provide valuable top-up pension benefits to key personnel where the earnings cap is a problem.

A funded unapproved scheme is known as a FURB, and the position is:

(*a*) no tax relief on employee contributions;

(*b*) employee taxed on employer contributions, via a P11D entry (and possible use of a restricted PAYE code number), but no NIC liability. [*ICTA 1988, s 595(1); Reg 19(1)(d) SI 1979 No 591*].

(*c*) employer gets tax relief when contributions made provided employee is taxed thereon with no spreading of relief for large contributions. [*FA 1989, s 76*];

(*d*) income and gains of the scheme are taxed, at basic rate of 25% applying to a trust which provides relevant retirement benefits. [*ICTA 1988, s 686(2)(c)(i)*];

(*e*) no 10-year IHT charge on the discretionary trust. [*IHTA 1984, s 5*];

(*f*) no investment restrictions;

(*g*) no tax charge on lump sum benefits, which can be of the whole fund value;

(*h*) pensioner taxed on any pension received;

(*i*) no specific retirement date.

Employee contributions are not normally made. There is no tax allowance and the lump-sum obtained by reference to employee contributions may be taxable.

The set-up costs are likely to be around £1,500 with annual costs of £750. To achieve a saving compared with an investment with immediate access, the FURB requires an annual contribution of at least £5,000 or a single contribution of at least £35,000.

Funded offshore scheme

9.27   If the FURB is administered offshore, with the fund being wholly or partly exempt from tax on its income and capital gains, there is an income tax charge by reference to the lump-sum received by an employee where the fund is established for the employee after 30 November 1993. The charge is on the lump-sum less contributions made to the fund by the employer (taxed on the employee) and by the employee (if any). [*FA 1994, s 108*].

The deduction is reduced if the lump-sum is provided on the disposal/ surrender of a part of any asset, and the employee has the right (or expectation) to receive a further lump-sum. The reduction is on a pro rata basis.

Unfunded scheme

9.28   An unfunded scheme (known as an UURB) results in the employee being taxed on all benefits passing to him. It is really a promise by the company to pay a lump-sum on retirement and/or a pension, and there is no actual employer contribution for the employee to be taxed on.

PLANNING CHECKLIST — PENSION SCHEMES
company   • Consider self-administered scheme, for working shareholders, used as a tax saving vehicle.   • An OPS for all employees unlikely to give the best value within a family company environment.
working shareholders   • As for the company, but with due regard to obtaining benefits on retirement through the pension scheme.
other employees   • Personal pension scheme may be a better option than OPS.   • Money purchase OPS more appropriate than a final salary OPS if earnings could fluctuate.
non-working shareholders   • If a self-administered pension scheme is chosen, check contribution levels by reference to the likely levels to a traditional OPS.

Chapter 10

Raising Funds

Introduction

10.1   There are many ways in which a company can improve its finances. Some methods can be internally generated such as retaining profits or improving cash flow without any immediate tax consequence.

Externally generated funds may arise from the shareholders, from third parties or from third parties via the shareholders. In such cases the tax consequences can vary tremendously. The best method of raising finance from a tax viewpoint is often not apparent until the trading results have been established over a few years. Tax planning with the benefit of hindsight is of course impossible, but in this particular area there are often other factors which dictate the method of raising funds. The issue should be considered from all angles, with a combination of methods sometimes giving the optimum position.

Long-term funding will be in the form of share capital or loan. Short-term funding sometimes necessary to cover a fall in company generated working capital will normally be in the form of bank overdraft. Many companies make the mistake of funding long-term objectives with short term borrowings. If funding is required in excess of twelve months it may be well to discuss a term loan with the company's bankers and to agree favourable rates and conditions.

Company borrowings

Interest on a bank overdraft, bank loan, or other short-term loan of less than twelve months

10.2   Income for corporation tax purposes is computed in accordance with income tax principles. [*ICTA 1988, s 9(1)*]. There are no specific rules allowing the deduction of short interest against trading profits. Therefore it falls within the general deductibility of expenditure against trading profits included in *ICTA 1988, s 74(1)(a)*. For this to apply the interest must be wholly and exclusively laid out for the purposes of the company's trade. Interest paid to a non-UK resident in excess of a commercial rate together with interest relievable under MIRAS are specifically excluded. [*ICTA 1988, s 74(n) & (o)*].

If the interest augments or creates a loss for corporation tax purposes the loss can be carried forward to set against future profits of the same trade, *ICTA 1988, s 393(1)*, or set against any profits of the same accounting period, *ICTA 1988, s 393A(1)(a)* and if required then against any profits of the previous three years. [*ICTA 1988, s 393A(1)(b)*].

Other loan interest

10.3   If the interest is annual interest it is designated as a charge on income and is deducted from the total profits, *ICTA 1988, s 338(1)* after all other reliefs except group relief. If there are excess charges they can be carried forward to set against future trading profits from the same trade provided the loan is used wholly and exclusively for the purposes of the company's trade. [*ICTA 1988, s 393(9)*]. Excess trade charges cannot however be used in a *section 393A* claim against profits of the same or earlier accounting periods unles they arise in a cessation period. [*ICTA 1988, s 393A(7)*].

Charges on income include any yearly interest and any other interest payable in the United Kingdom on an advance from a bank carrying on a bona fide banking business in the UK or from a member of the Stock Exchange or a United Kingdom discount house. Interest which is deductible in computing profits or profits for the purposes of corporation tax cannot be treated as a charge on income. Thus bank interest incurred for trading purposes must be treated as a Schedule D Case I expense and not as a charge on income.

Interest for *ICTA 1988, s 338* purposes must be paid but for *ICTA 1988, s 74* it is deductible from profits on a normal accruals basis. *Minsham Properties Ltd v Price, Lysville Ltd v Price Ch D 1990, 63 TC 570, [1990] STC 718*. However under the new Gilts and Bonds régime, all corporate interest will be relievable on an accruals basis from 1 April 1996.

Practical considerations

10.4   Before embarking on a source of finance the company would be well-advised to consider its corporation tax position at the outset to make maximum use of interest relief. For example to maximise relief of a trading company with losses brought forward and non-trading income a term loan may be a better source of finance not only from a commercial point of view but also for corporation tax purposes.

10.4 *Raising Funds*

Example 1

Loan interest

The Wholesale Trading Company Limited has been trading at a loss for the past five years with accumulated trading losses brought forward at 30 September 1995 amounting to £5,000. Rather than sell the surplus business premises the company decided to let this out and the rent for the year ended 30 September 1996 is expected to be £3,000. The company requires additional finance of £50,000 on which the interest rate is expected to be 8%. Trading profits for the year are expected to amount to £6,000.

Draft Corporation Tax Computation for the year ended 30 September 1996.

	Assuming short-term loan £
Trading profits	6,000
Less interest	(4,000)
	2,000
Less Schedule D Case I loss brought forward, *ICTA 1988, s 393(1)*	(2,000)
	–
Schedule A	3,000
Profits chargeable to corporation tax	3,000
Loss available to carry forward £(5,000 − 2,000) =	£3,000

	Assuming long-term loan £
Schedule D Case I	6,000
Less loss brought forward, *ICTA 1988, s 393(1)*	(5,000)
	1,000
Schedule A	3,000
	4,000
Less interest, *ICTA 1988, s 338(1)*	(4,000)
Profits chargeable to corporation tax	Nil

If normal accounting principles would determine that the interest should be deducted from profits i.e. a bank overdraft taken out for the purposes of the trade, the tax treatment will follow suit. It would not be possible to claim such interest as an annual charge. *Wilcock v Frigate Investments Ltd [1982] STC 198.*

Relief already given under *ICTA 1988, s 338(1)* for trade charges will not be disturbed if subsequently a carry back claim for loss relief is made under *ICTA 1988, s 393A(8)* (see 4.11).

Shareholder borrowings

10.5   It is possible for the shareholder to borrow the funds himself and to lend these to the company which are used wholly and exclusively for the purposes of the company's business or that of an associated company. [*ICTA 1988, s 360*]. Relief from income tax will be available to the shareholder in respect of loan interest paid (but not in respect of bank overdraft interest) provided certain conditions are satisfied.

Material interest

10.6   First the shareholder must possess a material interest in the relevant company i.e. he must control either directly or indirectly through intermediate companies over 5% of the ordinary share capital of the company. This ownership can be alone or through associates. Alternatively he may possess or be entitled to acquire more than 5% of the assets on a winding up.

If an individual does not meet the material interest test he may still qualify for relief if he holds any number of ordinary shares in the company and in the period of applying the loan to the company to the payment of interest the individual has worked for the greater part of his time in the actual management or conduct of the company or associated company.

What constitutes 'worked for the greater part of his time in the actual management or conduct of the company' has been interpreted by the Revenue in November 1993 Tax Bulletin. The Revenue have drawn a distinction between directors and other individuals stating that the person must be a director or if not a director he must possess significant managerial or technical responsibilities. The Revenue interpret 'actual management or conduct of the company' to mean that the individuals must be concerned in the overall running and policy making of the company as a whole. Managerial or technical responsibility for just one particular area will not be sufficient. However the Revenue concedes that whether an individual does satisfy the 'actual management or conduct' test is a question which can only be answered by consideration of the full facts of the particular case.

Members of family companies whose management is divided between several individuals may have difficulty in claiming relief for interest if they do not have a 5% shareholding.

Qualifying close company

10.7   Secondly the company concerned must be a qualifying close company within the meaning of *ICTA 1988, s 13A(2)*. Consequently the company must exist either wholly or mainly to carry on a trade on a commercial basis or to let property to unconnected third parties. Alternatively the company concerned may own shares in a qualifying company or co-ordinate the activities of two or more qualifying companies.

Recovery of capital

10.8   When the interest is paid by the individual the company must continue to be a qualifying close company within the meaning of *ICTA 1988, s 13A(2)* and the individual must maintain a material interest in the company. [*ICTA 1988, s 360(2)*]. He must also be able to demonstrate that in the period from the application of the proceeds of the loan to the payment of the interest that he has not recovered any capital from the company. For this purpose any capital withdrawn (e.g. sale proceeds of shares or deemed market value on a gift) will be treated as repaying the loan and interest relief will be adjusted accordingly. [*ICTA 1988, s 363(1)*].

Where an individual makes the borrowing the bank or lending institution will normally insist upon security e.g. the applicant's house or insurance policy. Sometimes shareholders are of the opinion that this can be avoided if the loan is taken out by the company. So often this is not the case and the lending institution will again insist upon personal security being provided by the director shareholders.

Income tax relief for interest on the personal borrowing is given as a charge on income and for the full relief to be obtained the borrower must have sufficient total statutory income against which to set the charge. As a director/shareholder it will not be possible to carry excess personal charges forward nor back to set against total income of previous or prior years. Excess charges may only be carried forward where they constitute a business expense and there is a business source of income. [*ICTA 1988, s 349*].

If the taxpayer has a high level of taxable income it might be considered preferable for him to borrow personally as the tax rates are higher for an individual than for a company. This is of course unlikely to apply where the individual needs to extract income from the company to repay his borrowings; as this will create an additional personal tax liability. Relief for personal borrowings can be obtained on tax at 40% whereas on corporate borrowings the relief will only be at 25% or 33%.

The shareholder may also consider whether he has sufficient free capital not only for the company needs but also for his personal needs. At some stage he may need to make borrowings on which the interest does not qualify for income tax relief in which case borrowing now to pass funds to the company will give him some tax deductible borrowings.

If an individual lends funds to the company whether or not he borrows to enable him to do so, he may be unfortunate enough to find that the loan becomes irrecoverable. Provided the company has used the funds only for the purposes of its trade the individual can claim an allowable loss for capital gains tax purposes on the amount of the loan which is proved to be irrecoverable provided he retains the right to recover it. The relief also applies where the loan involves a guarantor who is called on to pay the debt such as where the individual shareholder personally guarantees the company's bank borowings. The guarantor then qualifies for the loss for capital gains purposes. [*TCGA 1992, s 253*]. Normally losses in respect of irrecoverable loans are deemed to arise when claimed but the Revenue will allow the claim to be backdated to an earlier period (see ESC D36). A similar situation applies to shares which have lost value (see ESC D28). (See also 15.18–15.21.)

Buying ordinary shares in the family company

10.9 Here the rules for income tax relief on loan interest to buy ordinary shares are the same as where the borrowings are used to pass funds to a qualifying close company, although there is no express stipulation that share subscription monies should be applied for trading purposes (see 10.5 above). The shares could be acquired by subscription or purchased from a third party. [*ICTA 1988, s 361*].

In the unfortunate event of the shareholder suffering a loss on selling the shares (or indeed on liquidation when a capital distribution is received, or when the shares have become of negligible value thereby being treated as a disposal under *TCGA 1992, s 24(2)*, the allowable loss established for capital gains tax purposes can often qualify for income tax relief. This is under *ICTA 1988, s 574* and applies in specific circumstances:

(*a*) the individual subscribed for the shares and did not acquire them after they had been issued;

(*b*) the company was a trading company for at least six consecutive years up to the disposal date, or for a shorter period provided that beforehand it was not trading in shares, land, commodities or futures. [*ICTA 1988, s 576(4)*].

The increased risk of injecting funds by way of shares being issued must be compared with the likely extra tax relief as a deduction from income rather than against chargeable gains. With a new family company, where prospects are encouraging, a balance between share capital and loans is likely to be the solution particularly as loans can easily be repaid.

Any individual can roll-over his chargeable gain on any disposal, where he reinvests in a qualifying company, under the CGT reinvestment relief. This is discussed in 14.25 above and it provides a useful incentive for investment in a family company whether the investment is passive or active.

Enterprise investment scheme (EIS)

Introduction

10.10   The aim of EIS is to provide a targeted incentive for new equity investment in unquoted trading companies, and of course nearly all family companies are just that. Business angels should be attracted to EIS as they can be employed by the company and draw reasonable remuneration. This naturally allows them to have a degree of 'hands on' involvement in the company and in turn gives their investment some security. [*ICTA 1988, s 289*].

Potentially, therefore, EIS has a major role to play when a family company requires funds. There are, however, several restrictions which may mean that investors will be difficult to find.

How EIS works

The tax relief

10.11   Income tax relief is available at the smaller of the lower rate which is currently 20% on investments up to £100,000 in each tax year or the amount that would reduce the taxpayer's liability to nil. The investment must be by a *qualifying investor* subscribing for eligible shares issued by a *qualifying company*. The investment can subsequently be realised free of capital gains tax after five years (see 10.21).

Carry-back election

10.12   If an EIS investment is made in the first half of a tax year (i.e. 6 April to 5 October inclusive), an election can be made to relate 50% of the investment to the preceding tax year. This is subject to a maximum carry-back of £15,000. [*ICTA 1988, s 289A(4)*].

Qualifying investor

10.13   This is an individual liable to UK income tax and who is not connected with the company in the period beginning two years before or period from incorporation if less and ending five years after the share issue. [*ICTA 1988, s 291(1), (5) and s 312(1A)(a)*]. This basically means that he must not directly or indirectly possess (or be entitled to possess) over 30% of:

(a)   the issued ordinary share capital of the company or any subsidiary; or

(b)   the loan capital and issued share capital of the company or any subsidiary; or (*c*)   the voting power in the company or any subsidiary.

[*ICTA 1988, s 291B(1)*].

Ordinarily an employee or a director is connected with the company but as explained in 10.15 that need not result in the debarring of EIS relief.

The investor should appreciate the risk element in view of the fact that he cannot hold over 30% of the issued ordinary share capital nor directly or indirectly possess or be entitled to acquire more than 30% of the assets on a winding up, *ICTA 1988, s 291B(1)*, for a period beginning two years before and ending five years after the share issue, but this may be balanced by his working for the company as a director (see 10.15). EIS relief is not obtained unless and until the company has carried on the qualifying trade for four months (an earlier winding-up or dissolution is acceptable provided it is for bona fide commercial reasons).

Eligible shares

10.14   These are new ordinary shares which for five years from issue do not carry any preferential right to dividends; or to asset distribution on a winding-up, or redemption. [*ICTA 1988, s 289*].

Qualifying company

10.15   A company is a qualifying company if:

(*a*)   it is an unquoted trading company carrying on a *qualifying activity* for at least three years. [*ICTA 1988, s 293(2)*];

(*b*)   the company must use the funds for a qualifying business activity within 12 months of receipt or, if later, within twelve months of commencing to trade;

(*c*)   there is an EIS raising limit of £1M per year, but this increases to £5M per year for a company engaged in certain shipping activities. [*ICTA 1988, s 290A(1)*];

(*d*)   the company must trade in the UK but does not have to be UK incorporated and resident. [*ICTA 1988, s 289(2)(ii)*];

(*e*)   a company will not qualify if it is under the control of another company. [*ICTA 1988, s 293(8)*]. The wide definition of control in *ICTA 1988, s 416* is applied for this purpose which looks at the rights of a controlling shareholder in the context of shareholder and loan creditor (see 3.19). Bank loan creditors are ignored for this purpose. This rule can often prohibit EIS relief where a company is mainly funded by institutional finance, as the company could be technically controlled by the venture capital company.

10.16   Raising Funds

Qualifying activity

10.16   A qualifying activity is:

(*a*)   a company, or any subsidiary, carrying on a *qualifying trade* or preparing to do so within two years; provided that the trade is carried on wholly or mainly in the UK throughout the three years from share issue or, if later, from commencement of trading;

(*b*)   also included is research and development or oil exploration, where such activity is carried on immediately following receipt of the EIS funds and it is intended that a qualifying trade will be carried on wholly or mainly in the UK.

Qualifying trade

10.17   All trades will qualify except those which fall within the special exclusions mentioned below at any time in the three years from the share issue or the three years from commencement of the trade, if later:

(*a*)   dealing in land, commodities, futures, shares, securities or other financial instruments;

(*b*)   dealing in goods otherwise than as wholesale or retail distributors;

(*c*)   banking, insurance, money-lending, debt-factoring, hire purchase financing, etc;

(*d*)   oil extraction activities;

(*e*)   leasing, letting pleasure craft ships on charter, letting assets on hire, receiving royalties or licence fees except generally where a film production company or research and development company is involved;

(*f*)   providing legal or accountancy services;

(*g*)   providing services or facilities for any trade, profession or vocation substantially falling within (*a*) to (*f*) which is carried on by a person who has a controlling interest in that trade and in that carried on by the qualifying company. [*ICTA 1988, s 297*].

Working for the company

10.18   The investor would ordinarily be connected with the company if he is a director, and therefore debarred from EIS relief. However, if that is the only reason for connection, he can obtain EIS relief provided he meets the following conditions:

(*a*)   director's remuneration is reasonable for the services performed;

(*b*)   when issued with eligible shares he was not and had never been connected with the company e.g. as an employee/director, or he had never been an employee (excludes director) of a person who previously carried on the company's trade or part thereof.

This is clearly an attractive feature to the investor, and it is imperative that his appointment as director is *after* the share issue.

The investor's tax relief

10.19 The relief reduces the investor's income tax liability, but not his income. His tax liability for the purposes of determining the EIS relief is calculated ignoring the following:

(*a*) personal allowances and maintenance payments which attract relief at a reduced rate;

(*b*) loan interest for main residence or life annuity;

(*c*) relief on medical insurance premiums;

(*d*) DTR or unilateral relief;

(*e*) basic rate tax relief deducted at source from certain payments.

Example 2

The investor's tax relief

Wheeler's 1995/96 income comprises earnings of £50,000. He makes an EIS investment of £100,000 on 1 September 1995. Wheeler is married.

income tax
On £46,475 (50,000 – 3,525 personal allowance)

	£		£
first	3,200 @ 20%	=	640
next	21,100 @ 25%	=	5,275
balance	22,175 @ 40%	=	8,870
	46,475		14,785

			£
less relief on:			
	MCA	1,720 @ 15% =	(258)
			£14,527

EIS relief is restricted to £14,785 (not £14,527) being less than 20% of £100,000 = £20,000.

Wheeler could carry back some of the EIS investment to 1994/95 and he may then obtain tax relief on the balance of £3,805. Indeed, a maximum carry-back of £15,000 may well give the optimum position.

Disposal of eligible shares — EIS relief position

10.20   If the disposal is within five years, the EIS relief is withdrawn if the disposal is not a bargain at arm's length.

Otherwise the relief is withdrawn or reduced by multiplying the consideration received by the lower rate tax for the tax year of issue. If this amount equals or exceeds the attributable relief, that relief is withdrawn. If less, the relief is reduced by that amount. If the EIS was restricted, the amount is multiplied by

$$\frac{\text{Reduced relief}}{\text{EIS at lower rate (20\%)}}$$

Example 3

Disposal of eligible shares — EIS relief position (1)

1995/96	Moore claims EIS relief due on £100,000 (= £20,000)
1997/98	Moore sells all the shares for £90,000

Reduction in relief = £90,000 × 20% = £18,000

EIS relief is reduced by £18,000

Example 4

Disposal of eligible shares — EIS relief position (2)

Same facts, except EIS relief on the £100,000 was restricted to £15,000

Reduction in relief = £90,000 × $\dfrac{£15,000}{£20,000}$ × 20%

= £13,500

Disposal of eligible shares — income tax & CGT positions

10.21   A disposal at a loss can entitle the shareholder to a CGT loss but the cost of the shares is reduced by the EIS relief. Any CGT loss can normally be set against income in the same or the preceding tax year under *ICTA 1988, s 574* — whether the disposal is before or after the five-year holding period.

A gain on disposal after the five-year holding period is not chargeable to CGT.

Example 5

Disposal of eligible shares — income tax and CGT position

Whymark subscribed for shares in January 1995 for £100,000. EIS relief obtained of £20,000.

Whymark sells the shares in January 1997 for £60,000.

EIS relief position

Withdrawal of relief = £60,000 @ 20% − £12,000

CGT/IT position

	£	£
Proceeds		60,000
Cost	100,000	
less EIS relief		
(20,000 − 12,000)	8,000	92,000
allowable loss		32,000

If the conditions in *ICTA 1988, s 574* are met, the relief can be set against Whymark's 1996/97 or 1995/96 income.

Combining EIS relief with CGT reinvestment relief

10.22 If the shareholder disposed of another chargeable asset and reinvests the proceeds in an unquoted trading company he could qualify under both sets of rules, resulting in a 40% tax deferral (via CGT reinvestment relief) and a 20% tax reduction (via EIS relief). The reinvestment relief rules are slightly more restrictive than usually apply, with *TCGA 1992, 5c Sch* covering the position. See also 14.25.

Venture capital trusts

Introduction

10.23 VCT investments are targeted incentives for investment in small to medium-sized unquoted companies carrying on qualifying trades in the UK. They represent a combination of an EIS company and an authorised investment trust company, with the VCT's shares being quoted on the Stock Market.

The VCT structure

10.24 Inland Revenue approval to a VCT is required under *ICTA 1988, s 842AA*. Many of the provisions of *s 842* applying to authorised investment trust companies also apply to an authorised VCT, but one of the exceptions is that there is no requirement that the VCT is resident in the UK.

At least 70% (by value) of the VCT's investments must be in shares and securities which are qualifying holdings. Furthermore, at least 50% (by value) of the qualifying holdings must comprise eligible shares which are ordinary share capital carrying no present or future preferential rights as to dividends or assets on a winding up or redemption.

No holding in any single company may exceed 15% of the VCT's total investments, but that restriction does not apply to investments in unit trusts, Government or local authority securities, or investments in other VCTs.

The unquoted companies in which the VCT invest must carry on a qualifying trade. The legislation defines what is *not* a qualifying trade and is much the same as for EIS.

The tax position

10.25 Income tax relief is given at a fixed rate of 20% on subscriptions for new ordinary shares in VCTs up to £100,000 in any tax year and then held for five years. After that period the market quote should help the investor to dispose of his shares if he so wishes.

CGT deferment is available on a gain on any disposal when the gain is reinvested in subscribing for new ordinary shares in a VCT (*TCGA 1992, 5c Sch* applies, as when using EIS relief with CGT reinvestment relief).

There is income tax exemption on dividends from VCTs and CGT exemption on a gain on disposal of shares in a VCT for investments of up to £100,000 a year.

When looking at the amount of tax relief available on a VCT investment, it is offset against the individual's tax liability for the tax year concerned in priority to other deductions and reliefs which are given in terms of tax offset. This order of priority means that VCT relief is given before EIS relief.

PLANNING CHECKLIST — RAISING FUNDS
company • Ensure interest on all borrowings qualifies for corporation tax relief. • Look to VCTs and EIS to obtain equity investment. • Look to individuals who have a CGT liability and can get reinvestment relief.
working shareholders • Consider whether it is advisable to use company borrowing (with personal guarantee) to acquire assets etc., particularly where additional tax would arise on extracting income to repay personal borrowing. • Use capital or borrowings to subscribe for further shares, striking a commercial balance between debt and equity. • Take account of greater risk in subscribing for shares rather than lending funds on loan.
non-working shareholders • As for non-working shareholders if owning over 5% of the ordinary share capital.

Chapter 11

Expanding Activities

Making a business acquisition

11.1　Companies can expand organically or by acquiring established businesses. The decision to make an acquisition should be based on a definite strategy. The company must have a clear idea of what it needs to achieve from the acquisition, for example, increased capacity and economies of scale, additional market share; new technology or diversification from new products or services. Sensible business acquisitions usually enable a company to grow at a faster rate.

However, the acquiring company must do a considerable amount of homework in identifying suitable targets and approaching selected prospects to draw up a short list. A considerable amount of scarce management time can be devoted to this exercise which may be detrimental to the running of the existing business. Management should therefore consider obtaining professional assistance from a reputable corporate finance department or firm.

11.2　The purchasing company must obtain full details about the financial performance and commercial operations of the target business, including details of its product range, position in the market, management team, customer base, intellectual property, properties, etc. A well advised vendor will require the purchaser to enter into a binding confidentiality agreement in relation to information disclosed during the negotiations.

The purchaser may instruct accountants and possibly other experts to undertake an investigation into the target company. The accountants report would typically cover the target's:

(*a*)　corporate structure;

(*b*)　management and personnel;

(*c*)　trading operations;

(*d*)　accounting policies;

(*e*)　financial, tax and trading position.

A surveyor may report on the properties owned by the target company and an actuary's report may be required on the target's company pension scheme. An environmental audit may be appropriate if there are potential risks inherent in the nature of the target's business.

11.3 An area often under-estimated is the integration of the new business within the purchasing company. In some cases, the vendor shareholders may need to be kept on in key managerial or technical positions.

Heads of agreement and final sale contract

11.4 After negotiations with the vendor (which, again, can be very time consuming), the parties will agree the heads of agreement. It is important that legal advice is sought before agreeing heads of agreement as this may prevent legal difficulties occurring later on. A purchaser should obtain an undertaking from the vendor not to negotiate with any other party.

Heads of agreement should be expressed to be 'subject to contract', pending preparation of the full sale and purchase agreement. It would normally cover the following areas:

(*a*)   the subject matter of the purchase i.e. is it a purchase of shares or assets?

(*b*)   the consideration for acquisition and the payment terms;

(*c*)   whether the price is to be satisfied by cash or shares/loan notes issued by the purchaser;

(*d*)   conditions;

(*e*)   warranties and indemnities;

(*f*)   consultancy and service agreements.

Agreement should be obtained as to the approach which will be taken on potentially contentious issues at this stage.

11.5 The purchase and sale agreement will build on the principles and terms agreed at the heads of agreement stage, the main areas being:

(*a*)   the detailed agreement for the sale;

(*b*)   the price payable, detailing any specific adjustments to it, and how it is to be satisfied;

(*c*)   conditions relating to the completion of the agreement and the completion procedure;

(*d*)   warranties and the deed of indemnity (see 11.27–11.29).

The acquiring company should also obtain a 'non-compete' covenant prohibiting the vendor company/shareholder from carrying on the same or similar business within a reasonable geographic area for a certain number of years.

Structuring an acquisition — assets or shares?

11.6 A business acquisition can basically be structured either as a purchase of the trade and assets of the target company as a going concern, or the shares of the company carrying on the business.

Asset purchase

11.7 As a general rule, the purchaser will often prefer to acquire the assets on which tax relief can be claimed, e.g. stock, plant. The purchaser may also benefit from an uplift in base values for capital allowances and capital gains purposes (i.e. exceeding the amount that would have been available to the target company). The purchaser also avoids responsibility for past actions of the company and the contingent liabilities etc.

An asset purchase is particularly useful if the acquiring company has generated capital gains on the sale of existing trading assets as they can be rolled-over against the cost of the new qualifying assets acquired.

Share purchase

11.8 In contrast, a purchase of shares carries the risk of taking over the target company's undiscovered or contingent liabilities. Carefully drawn warranties and indemnities are necessary to reduce the purchaser's potential liability. No immediate tax relief can be claimed for the cost of the shares purchased (relief only being given on a subsequent sale of the company).

If the company has unrelieved tax losses or surplus ACT, these amounts will remain within the company for the indirect benefit of the purchaser, subject to the potential application of certain anti-avoidance rules (see 11.21 and 11.22).

Asset purchase

11.9 The agreement for an asset purchase should identify precisely the assets and liabilities which will be taken over. This could comprise:

(*a*) freehold/leasehold premises;

(*b*) plant, machinery and vehicles;

(*c*)   leasing, hire purchase and other agreements;

(*d*)   intellectual property, trade marks, designs and know-how;

(*e*)   goodwill;

(*f*)   stock and work in progress;

(*g*)   debtors and creditors;

(*h*)   benefit of contracts;

(*i*)   employees (particularly key personnel);

(*j*)   business accounts and records.

In many cases, the target's debtors are not taken over by the purchaser. This saves stamp duty (see 11.11) and arguments about bad debts. The purchaser will often collect the debts as agent for the vendor. Similarly, liabilities are often retained by the target with the purchaser paying them as agent on the target's behalf, perhaps out of the proceeds of the book debts collected.

Fewer warranties are required on an asset sale as they only need to be given in relation to the particular assets (and liabilities) transferred.

11.10   It is important to include the 'breakdown' of the total purchase price against the various assets in the purchase contract. If the apportionment of the price is stipulated in the purchase agreement, the parties cannot argue about it after the contract has been signed. Although the Inland Revenue have the power to re-allocate the consideration on a just and reasonable basis, they are unlikely to interfere with any arm's length transaction between unconnected parties, unless it is clearly artificial. In any deal, there is usually a parameter of values of each asset which can be substantiated commercially.

11.11   The purchaser will be liable to pay stamp duty at the rate of 1% on dutiable assets, typically, property, goodwill, debts etc. Where the purchaser assumes liabilities, these will be treated as consideration for stamp duty purposes, in addition to the actual cash consideration.

11.12   The transfer of the trade should not be subject to VAT, as a result of the Transfer of Going Concern provisions in *Article 5* of the *VAT (Special Provisions) Order 1995*. If let property (upon which the vendor has opted to tax) is to be transferred under these provisions without VAT, the purchaser must elect to opt to tax the property before the transfer. Where the transfer of assets does not fall within these rules, the vendor should account for VAT on the purchase price. This VAT would be treated as input tax relating to the purchaser's general business overheads, which would be recoverable subject to any partial exemption status.

11.13   The integration of the acquired trade with the purchaser's existing business may be treated as merely extending its own trade or the commencement of a new trade (see, for example, *Cannon Industries Ltd v Edwards (1965) 42 TC 625* and *George Humphries & Co v Cook (1934) 19 TC 121*). If the Inland Revenue argued that a new trade had been commenced, any unused Schedule D Case I losses of the existing business would not be available to offset against future profits of the merged business. This problem might be avoided by treating the acquisition as a separate trade and preparing tax computations for the two trades.

11.14   It is generally easier to obtain tax relief for the interest or the other financial costs incurred in relation to the acquisition of a business or trade, rather than shares.

Tax treatment of assets purchased

Buildings

11.15   The purchase of a used *industrial* building with qualify for annual writing down allowances. The annual allowance will generally be the original construction cost (or purchase price, if lower), spread over the remaining period of the 25 year tax life of the building (50 years for pre 6 November 1962 buildings). [*CAA 1990, s 3(3)*]. No relief would be available on commercial buildings unless they were situated in an enterprise zone. (100% enterprise zone initial allowances can be claimed on industrial/commercial buildings purchased unused or within 2 years of first use.)

If the purchasing company or group has made capital gains on qualifying assets either within one year before or three years after the date of acquisition the expenditure on the freehold/leasehold property can be used to roll over these gains. [*TCGA 1992, s 152*].

Plant and machinery

11.16   Expenditure on plant and machinery acquired will rank for 25% writing down allowances at the rate of 25% per annum (strictly, the qualifying expenditure will be added to the purchaser's existing pool, with 25% WDA being claimed on the total balance).

Goodwill

11.17   No immediate tax relief is available for the purchase of good-will, although of course goodwill will have to be written off or amortised in the purchaser's accounts. The acquisition of goodwill will also qualify as qualifying expenditure for roll-over relief purposes (as in (a) above).

However, if the purchaser is acquiring valuable know-how, i.e. industrial information and techniques relating to the manufacture or processing operations, it may be possible to allocate some of the purchase price of goodwill to know-how. This will enable the purchaser to claim know-how allowances at the rate of 25% per annum on the cost (on a reducing balance basis). [*ICTA 1988, s 530(2)*]. However, as the know-how is being acquired with the trade, the vendor and purchaser must jointly elect for it to be treated as an acquisition of know-how. The election must be made within 2 years from the date of the acquisition. [*ICTA 1988, s 531(3)*].

Expenditure on purchasing patent rights is pooled with other patent expenditure and 25% allowances are available. [*ICTA 1988, s 520*].

Trading stock

11.18   The purchase of trading stock will be relieved as a Schedule D Case I expense, as and when stock is realised. The Inland Revenue would only be able to challenge the amount allocated for the purchase of stock if it is so artificial as to fall outside the protection of *ICTA 1988, s 100(1)(a)* (*Moore v R J Mackenzie & Sons (1972) 48 TC 196*). If the stock is sold to a connected party it will be valued at market value for tax purposes subject to an election to substitute the higher of the actual sale price or book value, where both exceed the market value. [*ICTA 1988, s 100(1A)(1C)*].

Example 1

Apportioning purchase consideration

Shilton's Plastic Mouldings Ltd is negotiating to purchase the trade and assets of a competitor for a total consideration of £500,000. The purchase price was initially allocated by the vendor as:

	£
Goodwill	200,000
Plant	135,000
Stock (book value)	165,000
	500,000

It is estimated that £150,000 of the goodwill could be attributed to technical information.

By allocating £150,000 of the goodwill to 'know-how', Shilton's Plastic Mouldings Ltd will be able to claim know-how allowances at the rate of 25% p.a. on a reducing balance basis. Both parties must elect for this treatment under *ICTA 1988, s 531(3)* otherwise it will still be treated as a disposal of goodwill. (On the other hand, if Shilton's Plastic Mouldings Ltd has generated chargeable gains within the previous three years or is likely to do so within the next year, it might prefer to maximise the amount paid for goodwill to enable a roll-over claim to be made.)

The stock could also be sold at a mark-up of 20% i.e. £198,000 which would reduce the purchaser's trading profit on sale.

The vendor company is agreeable to these proposals as this enables a substantial part of its unused Schedule D Case I losses to be absorbed (which would otherwise be lost on cessation) and reduces its capital gain on the sale of goodwill.

The final agreed allocation of the purchase price laid down in the sale agreement would therefore be:

	£
Goodwill	17,000
Know-how	150,000
Plant	135,000
Stock	198,000
	500,000

Share purchase

11.19 A purchase of shares does not produce any cessation of trade problems for the company — the business continues in its existing form albeit under new ownership. The purchaser, however, will inherit the target's previous history and any previous tax problems. Normally, the risk can be minimised by obtaining appropriate warranties and indemnities from the vendor (see 11.27–11.29).

If there is considerable risk, for example, a large continent liability, the purchaser may require the vendor to hive the trade down first into a newly formed subsidiary — which would then be acquired as a clean company with the unwanted liabilities remaining behind in the transferor company. (It is normally possible to ensure the continuity of trading losses and capital allowances on the hive-down under *ICTA 1988, s 343*.) Any gain deferred on the transfer of assets within the previous six years from group companies (including the assets hived down, such as goodwill) would be taxed within the new company on its sale under *TCGA 1992, s 179*, although it may be possible to reduce the tax liability with careful advance planning.

11.20 The consideration given for the shares together with other allowable costs of acquisition will establish the purchaser's base cost for the future capital gains purposes (note that shares are not a qualifying asset for business asset roll-over relief purposes). If the purchaser issues shares or loan notes, the market value of the shares/loan notes will be treated as the consideration given (which will normally be the value attributed to the transaction where the parties are at arm's length) (see *Stanton v Drayton Commercial Investment Co Ltd [1982] STC 585*). Stamp duty at 0.5% is payable on the acquisition of shares.

11.21 A share purchase may be particularly desirable if the target company has accumulated Schedule D Case I trading profits and surplus ACT which may be available for offset against future taxable profits and tax liabilities of the target company. However, there are anti-avoidance rules which prevent the carry forward of losses and ACT where there is a change in the ownership of a company and a major change in the nature or conduct of the trade/business. [*ICTA 1988, ss 245* and *768*]. The Revenue has indicated that these provisions will not apply where changes are made to increase efficiency or keep pace with developing technology or management systems (SP10/91). Because of the potential vulnerability of carried forward losses and ACT, a purchaser should only pay for them on a deferred basis after their offset has been agreed.

11.22 Any unused capital losses in the target company would effectively be 'ring-fenced' under the pre-entry loss rules in *TCGA 1992, 7A Sch* which apply to all companies acquired after 31 March 1987. These rules were introduced to prevent 'capital loss' buying i.e. where the acquiring company sheltered its own capital gains by routing the disposal of assets through the purchased capital loss company. Such pre-entry capital losses can only be deducted against gains arising on assets owned by the target company at the date of acquisition or on gains realised on assets subsequently acquired from third parties. Similar restrictions apply to the pre-acquisition element of a capital loss realised on a subsequent disposal of any assets held by the target company on acquisition.

11.23 An acquisition of shares is treated as a business activity for VAT purposes. The recovery of input tax on costs associated with the acquisition is based on the purchaser's VAT status and is regarded as a business overhead. If the purchasing company is fully taxable for VAT purposes, then all the input tax is recoverable. If the company is partially exempt, the input tax would be restricted. (If the shares are issued as part of the consideration, this being an exempt supply may also cause a restriction in the recovery of VAT.)

11.24 Because of its capital nature interest incurred on UK bank borrowing to finance the acquisition of shares is unlikely to be allowed as a Schedule D Case I trading expense. Instead, relief for all interest should be allowable as a charge on income when paid. There are, however, difficulties in obtaining relief for short-term interest if it is paid other than to a UK bank.

11.25 Once acquired, the purchaser will need to decide how the company will be integrated with its existing operations. The acquired company may be left as a separate subsidiary company, in which case the various reliefs available to groups will apply. Alternatively, the trade of the target company may be hived-up and integrated with the purchaser's existing trade or kept separate on a divisionalised basis (see 3.22).

11.26 A group income election should be made for the purchased company enabling dividends to be paid up without ACT etc. (see 3.23). Dividends paid up outside a group income election may cause the Inland Revenue to apply *ICTA 1988, s 703* if the dividend is abnormal and paid out of the target's pre-acquisition profits. Similarly, any ACT carry back against pre-acquisition tax liabilities may be denied if there has been a major change in the nature of the trade within three years.

Protection of the purchaser

11.27 The legal principle of *caveat emptor* is pre-dominant in the context of the sale of company's shares. The company retains responsibility for all liabilities and actions and therefore the purchasing company will inherit all these problems, subject to any express agreement with the vendor in the contract. The purchaser should therefore ensure that its inherited liabilities are limited to those which were known at the time of acquisition and hence were reflected in the price paid for the company.

In some cases, a full investigation by the purchaser's accountants may not be justifiable or practicable, particularly if there is time pressure to complete the deal. The prospective purchaser must therefore seek protection under the sale agreement, by means of obtaining adequate warranties and indemnities. The purchaser will normally do the first draft of the agreement to place the full burden on the vendor. The vendor will aim to make the purchaser aware of all relevant facts through the disclosure letter.

The basic aim of warranties and indemnities should be to allocate the financial risks between the purchaser and vendor. However, warranties and, to a lesser extent, indemnities play a vital role in forcing the vendor to think and make disclosure about relevant items and events. Such draft 'information seeking' warranties can then be used to draw up specific warranties applicable to the precise circumstances.

The warranties and Deed of Indemnity usually appear in separate documents. The warranties will appear in the sale agreement between the vendors and purchasers (often accounting for about two-thirds of the agreement!). A separate Deed of Indemnity should be drawn in favour of the purchaser, thus enabling any indemnity payments to be treated as adjusting the purchase consideration (see ESC D44).

Retention payments

11.28   It is not inconceivable that the vendor may become insolvent, be liquidated or simply vanish. Thus, if the vendor or warrantor is not available or has no financial resources, any claim for compensation under the warranties will be fruitless. It may therefore be appropriate for the purchaser to negotiate for a certain portion of the sale consideration to be 'retained' (as security for the payment of funds due on a breach of warranty). The retention monies will usually be held by one or both parties' solicitors in an 'escrow' account.

Warranties

11.29   The primary function of drafting comprehensive warranties is to flush out all relevant information about the target company through disclosure by the vendor in a disclosure letter. The enquiries and analysis involved in the preparation of the disclosure letter will concentrate the vendor's mind on any potential problems within the target company (or group). A disclosure may impact the terms of the transaction, which may cause the purchaser to change the price or ask for specific indemnities.

The production of a formal disclosure letter (together with other documents cited as disclosed) is therefore an important exercise. The danger for the vendor is the possibility of innocent non-disclosure. In practice, information contained in an accountants report is treated as disclosed.

The warranty provides a remedy for the purchaser to sue for damages for breach of contract to compensate for the loss. Where a warranty is breached or proved to be untrue, the vendor will compensate the purchaser for the financial loss he has suffered in consequence of the non-disclosure or inaccurate disclosure of problems affecting the target business/company at completion. Payment would normally be of such an amount as to place the purchaser in the position he would have been in had the warranty been true.

This will normally be less than the full amount of the loss/additional liability covered since the purchaser would have discounted the purchase price for remoteness etc. The quantum of damages will be decided upon by the court after hearing expert evidence which can be a costly and time-consuming exercise. A claimant is therefore encouraged to compromise even if he has a strong case. However, the use of a valid 'liquidated damages' clause in the agreement will avoid the need for the court to get involved.

A well advised vendor will ensure that no warranty claim arises under the sale agreement if the matter has been clearly disclosed to the purchaser before completion through the formal disclosure letter or where the purchaser does not in fact suffer any 'loss'. Furthermore, it is normal for the warranty claim to be limited to a specific figure, normally equal to the purchase consideration, and de-minimis limits will also be imposed to avoid trivial claims under the warranty.

A Deed of Indemnity will normally be given by the covenantors in favour of the purchaser under which they will indemnify the full amount of any tax liability which is suffered by the company and is covered by the indemnity. The trend in recent years has now moved to having a 'blanket' indemnity covering all or virtually all forms of taxation liability.

This contrasts with a warranty under which the warrantor compensates the purchaser for the amount of financial loss suffered by the purchaser in consequence of the breach. (The target company is not directly concerned.) The purchaser will therefore prefer to obtain an indemnity from the vendor to cover unprovided pre-acquisition tax liabilities.

It is reasonable for the purchaser to be indemnified also against all costs, interest on overdue tax and tax penalties which may arise on the tax liabilities covered by the indemnity. The covenantors may justifiably seek some control over the handling and negotiation of any pre-sale tax liabilities so as to ensure they are fully contested and defended whenever possible.

PLANNING CHECKLIST — EXPANDING ACTIVITIES

Company
- Asset purchase usually provides increased tax relief on acquired assets purchased — purchase price should ideally be weighted in favour of tax allowable assets.
- Share purchase provides continuity of trade in target company and retention of any unused tax losses, ACT etc.
- Integration of the target trade with the acquirers should be structured to avoid prejudicing tax losses.

Working shareholders
- Need to limit commercial exposure on purchase by obtaining appropriate warranties and indemnities, obtaining full disclosure on all material items affecting 'the target'.
- Obtain non-competition covenants from vendors.

Other employees
- Rationalisation of workforce can lead to high redundancy and compensation costs (employment contracts are automatically transferred on asset purchases).

Non-working shareholders
- Require controlling/working shareholders to protect their position (may need a shareholder's agreement to protect their interests).

Chapter 12

Reorganising Shares and Trading Activities

Introduction

12.1   Developments in the life of a family company may make it necessary for the company to change its structure by including new shareholders or to increase or decrease the number of shares in existence. An existing shareholder may wish to give shares to the next generation as part of succession or capital tax planning. The directors or shareholders may decide to provide a valuable 'key' manager or new manager as an incentive and to foster a sense of proprietorship.

12.2   The mechanics of providing shares, whether through a new issue or by a transfer from an existing shareholder may involve a CGT liability, although business asset hold-over gift relief is usually available (see 12.6 and 12.19). If shares are made available to an existing or new employee for less than full consideration, the employee will suffer a Schedule E income tax charge, except where it can be demonstrated that the shares do not derive from his employment or prospective employment. This can normally be demonstrated if the employee is a member of the family (see 12.20).

12.3   When it is necessary for the company to decrease the number of shares in existence, the ability of a company to buy in its own shares means that the shareholders can look to the company itself as a willing buyer for their shares. This provides a useful 'exit' route in a number of situations. For example, where the controlling shareholder wishes to realise the value of his shares and, at the same time, make way for the next line of management. A buy-in can also be used to buy-out a dissident or disinterested shareholder. The company law and tax aspects of an own share purchase are covered in 12.23.

12.4   Some family businesses eventually develop to the stage where various activities or trades are run by different members of the family. If the shareholders each have different aspirations and requirements about the running of their divisions this may lead to a need to separate out the various trades. The trades could be transferred to new companies so that they can be run independently by the relevant shareholders. This can be achieved by a reconstruction or demerger — the mechanics and tax implications are discussed in 12.29.

Gift of shares

Married couples

12.5 Where shares are transferred between husband and wife who are living together during the year of assessment in which the disposal takes place, no CGT liability arises. The transferee spouse automatically inherits the transferor spouse's indexed base cost which would be derived from his/her share pool without the need of an election. [*TCGA 1992, s 58*]. On subsequent disposals the transferor's acquisition is treated as the transferee's. Indexation allowance available to the transferor is automatically built into the transferee's base cost if the transfer occurs before 30 November 1993 but cannot be clawed back if the transferor subsequently sells at a loss.

However for post-29 November 1993 transfers, if the transferee spouse realises a capital loss on a subsequent sale of the asset, any indexation element built into the transferee's loss including that inherited from the transferor spouse will be deducted to give a no gain/no loss result. [*TCGA 1992, s 56(2)*]. A husband and wife are not considered to be living together if they are separated by court order or by deed of separation or they are separated in circumstances that are likely to prove to be permanent. [*ICTA 1988, s 282*].

Other individuals

12.6 In other cases, a gift or 'under-value' transfer of shares from an existing shareholder will normally represent a disposal at market value for CGT purposes. This will apply whether the parties to the transaction are connected or not. [*TCGA 1992, ss 17, 18*].

12.7 If the disposal is to a connected person and a loss results that loss is only available for set off against future gains from disposal to the same person. [*TCGA 1992, s 18(3)*].

Business asset hold-over relief

12.8 A non-arm's length transfer of unquoted shares in a trading company will normally be eligible for business asset hold-over gift relief under *TCGA 1992, s 165*. To qualify the shares in question must be unquoted shares in a trading company or holding company of a trading group. Relief can also be claimed for quoted shares in a *personal* trading company/holding company of a trading group. [*TCGA 1992, s 165(2)*]. A personal company is one in which the voting rights are exerciseable by no less than 5% by the individual. [*TCGA 1992, 6 Sch 2*].

12.9 The transferor and transferee must jointly elect for hold-over relief, except where the transfer is made to trustees, in which case only the transferor makes the claim. [*TCGA 1992, s 165(1)(b)*]. The election must be made within 6 years after the end of the tax year in which the shares are transferred. [*TMA 1970, s 43(1)*]. Where shares in an investment company are gifted, hold-over relief cannot be claimed and therefore the transferor will suffer a CGT liability. [*TCGA 1992, s 165(2)(b)*].

The transfer of shares by an existing shareholder to an individual or interest in possession trust or accumulation and maintenance trust qualifies as a potentially exempt transfer for inheritance tax purposes. [*IHTA 1984, s 3A*]. No IHT liability would therefore arise provided the transferor shareholder survives seven years. Where the shares are gifted such that they are transferred for no consideration or are transferred at an undervalue, hold-over relief or relief for gifts of business assets will be available. [*TCGA 1992, s 165*]. This will have the effect of eliminating the transferor's capital gain. The gain will in turn be deducted from the transferee's deemed market value acquisition cost. [*TCGA 1992, s 17*]. The held-over gain will therefore become chargeable if and when the transferee subsequently makes a disposal of the gifted shares. In effect, the transferee will inherit the transferor's indexed base cost.

Example 1

Hold-over relief on pure gift

In May 1995, Brian Clough gave his son, Nigel, 30% of the shares in the family company, Cloughies Breakfast Foods Limited, which he incorporated in August 1986. The value of the shares transferred in May 1995 has been agreed by the Inland Revenue Shares Valuation Division at £50,000.

	£
Consideration = MV	50,000
Less Part disposal cost (say)	(2,500)
Unindexed gain	47,500
Less Indexation £2,500 × 52.9%	(1,323)
Indexed gain	46,177
Less TCGA 1992, s 165 relief	(46,177)
Chargeable gain	£ –

Nigel's CGT base cost will be £3,823 (i.e. MV of £50,000 less gain held-over of £46,177). This is effectively the 'cost' of the shares transferred i.e. £2,500 plus Brian's indexation allowance £1,323.

12.10   Since the computational effect of a hold-over claim can be computed without reference to the market value of the shares, the Inland Revenue will in most cases permit a hold-over claim to be made without the need to prepare a computation of the chargeable gain or to agree a valuation of the gifted shares. This concessionary treatment provided by SP8/92, must be claimed in writing by both the transferor and the transferee. Both parties must confirm they are satisfied that the value of the shares exceeds its original indexed base cost and also provide full relevant details of the shares transferred including the date of their acquisition and the allowable expenditure.

12.11   If the shares are sold an undervalue for an amount exceeding the transferor's base cost or deemed March 1982 base value, *excluding* indexation, the gain eligible for hold-over relief will be restricted by the amount of the excess consideration. [*TCGA 1992, s 165(7)*]. The excess of the actual consideration received by the transferor shareholder over his base cost, therefore becomes chargeable, as this is effectively the realised part of his gain. It is therefore possible for shares to be sold at their original base cost (as extracted from the transferor's share pool or March 1982) value without incurring a capital gain, provided a hold-over election is made.

Example 2

Hold-over relief where actual consideration received

If Nigel had provided some *actual* consideration, of say £20,000, his held-over gain would be restricted by £17,500 which is the amount by which the actual cash received £20,000 exceeds the base cost of £2,500:

	£	£
Indexed gain (as above)		46,177
less TCGA 1992, s 165 relief		
Gain	46,177	
Amount restricted	(17,500)	(28,677)
Chargeable gain		17,500

Nigel's CGT base cost would then be £21,323 (i.e. £50,000 less held-over gain of £28,677). This represents the amount paid i.e. £20,000 plus Brian's indexation allowance of £1,323.

12.12   There are a number of potential traps which may restrict the amount of hold-over relief and therefore create unexpected tax liabilities. An important example is where a personal company holds chargeable non-trading/investment assets when the shares are transferred. In such cases the held-over gain is restricted by reference to the following formula:

$$\text{Relevant gain} \times \frac{\text{Market value of chargeable business assets}}{\text{Market value of chargeable assets}}$$

The above restriction means that a chargeable gain will arise to the extent that the value of the company's chargeable assets reflects non-trading or investment assets. [*TCGA 1992, 7 Sch 7*]. It is therefore necessary to examine the company's balance sheet *before* any transfer of shares is made.

Goodwill may not appear on the balance sheet. This does not mean that goodwill does not exist but merely indicates that no payment has been made for goodwill. Goodwill is the difference between the value of a business as a whole and the aggregate of the fair value of its separable net assets (SSAP 22). Separable net assets are those assets and liabilities which can be identified and sold or discharged separately without necessarily disposing of the business as a whole and include identifiable intangible assets. Fair value is the amount for which an asset could be exchanged in an arm's length transaction. The inclusion of goodwill will have a beneficial effect on the chargeable business asset/chargeable asset calculation of a trading company.

Retirement relief

12.13   Retirement relief is given automatically to individuals who have attained the age of 55 years on the disposal of shares in a personal trading company or personal holding company of a trading group. [*TCGA 1992, s 163*].

Relief is given if the shares have been owned for one year before the disposal. However, the maximum amount of relief is only available if the shares have been owned for 10 years.

Retirement relief is also available to persons aged under 55 who are retiring on grounds of ill-health. The claim must be made within 2 years of the end of the year in which the disposal occurs. [*TCGA 1992, 6 Sch 5(2)*].

12.14   If the transferor shareholder is eligible for retirement relief, this will be deducted *before* any business asset hold-over gift relief. Where a subsequent disposal of shares to a third party is contemplated, a prior gift could increase the transferor's overall tax liability. This is because valuable retirement relief may have been 'wasted' on the gift. Where this problem is likely to occur, the third party disposal should take place before the 'gift relief' disposal.

Issue of new shares

12.15   A controlling shareholder might be tempted to procure an issue of shares to the prospective shareholder in order to avoid a direct disposal out of his holding. However, where new shares are issued for less than full consideration, a deemed CGT charge may arise under the value shifting legislation in *TCGA 1992, s 29*. Broadly speaking, a deemed disposal will arise where:

(*a*)   a controlling shareholder exercises control; and

(*b*)   as a result, value passes out of shares owned (or rights over the company exerciseable) by him (or a connected person); and

(*c*)   value passes into *other* shares in or rights over the company. [*TCGA 1992, s 29(2)*].

A deemed CGT charge can also occur where a group of shareholders exercise control in concert to cause value to be shifted out of their shares into other shares (see *Floor v Davis (1978) STC 436*).

These rules apply even if there is no intention of tax avoidance.

12.16   A controlling shareholder would therefore be subject to a value-shifting charge where he procures an issue of shares to others which causes his own shares to depreciate in value. The shares acquired by the allottees would be worth more than the amount subscribed for them. A deemed CGT charge would also catch any value flowing out of the controlling shareholder's holding where there is a variation in the rights attaching to his or other shares.

12.17   Although *TCGA 1992, s 29* creates a deemed disposal by the controlling shareholder *without* deeming a corresponding acquisition by the beneficiary, in practice the Inland Revenue will accept a business asset hold-over relief claim under *TCGA 1992, s 29*. A joint election should therefore prevent a value-shifting charge crystallising in most cases.

Example 3

Effect of value shift on issue of shares

Alan owned the entire 1,000 £1 issued ordinary shares in Mullery Limited. His shareholding was worth some £150,000 in March 1982 and is currently worth £600,000. (The company has authorised share capital of 5,000 £1 ordinary shares.)

In March 1995, Alan arranged for the company to issue 800 £1 shares at par to a valued manager, Alf. This depreciated the value of Alan's holding to £250,000.

Since Alan has control of the company and had exercised it so that value shifted out of his shares into those held by Alf, Alan would be treated as making part disposal of his shares at market value under *TCGA 1992 s 29(1)*.

It is assumed that £100,000 would be paid for the shares if the parties had been dealing at arm's length.

1994/95 — March 1995 disposal

	£
Deemed consideration (MV) —	100,000
Less March 1982 base value (part disposal)	
£150,000 × $\dfrac{£100,000}{£100,000 + £250,000}$	(42,857)
Indexation £42,857 × 85.7%	(36,728)
Chargeable gain	20,415

Inheritance Tax

12.18   The IHT legislation contains similar provisions for value shifting out of a person's estate as a result of the alteration of share rights in an unquoted close company. The IHT provisions examine the diminution in value to the donor's estate. Thus, where the alteration reduces the value of the donor's shareholding this will be treated as a transfer of value by the relevant shareholders subject to the exemption for non-gratuitous transfers and business property relief etc. [*IHTA 1984, ss 10, 103*]. It is important to note that the IHT value shifting transfer does not qualify as a potentially exempt transfer. [*IHTA 1984, s 98(3)*].

Schedule E charge for employees or directors

12.19   As explained in 6.43, where shares are issued or transferred to an employee/director as a gift or at a reduced price, he will be subject to a Schedule E income tax charge on the amount of the undervalue element (*Weight v Salmon (1935) 19 TC 174*). There is no Class 1 NIC liability on the provision of shares. [*Social Security (Contributions) Regulations 1979, Reg 19(1)(m)*]. It is normally very difficult to refute a Schedule E charge where shares are being transferred to an employee or director. The acid test is to ask the question 'would the shares have been made available on these terms to the individual if he was not an employee of the company?' If the answer is 'no', the shares will be treated as a benefit derived from the employment.

12.20   Usually, the only realistic chance of avoiding a Schedule E assessment is where shares are gifted to a member of the family, as this would characterise the transfer of the shares as a personal gift.

Example 4

Calculation of Schedule E charge under 'Weight v Salmon' principle

In example 3, Alf subscribed for 800 £1 ordinary shares in Mullery Ltd as par when those shares were worth £100,000. As Alf is an employee of the company, he will be assessed under Schedule E on the undervalue element, as follows:

	£
Market value of shares	100,000
Less Actual price paid	
800 × £1	(800)
Assessable amount	99,200

12.21 A potential double tax charge can arise where shares have been gifted by an existing shareholder to an employer/director and a hold-over election under *TCGA 1992, s 165* has been made. The recipient employer/director will be subject to a Schedule E charge on the market value of the shares. However, his market value acquisition cost will be reduced by the held-over gain. The restriction in his CGT base cost will give rise to double taxation when the shares are subsequently sold by him. This problem can be overcome by using a share option because the legislation specifically provides that any amount assessed on the exercise of the share option is added to an individual's CGT base cost. [*TCGA 1992, s 120(4)*].

12.22 A similar double tax charge can arise where shares are acquired at an undervalue on subscription. As there is no corresponding disposal, *TCGA 1992, s 17(1)* cannot be used to impute a market value base cost. [*TCGA 1992, s 17(2)*]. The employee/director's CGT base cost will therefore be the amount (if any) paid for the shares, although he will have a Schedule E assessment based on the market value of the shares. Once again, this problem can be overcome by the use of a share option arrangement.

Purchase of own shares

12.23 The use of the family company as a willing buyer for the purchase of its own shares can provide a useful and tax efficient exit route for its shareholders. It can also be used on the death of a shareholder where his personal representatives or beneficiaries do not wish to keep the shares or even where the estate is illiquid and the main asset is the shares. The shares can be brought back by the company avoiding loss of control by the family.

12.24   It is vital that the own share purchase arrangements follow the various company law requirements. A failure to comply with all the relevant rules would mean that the share purchase would be void.

A summary of the main legal requirements for a purchase of own shares by a private company is set out in the *Table* below.

Table 1

Company law requirements for purchase of own shares by a private company

1. The company must have to express power in its Articles of Association (Note — Table A reg 35 (for companies incorporated after 30 June 1985) permits it). Older companies will normally need to amend their Articles (as old Table A does not provide requisite authority).

2. There is no limit to the number of shares which may be purchased back, although at least one irredeemable share must be held after the purchase.

3. The purchased shares are immediately cancelled.

4. Payment must be made on completion of the transaction. It is not possible for payment to be deferred.

5. The shares to be purchased can be bought by the company:
   (*a*)   out of its distributable profits; or
   (*b*)   out of the proceeds of a fresh issue of shares; or
   (*c*)   out of capital, *provided* all distributable profits are used first.

6. A capital redemption reserve (which is non-distributable) must be set up to the extent that shares are purchased from distributable reserves — the amount transferred being equal to the *nominal* value of the shares purchased. This facilitates the maintenance of the company's capital base.

7. A purchase of share out of *capital* requires, *inter alia*, a special resolution, a statutory declaration of solvency by the directors (accompanied by a 'concurring' auditor's report) and publicity in the 'London Gazette' and a national newspaper.

8. The 'buy-in' contract (for an 'off-market' purchase) must be approved by a special resolution of the shareholders (excluding the votes of those shares which are to be brought in).

Tax treatment

12.25   Where a company purchases its own shares, this will represent a distribution for tax purposes. The distribution will be the excess of the amount paid for the shares over the amount originally subscribed for them. [*ICTA 1988, s 209(2)(b)*]. Thus, if the vendor was not the original subscriber, the price paid by him to acquire the shares would be irrelevant for this calculation.

However, the distribution treatment is disapplied where the relevant conditions for treating the payment as capital are satisfied. [*ICTA 1988, s 219(1)*]. The vendor shareholder would then be subject to CGT on the amount received. The company is also treated as making a capital payment.

It is important to realise that these provisions were introduced in the *Finance Act 1982* to relieve the tax burden for individual shareholders at a time of relatively high income tax rates. However, following the assimilation of income and CGT rates in the *FA 1988*, CGT treatment will now be detrimental in many cases.

12.26 A checklist of the main conditions which must be satisfied for the vendor to obtain CGT treatment under *ICTA 1988, s 219* is given in *Table 2* below. In practice, a detailed review of the legislation in *ICTA 1988, ss 219–229* is essential to determine whether a proposed own share purchase scheme will be treated as a CGT disposal. It is possible to obtain advance clearance from the Inland Revenue for CGT treatment under *ICTA 1988, s 225(1)(a)*. A clearance under *ICTA 1988, s 707* (transactions in securities) should also be made.

Table 2

Main conditions for s 219 capital treatment

Conditions for company	Statutory references (all to *ICTA 1988*)
1. The company must be an unquoted trading company or an unquoted holding company of a trading group (shares quoted on the AIM or Third Market are treated as unquoted for this purpose).	*s 219(1)*
2. The purchase must be made wholly or mainly for the purpose of benefiting the company's trade (or the trade of any of its 75% subsidiaries).	
The Inland Revenue interpret 'for the purpose of benefiting a trade' fairly liberally — see IR SP2/82. The Inland Revenue would normally wish to see the vendor giving up his entire interest in the company, although the retention of a minimal 'sentimental' stake may be allowed.	*s 219(1)(a)*
3. The purchase must not form part of a scheme or arrangement to enable the owner to participate in the profits of the company without receiving a dividend or to avoid tax.	*s 219(1)(a)*

4. Conditions 2 and 3 above do not apply where 'all or almost all' (see IR SP2/82 para 6) the payment (excluding the CGT paid thereon) is applied by the personal representatives in discharging the IHT liability of the deceased shareholder within two years of death, provided the IHT liability could not otherwise have been satisfied without causing undue hardship.

   Also, in such cases, the conditions required to be satisfied by the vendor shareholder (see below) are ignored.   *s 219(1)(b)(2)*

Conditions for vendor shareholder

1. The vendor shareholder must be resident and ordinarily resident in the UK in the tax year of purchase.   *s 220(1)–(3)*

2. The shares must have been owned by the vendor for at least five years before the date of sale.

   If the vendor inherited the shares, the period of ownership of the deceased shareholder/personal representatives can also be counted and the ownership requirement is reduced to three years.   *s 220(5)–(8)*

3. The shareholder must sell all his shares. If he does not, his proportionate shareholding (including associates) must be substantially reduced, although the Inland Revenue would not normally accept that this benefits the trade (see condition 2 for company above).   *s 221*

4. The vendor must not be 'connected' with the company immediately after the purchase.   *s 221*
          s 223

   For these purposes, a person is connected with the company if, he (together with his associates — (see below) possesses or is entitled to acquire more than 30% of:

   (*a*) the issued ordinary share capital; (or)
   (*b*) the loan capital and issued share capital; (or)
   (*c*) the voting power of the company.   *s 228*

'Associate' is defined in *s 227* and includes an individual's spouse and *minor* children but excludes, for example, brothers and parents.

12.27   Where the relevant conditions in *ICTA 1988, s 219* are satisfied, CGT treatment will be automatic — it is not optional. Therefore, if distribution treatment is required it will be necessary to engineer a deliberate breach of (at least) one of these conditions. Some possibilities are given below:

(*a*)   the shares could first be transferred to a life interest trust for the vendor shareholder's benefit. The trustees of the life interest trust would not have held the shares for at least five years at the date of the share repurchase and the condition in *ICTA 1988, s 220(5)* would therefore be broken. The transfer of shares to the life interest trust would be a disposal for CGT purposes but the gain can be held-over under the business asset gift relief provisions (see 12.9). [*TCGA 1992, s 165*];

(*b*)   *ICTA 1988, s 220(1)* states that if the shares are held through a nominee, the nominee must be a UK resident. This rule could therefore be broken by transferring the shares to a non-resident nominee. The transfer to a nominee would not involve any disposal for CGT purposes. This route may be vulnerable to a challenge by the Inland Revenue under the dicta in *Furniss v Dawson*;

(*c*)   it may be possible for the vendor shareholder to immediately lend back some of his proceeds to the company to break the 'connected with company' test in *ICTA 1988, s 223(1)*. The aim here is to ensure that the amount left outstanding as a loan exceeds 30% of the combined share and loan capital (the Inland Revenue treat an ordinary loan as loan capital). In many cases an immediate loan back to the company of only a small amount would break this condition;

(*d*)   a transfer of shares to/from a spouse prior to the share purchase or a termination payment to the vendor will usually be regarded by the Inland Revenue as an arrangement to avoid tax. It has been reported that clearance for capital treatment is invariably refused in such cases;

(*e*)   it might be possible to put forward the argument to the Inland Revenue that the buy-in was not for the purposes of the trade but to provide cash for the shareholder.

A degree of certainty can be obtained in advance about the efficiency of the arrangements to provide a distribution treatment by invoking the 'negative clearance' procedure in *ICTA 1988, s 225(1)(b)*. This requires the Inland Revenue to confirm within 30 days they are satisfied that the purchase falls *outside ICTA 1988, s 219*.

A comprehensive example illustrating the tax effects of a proposed buy-in under *ICTA 1988, s 219* and as a distribution is provided below.

Example 5

Capital v distribution treatment for own share purchase

Mr Ramsay is the controlling shareholder of Wembley Ltd, a company which he formed in 1966. Mr Ramsay is 50 years old and would like to retire from the company. He owns 700 of the issued £1 ordinary shares. His two sons, Ron and Terry own the remaining 300 shares between them.

Mr Ramsay needs to realise the value of his shares as he has no other major assets. He has agreed with his sons that control of the company should remain in the hands of his family and outside shareholders should not be brought in. However, his sons cannot personally afford to buy him out. Mr Ramsay has been advised that all these objectives can be satisfied by Wembley Ltd purchasing his shares. His shares will then be immediately cancelled, leaving the company under the control of Ron and Terry, without any direct personal cost to them. The company's auditors have determined that Mr Ramsay's shares should be sold at their fair value of £700,000.

Mr Ramsay subscribed for his 700 £1 ordinary shares at par in 1966 and they were worth around £60,000 in March 1982. *Prima facie*, Mr Ramsay and Wembley Ltd would be able to satisfy the conditions for capital treatment in *ICTA 1988, s 219* (see *Table 2* on page 178).

(i) Tax implications for Mr Ramsay

CGT treatment can be expected to apply to the proposed buy-in of Mr Ramsay's shares. If the share purchase took place in June 1995, Mr Ramsay's estimated CGT liability would be £232,336 calculated as follows:

June 1995 — CGT disposal

	£
Sale proceeds	700,000
Less March 1982 value	(60,000)
Indexation at 88.6%	(53,160)
Indexed gain	586,840
Less Annual exemption	(6,000)
Chargeable gain	580,840
CGT @ 40%	£232,336

However, if Ramsay's disposal could be treated as a distribution, a tax liability of only £174,825 would arise, calculated as follows:

June 1995 — Distribution

	£
Amount received	700,000
Less Amount subscribed on issue	(700)
Net distribution	699,300
Add: Tax credit (20/80)	174,825
Gross distribution	874,125
Income tax thereon £874,125 × (40% − 20%)	£174,825

The 'distribution route' reduces Mr Ramsay's tax liability by £57,511 (£232,336 − £174,825).

If the transaction is treated as a distribution for tax purposes, this does not prevent a disposal arising for CGT purposes. However, *TCGA 1992, s 31* prevents double taxation by eliminating the element of the consideration taxed as distribution 'income' from the charge to CGT. This means that the vendor shareholder will be treated as selling his shares for an amount equal to the subscription price and therefore no gain arises. A loss may arise if March 1982 rebasing applies (see below) or where shares were purchased for an amount exceeding the subscription price. Indexation relief cannot be used to create or increase a capital loss on a post-29 November 1993 buy-in, although limited transitional relief was available for 1993/94 and 1994/95. Individuals and trustees (of pre-30 November 1993 trusts) were able to set indexation losses of up to £10,000 against their net chargeable gains (after deducting the annual CGT exemption).

As March 1982 rebasing applies, Mr Ramsay will also have a capital loss under the distribution route, as demonstrated below:

	£
Sale proceeds	700,000
Less taxed as 'distribution' income	(699,300)
CGT proceeds	700
Less March 1982 value	(60,000)
Capital loss	(59,300)

The Inland Revenue accept that where a company buys in its own shares there is no acquisition by the company as those shares are immediately cancelled under *Companies Act 1985, s 160(4)*. Consequently, the capital loss restriction on disposals to connected persons in *TCGA 1992, s 18(3)* does not apply so that the capital loss is freely available. It may be possible to relieve the capital loss against the individual's income (including the distribution) under *ICTA 1988, s 574*. *ICTA 1988, s 574* relief can only be used where, *inter alia*, the loss was incurred 'by way of a bargain at arm's length for full consideration'. Relief may therefore be claimed by a minority shareholder but the Revenue are likely to be difficult where the buy-in is from a controlling shareholder.

(ii) Tax consequences for Wembley Ltd

If the transaction is treated as 'capital' under *ICTA 1988, s 219*, Wembley Ltd would be treated as having made a capital payment on which no tax relief is available — it would *not* be a distribution and therefore no ACT would arise.

If the CGT rules are *not* brought into play, Wembley Ltd would be treated as having made a distribution. It would therefore have to account for ACT of £174,825 (i.e. 20/80 × £699,300) under the quarterly CT61 accounting procedure. If the company cannot offset the ACT against its current year liability, then it can elect to recover the surplus against its tax liability for the previous 6 years. [*ICTA 1988, s 239(3)*].

(iii) Conclusion

Provided Wembley Ltd can recover its ACT promptly, it would clearly be beneficial for Mr Ramsay's disposal to be treated as a distribution as it gives him a lower tax liability. However, as the relevant conditions for CGT treatment appear to be satisfied the buy-in would automatically be treated as a capital transaction. Consequently, one of the conditions for CGT treatment must be broken (see 12.27).

12.28   In some cases, the vendor shareholder may be entitled to retirement relief or may have a substantial March 1982 base value which would result in a low CGT liability. Before proceeding with any buy-in transaction, initial calculations must always be prepared to determine the most beneficial route — CGT or distribution. This will then dictate the required arrangements and the relevant tax planning steps.

Company partitions and demergers

12.29   When two or more influential shareholders have a fundamental disagreement about the direction of the business, the company or one of the shareholders may buy the other out. However, if each shareholder manages separately identifiable parts of the business, the preferred route may be to 'partition' the company so that each shareholder takes over the relevant part of the business.

This could involve significant tax liabilities for the company and the shareholder. However, the division of the relevant business activities can usually be achieved on a tax-neutral basis by winding up the company and distributing the relevant assets to new companies owned by the shareholders under the procedure laid down in *Insolvency Act 1986, s 110*. Alternatively, one or more of the trades (or companies) can be distributed out under the demerger provisions. Although the demerger provisions avoid the need to put the company into liquidation, they contain more restrictions, for example, there must not be any intention to sell the demerged trade company (see 12.29).

The detailed procedure and tax consequences of a company partition under a *IA 1986, s 110* scheme will be explained through the use of a comprehensive case study example.

Example 6

Company partition scheme

Barnes (Transport & Haulage) Ltd carries on two separate businesses which are considered to be of similar value.

12.29 *Reorganising Shares and Trading Activities*

The transport and warehouse business is run by John Barnes and the haulage business is run by Paul Barnes. It has been decided that the two businesses would be better operated if John and Paul owned their respective businesses, to develop them as they wish. The company's tax advisors have recommended that this be effected by a reconstruction under *IA 1986, s 110*.

The various steps would be as follows:

(*a*)   the share capital of Barnes (Transport & Haulage) Ltd would be converted into two classes of ordinary shares — 'A' and 'B' shares split according to the respective values of each trade — in this case of similar value. (If the businesses were of unequal value, they could be equalised through the apportionment of liabilities and/or an equalisation payment — although this would be chargeable to CGT on the recipient shareholder.);

(*b*)   John will form 'Barnes Transport Ltd' to take over the transport and warehouse business and Paul will form 'Barnes Haulage Ltd' to take over the haulage business;

(*c*)   Barnes Ltd is then liquidated. Under *IA 1986, s 110*, a scheme of reconstruction takes place under which the liquidator:

   (i)   transfers the transport and warehouse business to Barnes Transport Ltd which, in turn, issues shares to John as consideration;

   (ii)   transfers the haulage trade to Barnes Haulage Ltd which, in turn, issues shares to Paul as consideration.

The various transactions are illustrated diagrammatically overleaf.

(i) Position of Barnes (Transport & Haulage) Ltd

Provided *TCGA 1992, s 139* applies, Barnes (Transport & Haulage) Ltd (being the transferor company) will be treated as disposing of its chargeable assets (included in the transfers to the two new companies) on a no gain/no loss basis i.e. the transferee companies will be deemed to have acquired the assets at their original cost (rebased to March 1982, where relevant) together with the accrued indexation allowance. [*TCGA 1992, s 139(1), 3 Sch 1*].

These provisions only apply if there is a scheme of reconstruction (or amalgamation). The most authoritative definition of a 'reconstruction' comes from Buckley J in an old stamp duty case (*South African Supply and Cold Storage Co Ltd (1904) 2 Ch 268*).

'What does 'reconstruction' mean? To my mind it means this. An undertaking of some definitive kind is being carried on, and the conclusion is arrived at that it is not desirable to kill that undertaking,

Barnes (Transport & Haulage) Ltd — diagram of transactions

Reconstruction

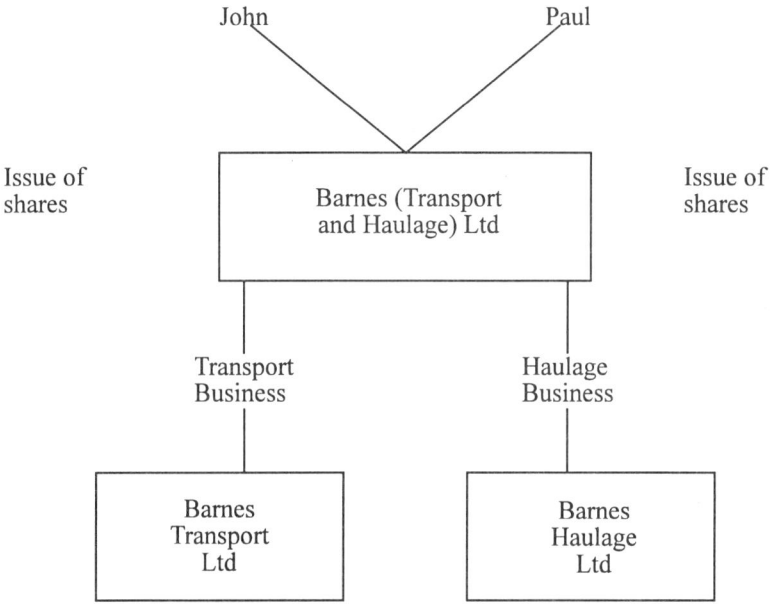

John   Paul

Issue of shares   Barnes (Transport and Haulage) Ltd   Issue of shares

Transport Business   Haulage Business

Barnes Transport Ltd   Barnes Haulage Ltd

The position will therefore end up as follows:

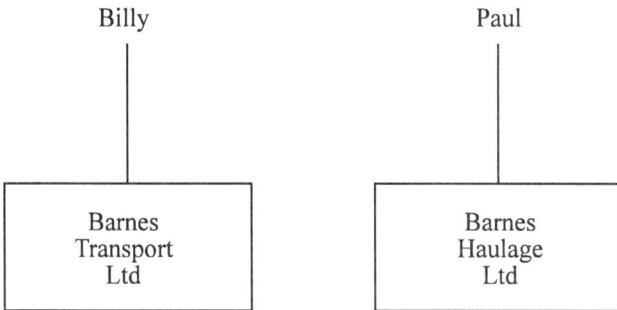

Billy   Paul

Barnes Transport Ltd   Barnes Haulage Ltd

but that it is desirable to preserve it in some form, and to do so, not by selling it to an outsider who shall carry it on — that would be a mere sale — but in some altered form to continue the undertaking in such a manner as that the persons now carrying it on will substantially continue to carry it on. It involves, I think, that substantially the same business shall be carried on and substantially the same persons shall carry it on. But it does not involve that all the assets shall pass to the new company or resuscitated company, or that all the shareholders of the old company shall be shareholders in the new company or resuscitated company. Substantially, the business and the persons interested must be the same'.

As far as Barnes (Transport & Haulage) Ltd is concerned, it has split its business and transferred its two trades to *different* shareholders which would appear to fall outside the above case law definition of a reconstruction. However, in practice, the Inland Revenue are prepared to extend the meaning of 'reconstruction' under SP5/85 to allow a division of a company's undertaking into two or more companies owned by different sets of shareholders, provided it is carried out for commercial reasons. (This type of reconstruction is sometimes referred to as a 'press release reconstruction'.) There must be a segregation of trades or businesses and not merely the segregation of its assets.

The operation of no gain/no loss rule in *TCGA 1992, s 139* for the transfer of assets on a reconstruction requires a number of other conditions to be satisfied:

(*a*)   the scheme must involve the transfer of the whole or part of one company's business to another company;

(*b*)   the scheme must be effected for bona fide commercial purposes and not for the avoidance of corporation tax, CGT or income tax. Advance clearance can be obtained from the Inland Revenue to confirm this is satisfied. [*TCGA 1992, s 139(5)*];

(*c*)   both the transferor and transferee companies must be UK resident at the time of transfer. [*TCGA 1992, s 139(1)*];

(*d*)   the transferor must not receive any part of the consideration for the transfer other than the assumption of its liabilities by the transferee companies. [*TCGA 1992, s 139(1)(c)*].

The reconstruction transactions contemplated by Barnes (Transport & Haulage) Ltd and its shareholders should therefore enable capital gains to be deferred at the company level.

(ii) Other tax consequences

The reconstruction provisions would not prevent the normal corporation tax consequences of a cessation of trade unless the succession provisions of *ICTA 1988, s 343* could be brought into play. If the succession provisions apply, this will enable any trading losses and the tax written-down value of plant, industrial buildings etc. to be carried over into the transferee company. In this particular example the common 75% beneficial ownership test required for an *ICTA 1988, s 343* transfer may not be satisfied after the reconstruction (prior to the transfer each trade is owned equally by John and Paul whereas after the transfer, each trade is owned separately by John and Paul). There may be an argument for saying that as 'associates', John and Paul are regarded as one person (under *ICTA 1988, s 344(4)*) which would then enable *ICTA 1988, s 343* to apply but the Inland Revenue might resist this approach. As trading stock is distributed *in specie* (i.e. not for valuable consideration), this will be deemed to pass at market value for tax purposes. [*ICTA 1988, s 100(1)(b)*].

The transfer of the trade and assets would not normally be subject to VAT as The Transfer of Going Concern provisions would apply. [*VAT (Special Provisions) Order 1995, Art 5*]. Stamp duty will normally be payable on the transfer of dutiable assets.

(iii) Position of John and Paul

Potentially, where shareholders of an existing company receive shares in another company on a reconstruction, this would be regarded as a distribution (being an indirect transfer by the company to its members). This is why it is essential for the disposing company — Barnes Ltd in this case — to be liquidated *before* the reconstruction exercise. Amounts received during the course of a winding-up do *not* constitute an income distribution (see 15.11). [*ICTA 1988, s 209(1)*].

The value of the shares acquired by John and Paul would therefore fall to be treated as a capital distribution. [*TCGA 1992, s 122(1)(5)*].

However, John and Paul will be protected from any CGT liabilities under *TCGA 1992, s 136* provided the shares are issued as part of the arrangements for a scheme of 'reconstruction'. Here again, the Revenue will permit the activities of a company to be divided between different shareholders under SP5/85 (provided the division is for bona fide commercial reasons).

Under *TCGA 1992, s 136* John and Paul will be treated as making no disposal for CGT purposes as regards their shares in Barnes Ltd with the result that the shares they acquire in their respective new companies — Barnes Transport Ltd and Barnes Haulage Ltd — will be treated as the same asset acquired at the same time as their old shares. (If the original shares are retained, they will be regarded as having been cancelled and replaced by a new issue. The original base cost will then have to be apportioned between the various shareholdings.)

TCGA 1992, s 136 requires the following conditions to be satisfied:

(*a*)   there must be an arrangement between the disposing company and its shareholders;

(*b*)   the shareholders must receive shares (and/or debentures) in the 'new' company in respect of and in proportion to their shares in the disposing company. (These shares must either be retained or cancelled.) This would not strictly be satisfied where a company's business is split between two or more companies owned by different sets of family shareholders. However, SP 5/85 would assist here as it does not insist on identity of shareholders in the old and new companies. [*TCGA 1992, s 136(1)(b)*];

(*c*)   the reconstruction must be effected for bona fide commercial reasons and not for the avoidance of tax. The advance clearance procedure in *TCGA 1992, s 138* will normally be used to confirm the Revenue are satisfied. [*TCGA 1992, s 137(1)*].

(iv) Position of recipient companies — Barnes Transport Ltd and Barnes Haulage Ltd

The new companies will acquire the relevant chargeable assets at the transferor's base cost (rebased to March 1982, if appropriate) with accrued indexation allowance. [*TCGA 1992, s 139*]. It should be noted that the de-grouping charge in *TCGA 1992, s 179* or *s 178* cannot apply in this situation as the chargeable assets were not transferred to a '*group*' company.

Permitted types of demerger

12.30   A reconstruction using *TCGA 1992, s 139* requires the transferor company to be liquidated to avoid the shareholders being subject to tax on an income distribution. This may not always be feasible or desirable. The *FA 1980* facilitated alternative methods of 'demerging' one or more trading activities carried on by a company or group, without the need to liquidate the transferor company.

In essence, a demerger is the division of a company or group into two or more companies or groups, with the ultimate shareholding ownership either being maintained or separated.

Three types of demerger are permitted by the *FA 1980* provisions. Each take the form of a distribution *in specie* of one or more trades or shares in one or more 75% subsidiaries.

Type I   — The direct distribution by a company to all or any of its members of shares in a 75% subsidiary (or subsidiaries).

Type II — The transfer of a company's trade or trades to one or more 'transferee' companies in consideration for the issue of shares in those companies to all or any of the members of the distributing company.

Type III — The transfer of shares in a 75% subsidiary (or subsidiaries) to one or more 'transferee' companies in consideration for the issue of shares in the companies to all or any of the members of the distributing company.

Demerger reliefs for shareholders

12.31 Provided the various qualifying conditions are met, the shares or trading assets received by the shareholders will *not* rank as an income distribution. The distribution is termed an 'exempt distribution'. [*ICTA 1988, s 213(2)*].

On a Type I demerger the distribution is not treated as a capital distribution, which would have been treated as part disposal for CGT purposes. The shares in the 75% subsidiary are treated as received in a 'new for old' reorganisation for CGT purposes. [*TCGA 1992, ss 127, 192(2)*]. A Type II or III demerger would normally qualify as a scheme of reconstruction so the 'new for old' reorganisation relief would apply (with reliance on SP5/85 if the original share ownership is split). [*TCGA 1992, s 136*].

Demerger relief for distributing companies

12.32 As the distributing company is treated as having made an 'exempt distribution' no ACT is payable. [*ICTA 1988, s 213(2)*].

In a Type I and Type III demerger a de-grouping charge could arise under *TCGA 1992, ss 178, 179* in consequence of assets transferred intra-group to the demerging company within the previous six years. However, a specific exemption is given for any de-grouping charge. [*TCGA 1992, s 192(3)*].

Type II and III demergers will usually qualify for 'reconstruction' relief under *TCGA 1992, s 139* to prevent capital gains being generated (by reference to market value consideration). A Type I demerger does not qualify for *TCGA 1992, s 139* relief (as the assets are not transferred to a company). This means a chargeable gain may be triggered on the disposal of the demerged subsidiary's shares, unless it can be mitigated in some way (e.g. by paying a pre-sale dividend).

The demerger provisions do not offer a complete tax-free basis for demergers. The *FA 1980* legislation mainly prevents the demerger distribution from being taxed in the shareholders' hands. Reliance must therefore be placed on the other 'succession' or reorganisation legislation to obtain exemption or carry-over of reliefs.

12.33 A demerger will only qualify for the exempt distribution treatment and the special reliefs mentioned above if it satisfies all the relevant conditions. These conditions are more onerous than for a reconstruction by liquidation agreement and reference must always be made to the detailed legislation in each case. The main conditions for a qualifying demerger are summarised below:

(*a*) all companies participating in the demerger transaction (the 'relevant companies') must be UK resident. [*ICTA 1988, s 213(4)*];

(*b*) the distributing company must be a trading company or member of a trading group. [*ICTA 1988, s 213(5)*];

(*c*) at the time of its distribution, a demerged 75% subsidiary must be a trading company or member of a trading group. [*ICTA 1988, s 213(5)*];

(*d*) the distribution must be made wholly or mainly for the benefit of some or all of the trading activities formerly carried on by the company/group. [*ICTA 1988, s 213(10)*];

(*e*) the distribution must not form part of a scheme or arrangement for:

　(i) the avoidance of tax or stamp duty. [*ICTA 1988, s 213(11)(a)*];

　(ii) the making of a 'chargeable payment' (see below). [*ICTA 1988, ss 213(11)(b), 214(2)*];

　(iii) the transfer of control of the demerged company to persons other than members of the distributing company. [*ICTA 1988, s 213(11)(c)*].

There are further pre-conditions for each type of demerger. [*ICTA 1988, s 213(6), (8)*].

Advance clearance can be obtained from the Inland Revenue to ensure they are satisfied that the demerger has been carried out for bona fide commercial reasons and not for the avoidance of tax. Indeed, tax clearances under *TCGA 1992, s 138* for the CGT reconstruction relief and *ICTA 1988, s 707* (*Transaction in Securities* legislation) will also be necessary.

Company law aspects

12.34 The company law implications must always be considered when structuring a demerger. For example, the distributing company must have sufficient distributable reserves to declare a dividend *in specie* equal to the book value of the assets/subsidiary transferred. *CA 1985, s 276* effectively enables any unrealised revaluation reserve (i.e., the difference between the revalued amount and cost of the transferred asset or shares) to be treated as realised for this purpose.

The distributing company must have the power in its Articles to make an *in specie* distribution.

PLANNING CHECKLIST — REORGANISING SHARES AND TRADING ACTIVITIES
Company • Several businesses can normally be partitioned without tax cost amongst different shareholders under a liquidation scheme of reconstruction or a demerger. • A reconstruction will involve winding the company up where it has insufficient reserves to declare a dividend *in specie* of the demerged trade.
Working shareholders • Shares can normally be transferred or trades moved to different companies via a reconstruction, without any immediate tax costs. • Funds can be extracted from the company on the shareholder's retirement in a tax efficient manner by arranging for the company to buy shares.
Other employees • Employees receiving shares are taxable on the 'benefit' under Schedule E.
Non-working shareholders • Can look to the company to buy their shares where they wish to cease their involvement with the company. • Must participate in a reconstruction.

Chapter 13

Valuing a Family Company

Introduction

13.1   Share valuations are required in a variety of situations. Commercial valuations fix the price at which shares in unquoted companies should change hands in actual transactions or where a valuation is sought for the purposes of a divorce settlement or financing arrangement. Tax legislation also requires shares to be valued in various circumstances giving rise to the need for fiscal or tax-based valuations. This chapter discusses commercial and tax based valuations. It will be seen that although similar concepts apply to both these types of valuation, there are marked differences in approach.

Commercial valuations

13.2   Commercial share valuations determine the price to be paid for the shares where, for example:

(*a*)   the shareholders wish to sell the company or a prospective purchaser wishes to make an offer for the company;

(*b*)   a shareholder is retiring and is required to sell his shares to the other shareholders or back to the company under an own share purchase (see 12.23–12.28).

13.3   A commercial value must reflect the circumstances of both the vendor and the purchaser in that it seeks to arrive at a fair value between what the vendor is giving up and what the purchaser acquires as a result of the acquisition.

13.4   Where a shareholder wishes to retire, the Articles of Association may provide a formula to arrive at the fair value at which shares must be offered to the other shareholders.

Value of company

13.5   Where the shareholders are seeking to sell the entire company, they will require an indication of how much the company is worth. Assistance can be obtained from the knowledge of reported disposals of comparable businesses, such as those listed in *Acquisitions Monthly* or trade journals. The general economic climate, the state of the particular industry in which the company trades and its particular position within it will also influence the valuation.

In many ways, a company is worth what somebody is prepared to pay for it. Consequently, the 'price' can also reflect the prospective purchaser's rationale for acquiring the business, e.g. to achieve increased market shares, economies of scale and so on. An attempt should be made to quantify the financial benefits accruing to the purchaser.

13.6   The commercial valuation of a company or business is essentially a matter for negotiation between the vendor and the purchaser. The basic approach is to determine what the company or business can earn or realise. The majority of company and business valuations are based on earnings. A capitalised earnings valuation requires an estimate of the business's future maintainable earnings and the application of an appropriate rate of return or price/earnings (P/E) multiple.

13.7   Some would argue that the value of a controlling interest should be based on discounted cash flow as the purchaser/investor is ultimately only interested in cash generation (which is not affected by accounting policies). This approach would require details of the forecast cash flows over a substantial period of time, which would then be discounted at an appropriate interest rate. (The interest rate would reflect the time value of money and the investor's perception of the risk inherent in the investor.) The sum of the discounted cash flows would give the net present value of the investment. Although this is a theoretically defensible approach in practice the purchaser/investor will normally have insufficient details to perform this type of calculation.

Maintainable earnings

13.8   Historic profits are generally taken as a starting point for determining a company's sustainable earnings as they are based on actual trading results and provide readily ascertainable figures. However, historical profits will only provide a guide to the business's future maintainable earnings. A rigorous assessment of the company's reported accounting profits will be required to assess the impact of any exceptional or non-recurring items and also any transactions which are not at arms length. Typically, adjustments may be required for items such as:

(*a*)   excessive director's remuneration and pension costs — i.e. the quasi-profit distribution element in a family company which reflects the director's proprietorial rewards and would not be paid to an arm's length management team;

(*b*)   income and expenses relating to discontinued or new operations and products;

(*c*)   profits and losses on the sale of fixed assets.

13.9   *Valuing a Family Company*

As the earnings basis values a company's ability to generate earnings, income from 'surplus' assets and investments which are not required for generating the principal trading profits must be excluded from the 'earnings' figure. The market value of surplus assets is then added to the earnings based figure to arrive at the total valuation of the company.

A prospective purchaser will assess what the business would earn after the acquisition, after adjusting for the financial impact of proposed changes. For example, the earnings could reflect the anticipated cost savings of fewer directors/managers being required after the acquisition and certain other economies of scale. Further adjustments may be necessary to reflect different financing structures and judgement about future trading conditions etc.

Forecasts or projections may be used as an alternative to the historic profits provided it is recognised that they are based on certain assumptions and are potentially unreliable.

Once the maintainable profits have been determined an appropriate future tax rate is applied to arrive at the maintainable earnings.

Price/earnings (P/E) multiple or rate of return

13.9   The purchaser's/investor's required rate of return must then be determined. This will generally consist of a 'risk-free' rate plus a premium which recognises the risk inherent in the particular business. The conventional approach is to apply an appropriate price/earnings or P/E ratio, which is calculated as follows.

$$\frac{\text{Price per share}}{\text{Net earnings per share}}$$

The P/E ratio can be thought of as the number of years earnings per share represented by the share price. The P/E ratio is, in fact, the reciprocal of the required rate of return or earnings yield.

Considerable judgement is required in selecting an appropriate P/E multiple. It may be possible to find the P/E multiple obtained on recent comparable business sales and acquisitions, such as those reported in *Acquisitions Monthly*. If such details are not readily available, published P/Es for comparable quoted companies can be used. If a comparable company cannot be found, the average P/E for the industrial/business sector in which the company operates can be taken from the *FT Actuaries Share Indices* ('FTASI') published in the *Financial Times*. (The industry sector P/E index is a weighted average of the P/E multiples of the major companies in the sector.)

Published P/E ratios are generally derived from the price obtained from a high volume of transactions in very small holdings (although at times

Private company price index

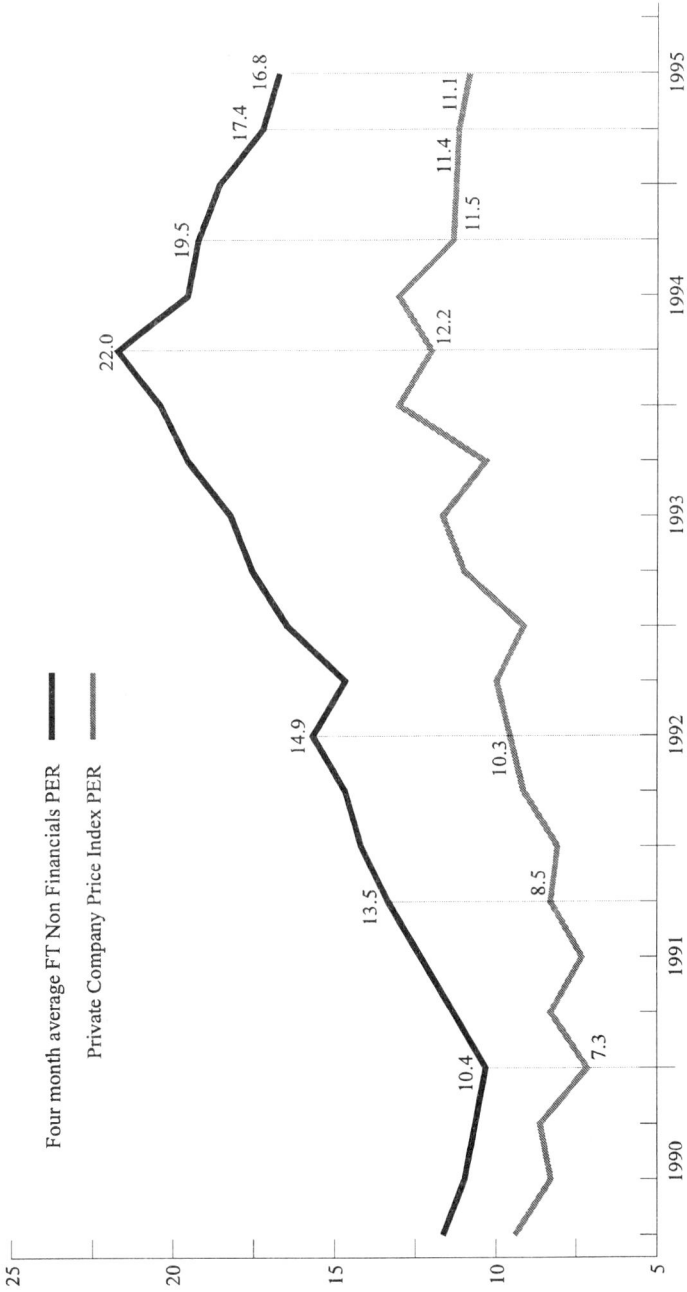

Four month average FT Non Financials PER

Private Company Price Index PER

22.0

19.5

17.4

16.8

14.9

13.5

10.4

12.2

11.5

11.4

11.1

10.3

8.5

7.3

1990   1991   1992   1993   1994   1995

25

20

15

10

5

Reproduced by kind permission of Acquisition Monthly August 1995 page 34 the market price may be heavily influenced by institutional investors and potential take over bids). A published P/E may therefore need to be increased to value the entire company. On the other hand, P/E ratios are often based on historical earnings figures although the share price anticipates market expectations. As companies emerge from the effects of a recession, the effect of the lag between low historical earnings and share prices based on future expectations can be quite pronounced and the P/E multiple would need to be discounted for this.

An interesting graphical comparison between quoted P/Es and unquoted P/Es (derived from actual transactions) from the August 1995 issue of *Acquisitions Monthly* is reproduced on page 195.

Net asset valuations

13.10   A valuation based on 'net assets' is not a true method of determining a going concern value for a trading company. Net asset values are really only applicable for pure asset-based companies, such as property or share investment companies or in the context of a 'break-up' situation.

After computing an earnings based valuation, further comfort is usually obtained by computing a net asset valuation. A net asset valuation is based on the company's balance sheet values, adjusted to reflect the current market value of properties, intellectual property etc. The difference between the earnings based valuation and the net asset value of the company will be goodwill. The purchaser will then ask whether the amount effectively being paid for goodwill is appropriate, giving the nature of the business and the current economic climate.

Special considerations

13.11   The basis of valuation will primarily depend on the vendors' reason for selling and the purchaser's rationale for making the acquisition. In practice, the skill is to determine the correct basis of valuation. In certain cases, the valuation would also need to reflect the benefits of synergy with the purchaser's existing business, the costs of merging with the purchaser's existing business etc.

If a company is loss-making, the value will be based on the future perception of the business and its prospects for recovery i.e. is it only a temporary downturn or will the company cease to exist. In the latter case, a break-up value of the assets would be appropriate with adjustments to reflect the forced sale value of assets, irrecoverable debts and termination costs, etc.

There is likely to be difficulty in assessing the maintainable earnings of companies with little or no track record. Forecast profits are likely to be used as a basis for valuation, but a purchaser would need to be comfortable with the underlying assumptions. In practice, a purchase is likely to make part of the sale price contingent on profit warranties or value the business in 'hind-sight' by using an earn-out (see 14.18).

Example 1

Valuation of company — case study

Cottee Ltd manufactures precision parts for the automotive industry. It is necessary to value the company in June 1995 to gauge the price that could be expected on a future sale. The most appropriate basis of valuing the company is by reference to its earning capacity.

The recent results of Cottee Ltd (all audited) are summarised as follows:

	Year ended 31 March		
	1993 £'000	1994 £'000	1995 £'000
Turnover	725	840	920
Profits before directors' remuneration	218	320	410
Director's remuneration	(78)	(90)	(116)
Trading profit before interest	140	230	294
Interest	(22)	(13)	(32)
Profit before taxation	118	217	262
Taxation	(32)	(56)	(68)
Profit after taxation	86	161	194
Effective tax rate	27%	26%	26%

Maintainable earnings

13.12   Given the trend of results and the fact that the company's order book is booming as a result of increased car sales, the historical profits may not provide a realistic assessment of the company's future earnings, as difficult trading conditions were experienced in 1993/94. The profits for the year ended 31 March 1995 can be taken as the starting point for maintainable profits plus (say) a prudent 5% increase to reflect management's expectations.

13.13 *Valuing a Family Company*

The accounts would then be analysed for any unusual items etc. and for adherence to standard accounting policies, which give rise to the following adjustments:

Example 2

	£'000	£'000
Maintainable profits		
Pre-tax profits for the year ended 31 March 1995	262	
Plus 5% increase	13	275
Adjustments		
Reduction in depreciation charge (company's rates more prudent than the norm)		15
Excessive directors' remuneration (based on prevailing industry rates for 2 directors) (£116,000 – £75,000)		41
		331
Less Taxation (£331,000 × 26%*)		(86)
MAINTAINABLE EARNINGS		245

* The tax charge reflects the influence of marginal rate

Selecting an appropriate P/E ratio

13.13 Assume on 3 June 1995 the majority of the quoted P/Es in the engineering vehicles sector fell within the range of 15 to 30, based on historic results (although the *FT Actuaries All Shares* P/E index for the sector was 59.87 — a temporary blip!). However, deals recorded in the private sector indicated lower P/Es in the order of 8 to 15 (there is a large gap between quoted and unquoted P/Es — see 13.9). Furthermore, approximately 60% of the company's turnover is with one major car manufacturer in the West Midlands and the P/E would need to be discounted to take account of the significant dependence on one supplier.

The assessment of an appropriate P/E multiple is obviously a subjective exercise. Based on all the relevant circumstances, this is taken to be 7.

Example 3

Value of Cottee Ltd

Maintainable earnings (per 13.12)	—	£245,000
P/E (per 13.13)	—	7
Value of the whole of the issued share capital of Cottee Limited £245,000 × 7	—	£1,715,000

Given the limited information available the shares could be valued in the range of £1,600,000 to £1,800,000.

Fiscal or tax-based valuations

Why fiscal valuations are required

13.14 Fiscal or tax based valuations are required by the tax legislation in various situations, for example:

(*a*) shares held at 31 March 1982 must be valued at that date for rebasing purposes;

(*b*) shares transferred otherwise than at arm's length must be valued (although if hold-over relief can be claimed both parties can elect to dispense with the valuation — see (12.9);

(*c*) determining the value of shares chargeable to inheritance tax on death or by reason of a lifetime transfer becoming chargeable on a death within seven years;

(*d*) determining the Schedule E benefit on shares made available to employees (see 6.43 and 12.19).

Basic concepts

13.15 The statutory rules for determining market value are deceptively simple. In *TCGA 1992, s 272(1)* and *IHTA 1984, s 160(1)*, the market value is the price which those assets/the property might reasonably be expected to fetch if sold in the open market. There is of course no open market for unquoted shares. A considerable body of case law and practice has therefore been built up over the last hundred or so years to provide the conceptual framework for valuing unquoted shares. Although valuations are carried out on an academic basis, it must always be remembered that share valuation is an art not a science; or 'intelligent guesswork' as Mr Justice Dankwerts called it in *Holt v CIR [1953] 1 WLR 1488.*

The value of a share is therefore what the valuer can successfully argue it to be. The tax or taxes on which the valuation turns will have a bearing on the situation. For example, if the shares are being valued for March 1982 rebasing purposes, as high a value as possible will be negotiated. If the same shares were being valued on death for IHT, a (much) lower valuer is likely to be argued for!

The main principles were succinctly summarised by Mr Justice Plowman in *re Lynall (deceased) (1971) 47 TC 375.* Unquoted shares are to be valued on the basis of a hypothetical sale, based on a price that could be reasonably expected to be paid:

(*a*)   by a hypothetical willing purchaser;

(*b*)   to a hypothetical willing vendor;

(*c*)   in the open market.

The hypothetical willing purchaser is assumed to be reasonably prudent and will therefore obtain all information relevant to the size of the shareholding and the amount of capital invested (see *TCGA 1992, s 273(3)*). A prudent hypothetical purchaser is likely to require detailed knowledge about the company's financial position and prospects etc. before he acquires a controlling interest. On the other hand, less information would be available to a purchaser of a minority stake, unless a substantial sum was being invested. The Revenue's view is that if the holding is less than 5% and the value is below £50,000, a prospective purchaser would only have access to published information. Inside information available to a director/employee purchaser is ignored — remember, it is an imaginary purchaser. Of course, this is where the (academic) assumptions upon which fiscal valuations are based differ from transactions in the real world.

The value has to be the best price that could be obtained by the vendor in an arm's length bargain in the open market. For this purpose, the restrictions on the transfer of shares normally found in most Articles of Association are disregarded in the hypothetical open market, although the purchaser is deemed to take the shares subject to those restrictions.

13.16   The valuation will primarily be influenced by the relative size of the shareholding. Majority/controlling shareholdings confer greater rights and power than minority/non-controlling shareholdings and are therefore worth more per share. It is usually helpful to allocate the shares being valued into one of the following categories.

Voting power%	Rights of shareholder
90% or more	Has right to sell shares and can give purchaser compulsory power to acquire remaining shares. Enjoys total control of the company (including right to wind up the company).
75% to 89.9%	Has effective control of the company. Has requisite votes to pass a special resolution and can put the company into liquidation or sell it as a going concern.
50.1% to 74.9%	Enjoys day to day control (but cannot pass special resolution).
50%	May have shared control or a deadlock situation. Value would depend on spread of other shareholdings.
25.1% to 49.9%	Influential minority — has right to block a special resolution (which requires 25% of the votes). Value would depend on spread of other shareholdings.
10.1% to 25%	Small minority but cannot be bought out by majority.
Up to 10%	Small minority liable to forced sale by majority.

13.17 A majority shareholder (having more than 50% of votes) can pass an ordinary resolution. He therefore enjoys practical command of the company, being able to decide the company's dividend policy, level of directors' remuneration and can often determine whether the company should be sold, floated, or wound-up. A control holding will therefore be based on the value of the entire company. In the case of a going concern, the value will be based on the company's underlying profitability and hence the earnings basis of valuation is normally used (see 13.8, 13.9 and 13.20).

In contrast, a minority shareholder is relatively impotent, he does not have control and the value of his holding would be primarily determined by the rights in the company's Articles of Association, the size of his own holding and the spread of other shareholdings. Frequently the Articles will impose a restriction on the right to transfer shares, subject to the Board's discretion. The minority shareholder will normally therefore be locked in and would not have any effective sanction against the Board of Directors. The restricted rights of a minority shareholder therefore produce a much lower valuation.

As dividends generally constitute the return for the minority shareholder, such holdings are often valued on a dividend yield basis, particularly where the taxpayer wishes to establish a low valuation. However, many unquoted companies do not pay dividends even though there are sufficient earnings to do so or their dividend payment record may be erratic. In such cases, the preferred approach would be to value the holdings on an earnings yield basis, although a lower (i.e. discounted) P/E ratio would be applied than for a control holding. The level of discount varies according to the size of the holding and the spread of the other shareholdings (e.g. a 40% shareholding may give practical control if the remaining shares are spread amongst ten shareholders).

There are no published formulae for discounts and Shares Valuation Division (SVD) usually succeed if the negotiations turn on the level of discount to be applied. Generally, discounts of between 45–75% are sought by the SVD for small minority holdings, with lower discounts of 30–40% for larger minority holdings of up to 49%. Use of the earnings basis avoids the use of notional dividends, which are less easy to support in negotiations with SVD. Earnings based valuations have become popular when valuing minority shareholdings for March 1982 rebasing purposes as this generally enables higher values to be negotiated with SVD.

Dealing with Shares Valuation Division — (SVD)

13.18   It is important to appreciate that Inspectors of Taxes and Examiners at the Capital Taxes Office must refer all share valuations to the Inland Revenues Shares Valuation Division ('SVD'). Although some valuations incorporated on a tax computation slip through 'on the nod' without referral to SVD, it is unwise to assume this will happen.

Once referred, the SVD will request basic information relevant to the shares being valued in form VAL 40. The writer's preferred approach is to submit a realistic share valuation report to SVD at the outset. The report would clearly set out all the relevant background information and the principles upon which the share valuation is based.

The main items covered in the report would be:

(*a*)   the purpose of valuation indicating which tax or taxes are involved;

(*b*)   the date on which the shares are being valued (this is critical as information which cannot be established at that date is not admissible);

(*c*)   the statutory principles upon which the value is based;

(*d*)   financial and trading background, this would include a summary of past results, trends, profit forecasts, shape of the company's order book, state of the industry in which the company operates, economic background and other factors affecting the valuation;

(*e*)   a clearly reasoned valuation, showing detailed calculations and the reasons for the various steps.

The Examiners at SVD should not be underestimated — they have considerable experience and expertise and are armed with an extensive database. Examiners will always consider realistic valuation submissions carefully. It is unwise to submit an unrealistic valuation in anticipation of SVD starting from the opposite side, with a view to meeting somewhere in the middle. This approach usually signals a weakness to the SVD which makes it easier for them to commence negotiations on very strong ground and the taxpayer will find it very difficult to recover from this position.

Share valuation methods

13.19   Share valuations are normally based on one of the following methods (or a weighted combination of two or all three of them).

(i)   Earnings (Capitalised earnings) basis
Maintainable earnings per share × P/E ratio.

(ii)   Net assets basis
Balance sheet value of net asset (after deducting liabilities), adjusted to reflect current open market value of assets (divided by number of shares in issue).

(iii)   Dividend yield basis.
$$\frac{\text{Gross dividend }\%}{\text{Required Gross Dividend yield}} \times \text{Nominal value per share}$$

Earnings basis

13.20   The earnings basis was discussed in 13.8 and the same considerations apply where shares are valued in for fiscal reasons. The general approach is to look at the company's profit record for the last three years although a longer period may be necessary if the trade is cyclical. The profit record is used to give a guide to the company's future performance and various adjustments may therefore be required (see 13.8). A 'notional' tax charge is then applied to arrive at the maintainable or sustainable earnings. The information assumed to be available to a prospective purchaser would be based on the size of the shareholding and the value of the transaction. For a controlling interest (of 50% or more) the purchaser would be deemed to have access to all the available financial information, including management accounts and the order book etc. A purchaser of an influential minority stake would be expected to have similar information but in less detail. The details provided for a small minority (5% to 25%) would be dictated by the transaction value, ranging from full disclosure to the basic information contained in the published accounts etc.

Hindsight information which becomes available after the date on which the value is being determined cannot be used to influence the valuation. In the context, published accounts are only assumed to be available when signed.

13.20 *Valuing a Family Company*

The P/E ratio applied to the maintainable earnings would be assessed by looking at the ratios of comparable quoted/unquoted companies, ideally based on recent known company sales/takeovers. If comparable reported transactions cannot be found, the P/E ratio for an appropriate comparable quoted company or industry sector is used (see 13.9).

The P/E may need to be adjusted downwards if the relevant company is smaller or has less geographical coverage etc. than the quoted company or sector. Unless the company is wholly-owned, the value would be discounted to reflect the size of the controlling interest, which would normally be in the following regions:

Voting power	Discount %
99% to 75%	5% to 10%
below 75%	15% to 20%

Example 4

Valuation of controlling interest on earnings basis

Hunter's Butchers Ltd has carried on a long established family business of retail butchers and manufacturers of meat based products. Mr Hunter, who owns 80 of the company's 100 £1 ordinary shares, has received an offer for the company. He acquired his shareholding in 1971 on the death of his father and wishes to estimate the March 1982 value of the holding to compute his likely CGT liability.

The company's pre-tax profits for the three years to 31 December 1981, (adjusted for excessive director's remuneration) were as follows:

	£'000
y/e 31/12/79	238
y/e 31/12/80	207
y/e 31/12/81	382

Prospects for the business were good in March 1982 and management accounts increased monthly profits to that date. A supportable figure of maintainable profits would be £400,000.

The company's tax charge between 1979 and 1981 ranged between 25% and 30%, as a result of stock relief claims. It would therefore be appropriate to apply a tax charge of 30%.

Maintainable earnings:	£'000
Maintainable pre-tax profits	400
Less Tax at 30%	(120)
Maintainable earnings	280

Relevant P/E's for the food sector at 31 March 1982 were:

Food manufacturing (average)	7.85
Food retailing (average)	13.77

Given that a control holding is being valued, a P/E of 12 could prudently be taken.

Valuation of company:

= Maintainable earnings × P/E ratio
= £280,000 × 12
= £3,360,000

Value per share:

$$\frac{£3,360,000}{100} = £33,600 \text{ per share}$$

Value of Mr Hunter's shares at 31 March 1982:

£33,600 × 80 = £2,688,000

Net assets basis

13.21   Asset based valuations are adopted where a company has substantial asset backing (such as property and investment companies), where the company is about to go into liquidation, or where a purchaser is likely to strip the assets out of the company and wind it up (where the assets are under utilised). Furthermore, although a going concern value will normally be calculated by reference to earnings, it is always worthwhile valuing the business on an asset basis as a cross check. Material differences may need to be explained or investigated. Normally, the capitalised earnings basis should exceed the value of the tangible net assets with the difference being the goodwill element. Is the goodwill figure reasonable in the circumstances? However, if the asset value exceeds the earnings basis, this could indicate that the earnings have been under-capitalised.

There are various types of asset based valuations. If the company is being valued as a going concern, then the open market value of its assets at the valuation date would be taken. The book value of the assets may therefore require adjustment. Although the balance sheet may fairly reflect the value of stock, debtors and possibly plant, a revaluation adjustment may be required in the case of land and buildings.

If a 'break-up' basis of valuation is applicable (i.e. the value that would be realised on a liquidation), then the realisable value of the assets will be taken. Furthermore, the closure would also involve redundancy payments and other termination costs (e.g. cancellation of lease agreements etc.), costs of liquidation and tax charges arising on the disposal of assets. For these reasons, the break-up value of the business will be much lower than either a going concern or infeed balance sheet value.

Example 5

Net asset valuation

An extract from the balance sheet of Hunter's Butchers Ltd at 31 March 1982 (see Example 4), together with estimated market value, shows:

	Net book value £'000	Market value £'000
Freehold shop premises	430	900
Leasehold shop premises	210	250
Factory	100	450
Net current assets	980	
	1,720	

Net asset valuation

	£'000
Current market values of	
Freehold shops	900
Leasehold shops	250
Factory	450
Net current assets	980
	£2,580

Value per share

$$= \frac{\text{Net asset value}}{\text{No. of shares}}$$

$$= \frac{£2,580,000}{100}$$

$$= £25,800 \text{ per share}$$

The SVD may seek a discount against this value to take account of the contingent CGT in the asset values. This would be a maximum of 30%

of the gain inherent in the shops and factory, reduced to reflect the remote probability of the tax becoming payable.

Dividend Yield basis

13.22   As indicated above, a small minority shareholder's return will be based on the company's dividend policy. If the company has a reliable track record of dividends which are either constant or show a steady increase or decrease, a dividend yield basis can be used (if the company is about to go into liquidation, a break up asset basis would be used with a significant discount for lack of control etc.).

An earnings based value can be used for an influential minority shareholder, particularly where the other shares are thinly spread and he is able to exert some degree of influence. It is important to remember that a fiscal valuation can take no account of the personal qualities or actual influence of the individual shareholder on dividend policy etc. The transaction is assumed to be an imaginary one in the assumed open market between a hypothetical willing vendor and hypothetical willing purchaser.

An earnings valuation may also be more appropriate if the company's dividends widely fluctuate or it does not pay dividends. Although it is possible to assume a notional dividend, this is very subjective. In the writer's view, it is better to adopt an earnings valuation which can be argued with greater certainty (particularly if a March 1982 rebasing value is sought), although a greater discount would be required to reflect the impotence of a small minority holding.

A dividend yield is calculated as follows:

$$\frac{\text{Nominal value of shares} \times \text{Dividend (as \% of nominal value)}}{\text{Value of share}} = \text{Dividend yield}$$

Thus, to calculate the value of the shares, the formula becomes:

$$\frac{\text{Nominal value of shares} \times \text{Dividend (as \% of nominal value)}}{\text{Dividend yield}} = \text{Value per share}$$

The starting point is to determine the required dividend yield. In practice, the SVD will normally start by applying the dividend yield from a comparable quoted company. It is usually difficult to find a true comparison particularly for small family businesses who typically carry on a limited range of activities (quoted companies often have a diverse spread). Consequently, the average dividend yield from the most comparable sector of the *Financial Times Actuaries Shares Indices* is normally taken. This average yield would then be increased to recognise the increased risk associated with investment in unquoted companies, such as the lack of marketability of the shares, smaller size, and limited activities. However, if the unquoted company has features which reduce risk to an investor, such as high asset backing, quality products, enjoys a niche market high level of dividend cover etc., then the required yield should be adjusted downwards.

An alternative approach which is sometimes taken in practice is to take a risk free rate of return (e.g. the yield on Gilts) and then add a premium for the degree of risk associated with the investment. This would give the investor's required rate of return.

Example 6

Value of shares on a dividend yield basis

Frank owns 50 £1 shares (representing a 5% holding) in Lampard's Electricals Ltd which trades as a retailer of electrical goods.

The SVD have agreed that the 5% holding can be valued on a dividend yield basis as follows:

Net dividend per share	$= £1.60$
Gross divided per share	$= £2.00 \left(£1.60 \times \dfrac{100}{80} \right)$
Gross dividend percentage	$= \dfrac{£2}{£1} \times 100 = 200\%$
Comparable quoted dividend yield	$= 6\%$

Adjustment for:

Non-marketability, reduced size of company, etc.	4%
High asset backing	(2%)
	8%

Value per share

$$\frac{\text{Dividend percentage} \times \text{Nominal value per share}}{\text{Dividend yield}} = \text{Value per share}$$

$$\frac{200\% \times £1}{8\%} = £25 \text{ per share}$$

March 1982 rebasing valuations

13.23 The valuation of shares at 31 March 1982 is now a key area of share valuations, being performed for the purposes of CGT rebasing.

The March 1982 rebasing legislation assumes that the shareholder has notionally sold and reacquired his shareholding at its market value at 31 March 1982. Each shareholder is looked at separately for rebasing purposes, which often gives an unfair result for minority shareholders (see below).

On a sale of shares held at March 1982, the shareholder can deduct the March 1982 value of the shares together with the indexation allowance thereon in arriving at his capital gain. (Unless an election for global rebasing is made, it will still be necessary to compute the capital gain/loss on the shares under the old rules, using historic cost. This result will be compared with that arising with March 1982 rebasing, and the lower gain or loss is taken.)

Given that indexation from March 1982 is now running in the region of 90%, it is worth noting that every £100 agreed in the March 1982 share valuation will produce a £190 deduction against the sale proceeds.

13.24 The value of a controlling interest held at March 1982 will be based on the value of the company at March 1982, with a small discount if the company is not wholly owned (see 13.20). The notional acquisition at March 1982 is based on the proportion of the shares held at that date. It is important to remember the CGT identification rules where shares have been acquired over a period of time. Generally, disposals of shares are first identified with the 'new holding' (i.e. shares acquired after March 1982), then with the March 1982 holding, and lastly with any non-pooled pre-6 April 1965 acquisitions (separately on a LIFO basis). March 1982 rebasing will therefore only be available once any new holding has been completely sold. By concession, the Revenue have indicated that where shares of the same class in a company have been acquired at different times, they will be treated as a 'single holding' for the purposes of rebasing (and indexation) valuation at 31 March 1982 (ESC D44).

Where there is a part disposal of shares from a majority holding, the deductible March 1982 base value would be a pro-rata proportion of the value of the shares held in March 1982 (not the March 1982 value of the shares being sold), as illustrated in the example below.

Example 7

Part disposal of majority holding

In February 1994, Malcolm sold 250 out of the 700 shares he held in Macdonald's Foods Limited (which had an issued share capital of 1,000 £1 shares). The 700 shares were acquired by Malcolm at par in 1975.

13.25 *Valuing a Family Company*

Malcolm received £30,000 for the 250 shares. The relevant share valuations at March 1982 were:

Holding	Value per share
%	£
100	30
70	25
25	10

The chargeable gain would be calculated as follows:

	£
Sale proceeds	30,000
Less Part disposal — March 1982 base value	
£25 per share × 250 shares	(6,250)
(70% majority value)	
Unindexed gain	23,750
Less Indexation	
£6,250 × 79.4%	(4,963)
Chargeable gain	£18,787

13.25   Each shareholding is looked at separately when valuing shares at March 1982 — there is no aggregation principle. This rule works rather unfairly in the context of a family company where shareholdings are fragmented amongst different members of the family. A minority holding at March 1982 would be discounted to reflect the shareholders' inability to control, restrictions on transfer, and reliance on the directors for his dividend income. This means, for example, that a 25% holding would be worth substantially less than 25% of the value of the entire company.

On a sale of the entire company each shareholder will have a pro-rata share of the proceeds. However, the March 1982 value of a minority shareholding would not be a pro-rata share of the March 1982 value of the company. Thus, a minority shareholder will have a disproportionately large gain, even if the value of the company has kept pace with inflation since March 1982.

Example 8

Valuing minority shareholding at 31 March 1982

In June 1994, Lineker Sports Clothes Ltd was sold for £1,000,000. The company had an issued share capital of 1,000 shares, which had always been held equally by five shareholders (each holding 200 shares).

Based on the sale price, the following statistics can be derived:

Net earnings (i.e. post tax)	£80,000
Net earnings per share	£80
P/E ratio	12.5

The value of each individual's shareholding at 31 March 1982 is computed along the following lines:

Maintainable net earnings at March 1982 (say)	£20,000
Net earnings per share	£20

The FT Actuaries Textiles Sector P/E at 31 March 1982 was 13.42. After adjusting for non-marketability etc., a P/E ratio of 6.0 is taken. The value per share is therefore £120 (i.e. £20 × 6).

Each shareholder receives proceeds of £200,000, but will only have a deductible March 1982 base value (ignoring indexation) of £24,000 i.e. £120 per share × 200.

13.26   Where a company is controlled jointly by a husband and wife, although each separately has a minority holding, their shares must still be valued in isolation (there is no equivalent of the 'related property' rule which applies for IHT (see 16.6)). However, if the couple own shares in the same company (of the same class) at 31 March 1982 and the wife subsequently transfers her shares to her husband, those shares can be treated as held by him at 31 March 1982 for the purposes of the rebasing valuation. The same rule applies if the husband transfers shares to his wife and also to other no gain/no loss transfers (see *TCGA 1992, 3 Sch 1* and SP5/89). This concession provides a valuable tax saving opportunity where the sale of a 'husband and wife' company is contemplated. By arranging a transfer of shares from one spouse to the other, the recipient spouse may be able to substantially increase his/her March 1982 valuation by switching it on to a controlling basis. The transfer of shares should be executed before a purchaser is found to avoid the risk of the Inland Revenue countering the advantage under the *Furniss v Dawson* principle. (See the decision in *R v CIR (Ex parte Kaye [1992] STC 581)*.)

Example 9

Valuation at March 1982 — aggregation of spouse's holding

The March 1982 valuations for the shares in Hughes Builders Ltd were as follows:

	Shares	March 1982 value per share	March 1982 Valuation
		£	£
Mr Hughes	40	120	4,800
Mrs Hughes	40	120	4,800
Mr Emilyn	20	30	600
	100		

However, if prior to a sale of the company, Mr Hughes transferred, (say), 36 shares to Mrs Hughes, she would then have 76% holding. This holding (valued on an earnings basis) might be worth (say) £700 per share. Mrs Hughes' base value would then be increased to £53,200 (76 × £700 per share).

13.27   Where shares held at March 1982 are subsequently transferred between husband and wife, ESC D44 enables the transferee spouse to elect for his/her valuation to be calculated by reference to the size of the transferor's holding. (See Example 10 below.) (The election must be made within two years from the end of the tax year in which the shares are sold, or such later time as permitted by the Board of the Inland Revenue.)

Example 10

Application of ESC D44

Mariner's (Boats and Leisure) Ltd was incorporated in 1976 with 100 £1 ordinary shares, which were held as follows:

Mr Mariner	80
Mrs Mariner	20

Mr Mariner transferred a further 10 shares to his wife in May 1994.

On a subsequent sale, Mrs Mariner can elect under ESC D44 to compute her March 1982 valuation as 30/80ths of the value of an 80% shareholding in the company at that date (rather than a 30% holding in isolation).

Key rebasing issues

13.28   It is useful to highlight some of the main principles affecting March 1982 share valuations:

(*a*)   it is not possible to index back to March 1982 from the ultimate sale price (indeed this is specifically indicated on SVD's form VAL 40). On the other hand, the use of foresight is permissible and should be used to demonstrate that the trading prospects and future growth etc. were rosy before March 1982;

(*b*)   if there are any arm's length transfers of any shares within a year of March 1982, these may provide very persuasive evidence of a high March 1982 valuation.

If, on the other hand, low valuations have previously been established with SVD for CGT or capital transfer tax purposes close to March 1982, they should be distinguished, by reference to the size of the shareholding and other circumstances, particularly where the value was agreed with SVD reserving its position on a 'without prejudice' basis;

(*c*)   the size of the shareholding will influence the level of financial and other information deemed to be available to a prospective purchaser at 31 March 1982. Controlling shareholders have full access to in-house information, such as management's accounts, forecasts etc. leading up to March 1982. On the other hand, minority holdings may only be entitled to those published accounts which are signed before 31 March 1982. This may mean, for example, that if the accounts to 31 December 1981 were not available at 31 March 1982, only the 31 December 1980 and previous year's accounts could be taken;

(*d*)   the maintainable profits are normally determined from the last three years audited accounts, adjusted for excessive director's remuneration etc. The general recession in the early 1980s meant that most companies experienced a decline in profits between 1979 and 1982. This trend may work to the advantage of a minority shareholder bearing in mind the information standards mentioned in (*c*) above. On the other hand, this may be detrimental to controlling valuations which are based on up to date information;

(*e*)   many companies did not pay the headline corporation tax rate in the early 1980s, due to the availability of 100% capital allowances and stock relief. This can be used to substantiate a lower or even a nil tax charge, this increasing the maintainable earnings. (Note, however that P/E ratios (at 31 March 1982) published in the *Investors' Chronicle* reflect a full corporation tax charge and are higher than the FTASI. A consistent approach must therefore be taken);

(*f*)   March 1982 share valuations (only) can be submitted direct to the SVD (i.e. by-passing the Inspector of Taxes) after the disposal has occurred where the valuation is required for a number of shareholders.

All shareholders with similar holdings to be valued at March 1982 must be prepared to be bound by the value agreed. For these purposes, the SVD must be provided with a full list of the shareholders, giving the size of their holdings at both 31 March 1982 and the date of disposal, and supplying details of their individual tax offices (IR Press Release — 18 November 1991).

PLANNING CHECKLIST — VALUING A FAMILY COMPANY

Company
- Maintainable earnings are normally used to value a business as a going concern — the maintainable earnings must reflect the likely future circumstances of the business and therefore historic results may need to be adjusted.

Working shareholders
- Commercial valuations should be based on full knowledge of business results, conditions etc.
- Fiscal valuations are based only on details relevant to 'stake' in company (other gleaned information is ignored).

Other employees
- Exceptionally, when valuing shares for the purposes of a Schedule E benefit charge, all information known to individual employees is deemed to be available.

Non-working shareholders
- 'Minority' share values are heavily discounted — good news where tax is payable, bad news for March 1982 rebasing.
- Consider transferring shares to/from spouse to increase size of holding for March 1982 rebasing valuation retrospectively.

Chapter 14

Selling the Family Business or Company

Methods of selling a business

14.1   Basically, there are two ways in which the family business can be sold. The vendor-shareholders may either secure the sale of the trade and assets out of the company or they can sell their shares in the company. Each method gives rise to different commercial, tax and legal consequences, which therefore influences the way in which the transaction is structured.

In general, the vendor-shareholders prefer to sell their shares, whereas the purchaser will often prefer to buy assets, but there will be situations where one party requires the opposite method. In the writer's experience, there are often one or two key factors which will dictate the manner in which the business is to be sold. Although this is a matter of negotiation between the two parties, in some cases one of the parties will have the 'upper hand' in imposing the structure of the deal.

This chapter focuses on the tax implications and strategies for the vendor. The purchaser's position is considered in detail in Chapter 11.

Basic CGT rules

Date of disposal

14.2   The sale of the company's assets or shares will involve a disposal for CGT purposes. A disposal is recognised for CGT at the time an unconditional contract is entered into, and not the date of completion. The date of disposal under a conditional contract arises when the relevant condition precedent is satisfied or waived. [*TCGA 1992, s 28*]. A company will pay tax on an asset sale, within 9 months after the end of the corporation tax accounting period which will normally end on the sale of the trade and assets. Individuals are currently liable to pay their CGT on 1 December following the year of disposal and from 1996/97 under self-assessment on 31 January following the year of assessment. Where an individual vendor anticipates selling shares before the end of the tax year, consideration should be given to deferring the date of disposal until after 6 April, as this will delay the payment of the tax by one year.

Deferred consideration

14.3 If part of the consideration is deferred, this must initially be included in the CGT consideration, without any discount for the delay in receipt or the fact that it may not be paid. The same rule applies even if the deferred element of the consideration is conditional upon a specified event. The CGT assessment will only be revised if the taxpayer can satisfy the Inspector that part of the consideration has proved irrecoverable. [*TCGA 1992, s 48*]. The requirement to bring the full amount of the deferred consideration into the original CGT computation and pay tax on it can often give rise to cashflow difficulties. Where the Inland Revenue are satisfied that this will cause undue hardship, they may permit the tax to be paid in instalments. [*TCGA 1992, s 280*]. For these purposes the Revenue will accept that undue hardship arises where the tax on the entire consideration exceeds 50% of the initial consideration received by the tax payment date.

Sale of assets and trade

General legal consequences

14.4 The starting point in framing any agreement for the sale of the trade and assets is to identify precisely the assets and liabilities which will be taken over. This may also involve the assignment of leases and benefit of trading contracts. Employees will be transferred under the *Transfer of Undertakings (Protection of Employment) Regulations 1981*. In many cases, debtors and creditors will not be taken over by the purchaser as this saves stamp duty.

The legal documentation for an asset sale is likely to contain fewer warranties than under a share sale. Most sale agreements will require the vendor to covenant that he will not compete with the business being sold within a reasonable time scale and/or defined geographical limits.

General tax consequences

14.5 Under this method, the company will sell the trade, together with its various trading assets. This will inevitably create a cessation of the trade for tax purposes, which will bring an end to the accounting period for corporation tax purposes, unless the company is continuing another trade. [*ICTA 1988, s 12(3)(c)*]. Any unrelieved trading losses will be lost. [*ICTA 1988, s 393(1)*]. Capital gains may arise on the disposal of property and goodwill and balancing charges may arise on the sale of industrial buildings and plant.

Potential double tax charge

14.6 Probably the main disadvantage of an asset sale is the potential double charge to tax. The proceeds for the sale of the business will be subject to corporation tax. If the vendor shareholder needs the cash from the sale of the business, a further tax liability will be suffered on the extraction of the net proceeds from the company. The manner in which the cash is extracted will influence the tax liability. For example, it may be more tax efficient to extract some of the cash before winding the company up (see 15.15), provided the company can recover the ACT liability.

Apportionment of sale consideration

14.7 The tax payable by the company would depend upon the nature of each asset and the consideration which has been attributed to each one. In this context, it is important to achieve a sensible allocation of the total price paid for the business amongst the various individual assets and this should be specified in the sale agreement. For example, if the company has unused trading losses which would be lost on cessation, it may be possible to absorb them by allocating higher values to assets which would produce additional trading receipts, such as trading stock or plant and machinery which would produce a balancing charge.

Provided the vendor and purchaser have negotiated the price at arm's length and the allocation has been specified in the sale agreement, the Inland Revenue are unlikely to challenge the apportionment of the total price. However, it should be noted that the Inland Revenue do have a statutory power to re-apportion the consideration 'where necessary' for CGT purposes and for capital allowance purposes. [*TCGA 1992, s 52(4)* and *CAA 1990, ss 150, 151*].

In *EV Booth (Holdings) Limited v Buckwell (1980) STC 578*, it was held that a *party* to a sale could not resile from the apportionment in the contract for CGT purposes. Mr Justice Browne-Wilkinson also went on to say, by way of *obiter*, that the Inland Revenue might be able to look through the apportionment in some cases. In practice, the Inland Revenue are only likely to use the powers in cases where the allocated prices are blatantly unrealistic.

The detailed considerations which might apply in relation to the main categories of asset are set out in 14.8 to 14.11 below. Many of these factors will also influence the manner in which the price is apportioned.

It is particularly important to recognise that the indexation allowance cannot create or increase a capital loss (on post 29 November 1993 disposals). If the intended apportionment of the sale price produces a loss on one asset as a result of indexation, yet one or more of the other assets show capital gains, it should be adjusted. If the price of each 'loss making' asset is increased, this will reduce or eliminate the wasted indexation allowance.

Example 1

Minimising loss of indexation relief on asset sale

Royle Ltd is negotiating the sale of its hi-fi retail business as a going concern, involving the sale of its trade and assets. The company purchased the business in August 1982.

Both parties have agreed a price of £500,000 for the retail premises and goodwill (with stock being purchased at book value). The draft sale agreement has apportioned the price as follows:

	£
Retail premises	350,000
Goodwill	150,000

The net capital gain based on the above apportionment would be:

	Sale Price £	Cost £	Indexation £	Capital Gain £
Goodwill	150,000	(20,000)	(15,000)	115,000
Retail premises	350,000	(250,000)	(100,000)*	–
	500,000			115,000

* £250,000 × 75% = £187,500 but restricted to £100,000 to produce no gain. Indexation relief of £87,500 is therefore 'wasted'.

A more sensible apportionment (assuming the figures could be justified) would be:

	£
Retail premises	440,000
Goodwill	60,000

This would reduce the CGT liability to £27,500 as shown below:

	Sale Price £	Cost £	Indexation at 75% £	Capital Gain £
Goodwill	60,000	(20,000)	(15,000)	25,000
Retail premises	440,000	(250,000)	(187,500)	2,500
	500,000			27,500

Property

14.8   The disposal of freehold or leasehold property may give rise to a capital gain or loss. Where the property has been occupied and used for the purposes of the trade, it may be possible to roll-over any capital gain against the acquisition of qualifying re-investment expenditure, which may be useful if the company has other trading activities or is likely to begin a new trading venture in the near future. [*TCGA 1992, s 152*].

Gains on assets owned personally by a shareholder may also be rolled-over in this way provided the old and the new assets are used in the shareholder's same 'personal company'. [*TCGA 1992, s 157*].

If the property was owned at 31 March 1982, its value at that date can be deducted as the base cost in arriving at the capital gain. With indexation based thereon currently running at some 90%, the capital gain may be small or nil, given the current stagnation in property values.

Where a leasehold interest which has less than 50 years to run is being sold, the deductible base cost is restricted by a depreciation adjustment, *TCGA 1992, 8 Sch*, and a disposal at book value may therefore produce a taxable gain.

If industrial buildings allowances have been claimed on a factory, a balancing adjustment will arise. As a general rule, if an industrial building is sold above its original cost, there will be a taxable balancing charge equal to the total of the allowances previously claimed on the building. If the building is sold for an amount below the original cost, a balancing allowance would be given equal to the difference between the sale price and the tax written down value of the building. [*CAA 1990, s 4*]. There are two main points to note. If the industrial building or tranche of industrial building expenditure is older than its tax life of 25 years old or 50 years old for pre 6 November 1962 buildings, then no balancing adjustment will occur. [*CAA 1990, s 4(2)*].

Where the building is expected to produce a substantial balancing charge, it may be worthwhile considering granting a subsidiary interest in the building rather than selling it outright. For example, the building may be leased for, say, 125 years with an option to purchase the building after its tax life has expired. The company will not then suffer a balancing charge and can continue to claim industrial building allowances against the rental income.

However, for *enterprise zone* buildings purchased after 13 January 1994 the grant of subsidiary interest for a capital sum will be treated as giving rise to a balancing adjustment. However, only a balancing charge would be recognised (a balancing allowance would not). A balancing charge only arises if the capital sum is received within 7 years after the expenditure on the building is incurred. However, if guaranteed exit arrangements are in place at the time the expenditure is incurred, a balancing charge can arise at any time during the building's tax life i.e. the first 25 years.

Goodwill

14.9   The ability to deduct the March 1982 value of goodwill will be particularly beneficial if the company can show it was generating substantial profits prior to March 1982. If there is likely to be qualifying re-investment by the company, any capital gain arising on goodwill can also be eliminated by a roll-over relief claim.

There may also be advantages in allocating part of the disposal value of goodwill to know-how owned by the company. Know-how is defined in *ICTA 1988, s 533* and includes industrial information about manufacturing and processing. However, the sale of know-how on a disposal of the trade is treated as a sale of goodwill *unless* a joint election is made between the vendor and purchaser within 2 years following the sale. [*ICTA 1988, s 531(2)*]. It is therefore vital to ensure that a joint election is made where the transaction is to be treated as a sale of know-how and this should ideally be signed before the sale contract or be a binding condition of the contract. As well as producing a trading receipt for the vendor, the purchaser will be able to claim capital allowances.

Plant and machinery

14.10   In practice, plant often tends to be sold at its net book value. As the company is ceasing to trade, this will give rise to a taxable balancing charge, where the proceeds exceed the tax written down value ('TWDV') of the plant. (A balancing allowance arises if the TWDV exceeds the sale proceeds.) If the company wishes to minimise the balancing charge, it may prefer to sell the plant at TWDV. Provided the purchaser can claim capital allowances on the plant, the Inland Revenue cannot substitute market value. [*CAA 1990, s 26(1)(b)*].

It should not be forgotten that plant (used for trading purposes) will qualify as a chargeable asset for CGT purposes. Thus, if the plant is sold for an amount in excess of its indexed base cost, a capital gain will arise, although where the consideration for an individual item of plant is less than £6,000, the gain is not taxable. [*TCGA 1992, s 262*]. Where the vendor company is disposing of a large number of individual items of plant which qualify for the £6,000 chattel exemption, it will often be advantageous to specify the consideration allocated to each item in the sale agreement to ensure relief is obtained.

Capital gains arising on the sale of *fixed* plant and machinery may be held-over for a maximum period of 10 years or up to the date the plant is sold if earlier. [*TCGA 1992, s 154*]. It is possible to convert the held-over gain to a more permanent roll-over claim by purchasing a non-depreciating asset, such as goodwill or freehold property, within the hold-over period.

Plant is usually sold below its original cost, producing a loss. Because of a special rule, the base cost for CGT purposes must be restricted by the net capital allowances claimed on the asset, being the difference between cost and proceeds. [*TCGA 1992, s 41(1)(2)*]. This will invariably produce no gain. If the other assets cannot take full advantage of indexation (for example if there is no base cost) the vendor's overall tax position may be enhanced by selling plant for an amount at least equal to the cost plus accrued indexation (remembering that the sale proceeds are restricted to cost when computing the balancing adjustment for capital allowance purposes).

Trading stock and work in progress

14.11   Any profit arising on the sale of trading stock and work in progress will be treated as a trading receipt. Where the trading stock and work in progress is sold to another UK trader for valuable consideration, the Inland Revenue should accept the price agreed between the two parties. [*ICTA 1988, ss 100(1)(a), 101(1A)(a)*]. There may be some scope for flexing the price at which the stock etc. is sold in order to achieve the desired tax position. However, if the price attributed to the stock is substantially different from its market value, it is possible that the Inland Revenue may seek to argue that it had been taken out of trading stock prior to sale and therefore was not sold as trading stock, (using the principles in the case of *Petrotim Securities Ltd v Ayres (1963) 41 TC 389*).

If trading stock is sold to a connected person on cessation, it will be deemed to be transferred at market value, unless a joint election is made to treat the transfer at the higher of the actual sales price or book value (the election can only be made if both these amounts are less than market value). [*ICTA 1988, s 100(1A)(1C)*].

VAT — Transfer of going concern

14.12   In the vast majority of asset and trade sales, VAT will not be chargeable on the sale of the assets, as the transaction will be treated as a non-supply under *VAT (Special Provisions) Order 1995, Art 5*.

Example 2

Sale of trade and assets

Mr Platt (aged 50) has recently been approached by Lee plc to acquire the assets and undertaking of his profitable haulage business, Platt's Transport Ltd ('PT Ltd'). He incorporated the company in 1966 with £100 share capital and his shares were worth £1 million at 31 March 1982.

Lee plc have offered a total consideration of £3.5 million for the business.

PT Ltd's current summarised balance sheet (together with the relevant tax written down values (TWDV)) is as follows:

	£'000	
Warehouse property	400	TWDV = £200,000
Lorry fleet	700	TWDV = £600,000
Debtors	300	
Bank overdraft	(200)	
Creditors	(400)	
	800	

The warehouse property and goodwill were worth £400,000 and £500,000 respectively at 31 March 1982.

The prospective purchaser's accountants have performed a brief acquisition review and have supplied the following tentative valuations for the assets to be taken over:

	£'000
Warehouse property	1,000
Lorry fleet	700
Goodwill (balance)	1,800
	3,500

Mr Platt would like an indication of the net amount which could be paid out to him on the basis of the above deal.

Tax liabilities on sale of PT Ltd's assets

PT Ltd's tax liability on the sale of the relevant assets is computed as follows:

Chargeable gains

	Warehouse £'000	Goodwill £'000	Total £'000
Proceeds	1,000	1,800	
Less March 1982 value	(400)	(500)	
Indexation at (say) 90%	(360)	(450)	
	240	850	1,090

Tax on balancing charge

	Warehouse £'000	Lorry fleet £'000	
Cost/proceeds	400	700	
Less TWDV	(200)	(600)	
	200	100	300
Taxable profit on sale of assets			1,390
Tax thereon @ 33%			£459

Capital gains arising on capital distribution

PT Ltd's distributable reserves upon completion would be as follows:

	£'000
Per current balance sheet	800
Book profit on disposal:	
Warehouse (£1,000,000 − £400,000)	600
Goodwill	1,800
Liquidation etc. costs	(1)
Tax on disposal	(459)
Available to distribute	£2,740

If all the reserves were distributed as a capital distribution on liquidation the 'net proceeds' available to Mr Platt would be £2,404,000, computed thus:

	£'000
Capital distribution	2,740
Less March 1982 value	(1,000)
Indexation (say)	(900)
Taxable gain	840
Tax @ 40%	336
Post-tax proceeds	£2,404

It may be possible to reduce this tax liability by paying a dividend before the company is wound-up of £840,000 (i.e., the element of the sale proceeds which suffers tax at 40%). Mr Platt's tax liability would then be £210,000 increasing his net proceeds to £2,530,000, calculated as follows:

	Tax	Net cash received
	£'000	£'000
Dividend		
Cash		840
Tax thereon:		
£840,000 × 100/80 = £1,050,000 (gross) × 40%	420	
Less tax credit (20%)	(210)	
Higher rate tax on dividend	210	(210)
Capital distribution		
Cash (£2,740,000 − £840,000 dividend)		1,900
CGT thereon:		
Capital distribution	1,900	
Less March 1982 value	(1,000)	
Indexation × 90%	(900)	
Capital gain	−	
		£2,530

A pre-liquidation dividend will involve the payment of ACT which the company must be able to recover against its current/prior tax liabilities. In many cases, the dividend will be paid after the company has ceased trading but before the company is wound-up. The Inland Revenue have taken the view that this interim period does not constitute an accounting period for corporation tax purposes, which can prevent the company recovering its ACT under the six year carry back rule in *ICTA 1988, s 239(3)*. The answer here is to create a new corporation tax accounting period start by ensuring that the company acquires a source of income, such as purchasing gilts or opening a bank deposit account immediately after the cessation of the trade.

Sale of shares

14.13 Vendors generally prefer to sell shares in a company in order to avoid the potential double taxation which often arises with a sale of assets (see 14.6). A well advised purchaser may seek to negotiate a reduction in the price he pays for the company's shares to allow for the contingent tax inherent in the value of the company's assets, although the amount of the discount should depend on the likelihood and timing of the assets being sold.

Advantages of share sale

14.14   A share sale offers the following tax advantages:

(*a*)   the avoidance of the double tax charge, as the vendor receives the proceeds directly;

(*b*)   the ability to defer the capital gain on disposal where the acquiring company is able to satisfy the sale consideration through the issue of shares or loan stock;

(*c*)   the vendor may be in a position to obtain CGT retirement relief or reinvestment relief (by reinvesting the proceeds in shares of a qualifying company);

(*d*)   a share sale may enable some value to be received for the company's tax losses or surplus ACT (which could not be transferred to purchaser on an asset sale).

Legal aspects

14.15   As a purchaser of shares will effectively inherit all the company's liabilities and problems, a share sale agreement usually involves extensive warranties and indemnities given by the vendor, except perhaps in the case of a management buy-out. The function of warranties and indemnities is discussed in 11.29 above.

Company law can also impinge heavily on share sales, particularly the rules prohibiting the company providing financial assistance (such as a loan, guarantee, etc.) for the purchase of its own shares. However, it is usually possible for a private company to provide financial assistance out of its distributable profits if the directors provide a declaration of solvency and certain other conditions are satisfied. [*CA 1985, ss 155–158*].

Structuring the consideration for a share sale

Types of consideration

14.16   The vendor may sell his shares for:

(*a*)   a cash consideration;

(*b*)   loan notes issued by the acquiring company;

(*c*)   shares in the acquiring company;

(*d*)   a mixture of the above.

The consideration may be paid immediately on completion or on a deferred basis. Deferred consideration can either be structured as fixed or variable, for example, depending on the future profits under the so-called earn-out arrangement. In the current economic climate, there is much to be said for receiving all the consideration up-front as a guaranteed amount, despite the fact that it will attract an immediate tax liability.

Example 3

Post-tax proceeds on sale of shares

Mr Banks has received an offer from Stoke plc to sell his 100% shareholding in Banks Ltd for a consideration of £2 million (being the net asset value of the company with a small premium for goodwill).

Mr Banks' indexed base cost in the shares is £0.4 million and his company had distributable reserves prior to the sale of £1.5 million.

If he agrees to sell his shares for £2 million, the net post tax proceeds will be £1.36 million, as calculated below:

	£m	£m
Sale proceeds		2.00
Less CGT thereon:		
Sale proceeds	2.00	
Less Indexed base cost	(0.40)	
Chargeable gain	1.60 × 40%	(0.64)
Post tax proceeds		£1.36

Consideration satisfied in shares/loan notes

14.17   Where the vendor receives shares in the acquiring company in exchange for his/her shares, the CGT liability on the disposal can usually be deferred provided:

(*a*) the acquiring company ends up with more than 25% of the target company's ordinary shares. [*TCGA 1992, s 135*]; and

(*b*) the Inland Revenue are satisfied that the transaction was undertaken for commercial reasons and not for tax avoidance. [*TCGA 1992, s 137*]. It is usually advisable to obtain advance clearance on this point from the Inland Revenue under *TCGA 1992, s 138*.

If only part of the consideration is satisfied in shares, then only a pro-rata portion of the gain can be 'rolled-over'. Strictly, the shares received by the vendor in the acquiring company are treated as having been acquired at the same time and for the same amount as his old shareholding. [*TCGA 1992, s 127*].

Where the acquiring company satisfies the consideration by the issue of loan notes which constitute qualifying corporate bonds (QCBs) no immediate CGT liability arises. However, the capital gain or loss based on the deemed disposal of the shares at the time of the exchange is held-over and will become payable when the QCB is either paid or redeemed. Effectively, the vendor's tax position is frozen at the date of the exchange with the payment of the CGT being postponed on an interest free basis. [*TCGA 1992, s 116(10)(11)*].

Earn-out deals

14.18   Where the sale of the shares is structured as an earn-out, the vendor will be taxed according to the principles established in the case of *Marren v Ingles (1980) STC 500*. In addition to any immediate consideration received on the disposal of shares, the vendor will be taxed on the value of the right to receive the earn-out, as calculated at that date. (A right to receive earn-out consideration is frequently referred to as a 'chose in action'.) Further CGT liabilities may also arise on each subsequent payment made under the earn-out, each being treated as a part disposal of the right with the last payment being the final disposal. The calculation of the taxable gain on a subsequent earn-out payment is best explained by Example 4 below.

A particular difficulty arises if the earn-out turns out to be unsuccessful, so that the actual proceeds are lower than the value initially placed on the right. This will produce an allowable capital loss which cannot be carried back to offset the gain on the disposal of the shares in an earlier tax year.

Example 4

CGT treatment of earn-out payment

In October 1995, Mr Armfield sold his entire share capital stake in Pool Limited under a three year earn-out arrangement. At that date, the value of the likely payments to be made under the earn-out was agreed at £300,000.

In December 1996, he received his first earn-out payment of £80,000. At this date, the residual value of the earn-out was £250,000.

Mr Armfield's tax liability on the payment would be computed as follows:

£

	£
Amount received	80,000
Less Part disposal value of right	

$$£300,000 \times \frac{A\ (£80,000)}{A\ (£80,000) + B\ (£250,000)} \qquad (72,727)$$

Indexation (October 1995 — December 1996)	
£72,727 × (say) 4%	(2,909)
Capital gain	4,364

Retirement relief

14.19 Shareholders with a small equity interest in a family company should generally be able to secure valuable CGT retirement relief on disposal of those shares, provided:

(*a*) they are at least 55 years old at the date of disposal; or

(*b*) they have retired earlier on ill health grounds (provided it can be demonstrated that the illness has prevented the taxpayer from continuing his work and that it is likely to remain so). [*TCGA 1992, s 163(1), 6 Sch 3*].

14.20 For disposals after 29 November 1993, the first £250,000 of qualifying gains on shares are completely exempt with 50% exemption on the next £750,000. Thus, assuming the gain is £1 million or more, the maximum available relief will be £625,000 (i.e., £250,000 plus 50% of £750,000).

It is important to note that the full relief is only given where the taxpayer meets the qualifying conditions (in 14.21 below) for the full 10 year period. Where the conditions have only been satisfied for less than 10 years (but at least for the last 12 months, *TCGA 1992, 6 Sch 13*), the numerical limits for the two tiers of relief are scaled down on a pro-rata basis.

14.21 To obtain relief, the shareholder must be able to demonstrate that, throughout the 10 year qualifying period, he/she:

(*a*) was a full time working officer or employee of a trading company, holding company of a trading group, or a company which is part of a commercial association of companies. (A company is part of a commercial association of companies where, together with its associated companies, the respective businesses taken together, make up a single composite undertaking.) [*TCGA 1992, 6 Sch 1(1)*].

This requires the individual to devote the whole of their time to the company etc. in a technical or managerial capacity — 30 hours per week should be sufficient.

(*b*) owned at least 5% of the voting rights of the company (i.e., it is his personal company). [*TCGA 1992, s 163(3)*].

14.22 The gain on the sale of shares will usually qualify as an eligible gain except where the company has investments in the balance sheet at the date of disposal. In such cases, qualifying for relief will be restricted as follows.

$$\text{Gain} \times \frac{\text{Market value of chargeable business assets}}{\text{Market value of chargeable assets}}$$

Chargeable business assets are those chargeable assets including goodwill which are used for the trade. Items of plant and machinery will be counted as chargeable assets if both their original cost and market value exceeds £6,000.

Where the individual is disposing of shares in a personal holding company, this fraction is computed by reference to the chargeable assets of the group, with only an appropriate proportion being included if the subsidiary is wholly owned. The holding company's investment in its 51% subsidiaries is ignored. [*TCGA 1992, 6 Sch 8*].

Example 5

Retirement relief on sale of shares

On 31 May 1995, Mr Lineker (aged 59) sold all his shares in Goals Ltd for £750,000 realising an indexed gain of £520,000.

Mr Lineker inherited his 20% shareholding in Goals Ltd from his father in June 1972. He was appointed a director of the company in June 1976 and he worked for the company on a full time basis until 31 May 1995 when he retired.

The summarised balance sheet of Goals Ltd at 31 May 1995 was as follows:

	Book value £'000	Market value £'000
Land and buildings	350	650
Plant and machinery	302	350
Investment — (shares in Japan plc)	112	145
Net current assets	330	–
	£1,094	£1,145

14.23   Selling the Family Business or Company

The company's goodwill was worth about £500,000 at the end of May 1995.

Plant and machinery is analysed as follows:

	Book value £'000	Market value £'000
Plant costing and worth more than £6,000	152	165
Plant worth less than £6,000	85	120
Motor cars	65	65
	302	350

Mr Lineker's retirement relief would be calculated as follows:

(a) as he has held at least 5% of the voting rights and has been a full time working officer since June 1976 (i.e., more than 10 years) there is no restriction in retirement relief exemption;

(b) Goals Ltd has some chargeable 'non-business' assets and the gain qualifying for relief must therefore be restricted.

Market value of chargeable assets	Business £'000	Total £'000
Land and buildings	650	650
Goodwill	500	500
Plant and machinery:		
items worth more than £6,000	165	165
Investments:		
shares in Japan plc	–	145
	1,315	1,460

Gain qualifying for relief:	£
$£520,000 \times \dfrac{£1,315,000}{£1,460,000}$	468,356
Less Retirement relief	
First £250,000 — exempt	(250,000)
Next £218,356 — 50%	(109,178)
£468,356	109,178
Balance of gain not qualifying for relief (£520,000 − £468,356)	51,644
Chargeable gain	£160,822

Relaxation for switch for part-time status

14.23   Where an individual has ceased to work full time but continues to work for the company on a part time basis, he could still qualify for retirement relief on a subsequent disposal of his shares. Relief will be given provided he satisfied the conditions set out in 14.21 during a 10 year period ending on the date he ceased to be a full-time working officer/employee and the company continued to be his personal company up to the date he sold his shares. For this purpose, an individual would have to work at least 10 hours per week in a managerial or technical capacity and therefore careful records should be kept in order to substantiate a claim. [*TCGA 1992, s 163(5)(7)*].

Associated disposal

14.24   Any unused balance of retirement relief may be claimed on a qualifying associated disposal of a shareholder's personally owned asset which has been used for the company's business (for at least the last 12 months). The asset must be used by the company immediately before the sale of the shares and should therefore be sold at the same time or after the share sale. [*TCGA 1992, s 163(6)(7)*].

Furthermore, the gain which is eligible for relief will be restricted on a 'just and reasonable' basis, if the asset has only been used by the company for part of the shareholder's period of ownership or if a rent has been charged. If the asset has been let at full market rent, the gain will not qualify for relief. [*TCGA 1992, s 164(1), 6 Sch 10*].

Reinvestment relief (in relation to share sales)

Basic rules

14.25   Reinvestment relief applies to any gain realised (after 29 November 1993) by an individual or trustee, where the gain is reinvested in acquiring the shares of a qualifying unquoted trading company. Although the relief is available on the disposal of any type of chargeable asset, the comments here are confined to its use in relation to family company share sales.

An individual can roll-over his capital gain on a sale of shares (as well as other assets) by reinvesting the gain element of his disposal proceeds in 'eligible shares' of a 'qualifying company' ('Qualco'). [*TCGA 1992, s 164A(1)*]. Eligible shares are, broadly speaking, irredeemable ordinary shares which do not contain any preferential rights. [*TCGA 1992, s 164N*].

The individual must be resident in the UK when he makes his acquisition which must take place within one year before or three years after the disposal of the original asset. [*TCGA 1992, s 164A(9)*]. The reinvestment relief must be claimed within six years after the end of the tax year in which the disposal is made.

The individual can be a passive shareholder of Qualco if he wishes. He does not have to be a full-time working director or employee to obtain relief, although this will be necessary if he wishes to accumulate retirement relief on a subsequent disposal of Qualco. However, if he is an employee or director, the level of his remuneration should be kept to a modest amount in the first three years to ensure that this does not jeopardise the relief. [*TCGA 1992, s 164L(8)*].

Interaction with Enterprise Investment Scheme (EIS) relief

14.26 It is not possible for general reinvestment relief to be claimed if an EIS claim is made. [*TCGA 1992, s 164M*]. However *TCGA 1992, Sch 5B* provides a separate reinvestment regime for gains held-over against shares subscribed for in a qualifying EIS. An individual can defer the gain by *subscribing* for EIS shares (up to £100,000 per tax year) within one year before/three years after the gain arises. A claim is made to defer the gain by matching it with the expenditure on the EIS shares (to the extent that the expenditure has not been previously matched). The gain is then treated as postponed and will crystallise on certain events, such as:

(*a*)   where the EIS shares are sold or transferred (except to a spouse);

(*b*)   the individual becomes non-resident (except in certain cases where full-time employment is taken abroad);

(*c*)   the company ceases to qualify for EIS purposes.

Any disposal of the EIS shares after the 5 year qualifying period would itself be exempt (although the deferred gain would be triggered). A similar CGT hold-over régime applies to shares subscribed for in a venture capital trust (see 10.23 above).

Qualifying company

14.27 Under the general reinvestment relief régime Qualco must be a qualifying company at the date of acquisition and remain so throughout the relevant three year period (otherwise the relief will be clawed back). A Qualco is extensively defined in the legislation in much the same way as for the old BES/new EIS relief purposes and generally excludes financial, investment and property related business. [*TCGA 1992, s 164I*].

(*a*)   Qualco must usually be an unquoted UK resident company which:

(i)   exists wholly for the purpose of carrying on one or more qualifying trades (see (*b*)); and/or,

(ii)   is a holding company of a qualifying trading group holding at least one qualifying subsidiary (being a subsidiary which carries on a qualifying trade). [*TCGA 1992, s 164G*].

Relief will not be available if a holding company has a non-qualifying subsidiary.

(*b*) a qualifying trade is any trade except:

(i) land, commodities or share dealing;

(ii) banking, insurance, money lending and other financial services;

(iii) legal and accountancy services;

(iv) provision of administration services etc. to a commonly controlled company which carries on one of the above trades. [*TCGA 1992, s 164I(2)*].

Most retail, wholesale and manufacturing trades will therefore qualify.

Reference must always be made to the detailed legislation to determine whether a particular company will qualify. The problem here is that there is no formal advance clearance procedure to confirm whether Qualco satisfies the various tests (as there is for BES/EIS relief).

Operation of reinvestment relief

14.28 In contrast to the business asset roll-over relief (which requires the full amount of the proceeds to be reinvested to roll-over the entire gain), the reinvestment relief rules deem the gain on the sale of the original asset to be reinvested first. Consequently, the reinvestor only needs to reinvest the gain element of these proceeds to obtain full relief. Strictly, where relief is claimed, the proceeds realised on the disposal of the original asset and the base cost of the new Qualco shares will both be reduced by the relevant amount. [*TCGA 1992, s 164A(2)*].

The amount eligible for the reinvestment relief is taken as the lower of:

(*a*) the chargeable gain realised on the disposal of the original shares;

(*b*) the actual amount or value of consideration given for the acquisition of Qualco's shares;

(*c*) the market value of Qualco's shares, where acquired by gift or otherwise than at arm's length;

(*d*) the amount specified in the claim. [*TCGA 1992, s 164(2)(a)*].

This rule provides complete flexibility in the amount of relief taken. The claim can be restricted, for example, to preserve the annual CGT exemption. Exemptions for retirement relief generally take priority over reinvestment relief.

Example 6

Operation of reinvestment relief

In June 1995, Mr McDermott received £300,000 on the sale of his shares in Kop Ltd, realising an indexed gain of £143,000, calculated as follows:

	£
Net sale proceeds	£300,000
Less Original cost (September 1985)	(100,000)
Indexation (September 1985 to June 1995)	
£100,000 × 57%	(57,000)
Indexed gain	143,000

He subsequently purchased ordinary shares in Liverpool Ltd in June 1996 for £150,000 and rolled-over the gain on his Kop Ltd shares under the reinvestment relief provisions.

If Mr McDermott cannot use his annual CGT exemption for 1995/96, he can elect to restrict his relief to £137,000 (i.e. £143,000 less £6,000), leaving £6,000 in charge to be absorbed by the annual exemption. His final CGT computation would then be:

	£
Indexed gain (as above)	143,000
Less Reinvestment relief	(137,000)
	6,000
Less Annual exemption	(6,000)
Chargeable gain	Nil

The CGT base cost of his shares in Liverpool Ltd would be £13,000 (i.e., £150,000 less £137,000).

Clawback of relief

14.29   The general reinvestment relief contains a number of anti-avoidance traps which generally provide that the held-over gain becomes chargeable where one of the following events occur within three years after the acquisition of Qualco's shares:

(*a*)   the individual (or any associate of his) receives any payment or benefit from the company (other than reasonable remuneration or a normal return on dividends);

(*b*)   the Qualco shares are sold without being replaced within the relevant three year period;

(*c*)   the Qualco shares are exchanged for qualifying corporate bonds;

(*d*)   the reinvestor emigrates;

(*e*)   Qualco becomes a non-qualifying company. [*TCGA 1992, s 164F*].

Deferral of gain

14.30   In the right circumstances, reinvestment relief will provide a valuable CGT deferral and possibly a permanent saving if subsequently combined with retirement relief (or death!). However, there are numerous anti-avoidance restrictions, particularly with regard to the qualifying reinvestment and these will need to be carefully examined in each case to ensure the various statutory hurdles are cleared. In particular, the company in which the reinvestment is made must be carrying on a qualifying trade and certain subsequent events can trigger a clawback of the gain.

Pre-sale tax planning strategies

Pre-sale dividend

14.31   It is now frequently beneficial for the vendor to extract a pre-sale dividend. This should produce a commensurate reduction in the sale price (subject to negotiation) and the vendor's capital gain. The purchaser is likely to be agreeable as this would reduce his acquisition cost and saves stamp duty (at 0.5%). In determining the optimum level of pre-sale dividend a number of factors must be considered. The beneficial effect of a pre-sale dividend is demonstrated below.

Example 7

Tax saving produced by pre-sale dividend

Assume that Mr Banks (see Example 3) negotiated with Stoke plc to procure the payment of a dividend of £1.5 million (i.e. equivalent to the distributable reserves) and then sell his shares for a correspondingly lower price of £0.5 million. This would increase his net 'after tax' proceeds to £1.58 million.

	£m
Cash dividend	1.50
Sale proceeds from shares	0.50
	2.00
Less Higher rate tax on 'grossed-up' dividend 20% × £1.875m (i.e. 100/80 × £1.5m)	(0.38)

Less CGT on shares

Sale proceeds	0.50	
Less Indexed base cost	(0.40)	
	£0.10 × 40%	(0.04)
Post tax proceeds		£1.58

The tax saved by a pre-sale dividend in this case would be £0.22 million (i.e. £0.64 million see Example 3 less £0.42 million or effective saving of 15% on £1.50 million).

For a higher rate taxpayer, a dividend only carries an effective tax rate of 25% on the cash received, i.e. higher rate tax of £18.75 on every £75 cash received. (This is because of the 20% tax credit imputed to the shareholder.) This contrasts favourably with the 40% rate suffered by the shareholder if the amount is received on share sale proceeds. However, the company must be able to recover the ACT against its corporation tax liability, possibly using the six year carry-back rule.

Furthermore, the company must also have sufficient distributable reserves to provide for the dividend. If the company lacks the relevant cash resources, the vendor shareholder could lend the amount received on dividend back to the company. The purchaser would then undertake to procure the repayment of the vendor's loan, normally by injecting cash on loan account. The amount paid for the shares would therefore be correspondingly lower and the purchaser may seek a further discount to compensate for the delay in recovering the ACT. However the purchaser will obtain a 0.5% saving on the reduced amount paid for the shares.

The payment of a pre-sale dividend is specifically excluded from the legislation preventing a company from giving financial assistance for the purchase of its shares. [*CA 1985, s 151*].

Pre-sale stock dividend

14.32 If the company is not in a position to recover the ACT on a dividend, a pre-sale stock dividend could be used, which is a dividend satisfied by a bonus issue of shares. A stock dividend should be made well in advance of arrangements for the sale of the company to minimise the risk of challenge by the Inland Revenue under the *Furniss v Dawson* principle.

A stock dividend achieves a CGT saving by giving the shareholder an addition to his base cost equivalent to the appropriate 'amount in cash' (i.e. the dividend foregone or market value of the shares (if more than 15% different) by electing to take the bonus issue of shares. [*TCGA 1992, s 141*]. The effect is to convert a capital gain taxable at 40% to a dividend receipt for the shareholder effectively taxable at 25% on the net equivalent amount and therefore achieves a similar effect to a pre-sale dividend. However, a stock dividend does not attract an ACT liability or involve any cash payment by the company.

Providing the stock dividend is structured correctly there should be a minimal effect on reserves (e.g. cash dividend of £1,000 or 10,000 10p ordinary shares ranking *pari passu* with existing shares). In this case a base cost equal to the market value of the shares should be established (for an effective 25% income tax cost). However, only £1,000 of the cash dividend equivalent would be deducted from reserves.

Ex-gratia/termination payments

14.33   Many shareholder-directors are strongly tempted by the prospect of a £30,000 tax-free ex-gratia/termination payment prior to the sale. By arranging for a corresponding deduction in the share price, this would save them CGT at 40%. However, where such payments coincide with the sale of shares in a family company, the Inspector's almost automatic reaction is to disallow the payment on the basis that it is either a distribution or part of the consideration for the sale of the shares (thus denying the £30,000 tax-free exemption in the individual's hands) (*James Snook & Co. Ltd v Blasdale (1952) 33 TC 244*). In certain cases, it might be possible to argue that the termination payment was made for valid commercial reasons unconnected with the sale. It will be necessary to demonstrate that all shareholders received full market value for the shares and the termination payment was an independent transaction.

It is vital that the making of any ex-gratia payment should not be in the agreement for the sale of the shares and a Board resolution should be passed indicating that the payment is considered to be in the interests of the company.

Further dangers arise when the recipient of a termination payment is at or approaching retirement age. The Revenue now view such payments as an 'unapproved pension benefit' and seek to tax it under Schedule E. Where the individual is not a member of a pension scheme, it is possible to obtain approval from the Inland Revenue Pension Schemes Office to treat the termination payment as a tax free pension lump sum (see also 5.20).

Special pension contributions

14.34   Bearing in mind the risks associated with termination payments, it may be more efficient for the company to make a special payment to a pension scheme to enhance the proprietors pension rights.

The additional pension benefits and the cost of providing them would need to be quantified. If the individual is near retirement age, the benefits will be quite valuable, for example giving him an increased tax-free lump sum on commutation of the pension (although funding the enhanced benefits may be costly).

The Revenue have confirmed they will not seek to tax the contribution as a termination payment, provided the resulting pension benefits are within the permitted limits (SP2/81).

The company should be able to claim a trading deduction for the special pension payment, subject to the possibility that relief may be spread over a number of years with a maximum write-off period of 4 years (see 9.10 above).

Inter-spouse transfers

14.35   Where the vendor owns virtually all the shares, it may be possible to save tax by transferring some shares to his wife, who may then be able to use up her annual CGT exemption and available lower/basic rate band.

It will also be particularly beneficial to do this if his wife qualifies for retirement belief in her own right (i.e., owns at least 5% of the shares and is a full time working director/employee) and where she would otherwise have unused retirement relief (see also 14.36 below).

Maximising CGT base value at March 1982

14.36   Where the vendor held the shares at March 1982, he will be able to deduct the March 1982 value of the shares, together with indexation relief from the sale proceeds. While this may provide a significant relief for a controlling shareholder of a company which was profitable in 1982, a minority shareholder will typically have a low March 1982 base value (as the shares will be discounted for lack of control etc.).

This can be a problem in 'husband and wife' owned companies, if neither have control. However, by concession, it is possible to boost the March 1982 value by arranging for one spouse to transfer sufficient shares to give the other control before the onward sale of the company (see 13.26).

Becoming non-resident

14.37   Perhaps the most radical step, contemplated by many vendors (and achieved by few!) is to establish non-resident status in order to avoid paying UK capital gains tax on the sale of their company. The vendor must ensure that he is neither resident nor ordinarily resident in the UK throughout the tax year of disposal.

It is normally advisable to leave the UK before the tax year of disposal and remain outside the UK during the tax year of disposal. Visits back to the UK for the next two (preferably three) years should be kept to a minimum to ensure that the individual remains not resident and not ordinarily resident in the UK. Furthermore it is recommended that the UK family home is sold and a new home is purchased abroad. Where the individual goes to work under a full-time contract of employment abroad, he will be treated as not resident nor ordinarily resident from the day of departure provided the full-time employment abroad lasts at least one full tax year. Thus if a genuine full-time employment can be obtained abroad, it is easier to become non-resident for CGT purposes.

This is often impractical since the proprietor-shareholder may not be able to 'abandon' the company before it is sold, although this may be a feasible option for other shareholders. Although the Inland Revenue may by concession treat the individual as not resident and not ordinarily resident from the day of departure it is not prudent to rely on this where capital gains tax is being avoided. (See *CIR v R (Ex parte Fulford-Dobson) [1987] STC 344*).

The disruption caused by spending at least three years away from the UK is only likely to appeal to those selling out at the end of their business career. Others will seek more realistic solutions. It may be possible to defer the tax charge if the acquiring company is prepared to issue loan stock (or shares) in exchange for the vendor's shares. Some time later, the vendor may become non-resident and the gain on the redemption of the loan note could be realised tax free, although the Revenue are beginning to refuse clearance applications where the issue of loan notes is purely designed to avoid tax by non-residence as opposed to being dictated by the purchaser's commercial requirements.

It is vital to consider the vendor's tax position in the overseas country and it may be necessary to take a long holiday elsewhere to avoid being resident in that country if a material tax liability is likely to arise on the sale overseas.

Non-resident trusts structures

14.38   Following the changes made in the *Finance Act 1991*, the creation of a non-resident trust to avoid/defer UK capital gains tax will generally no longer be effective, unless the settlor is non-UK domiciled.

Various non-resident structures involving non-resident companies may be effective in deferring CGT on a company sale, but specialist advice must be sought here and inevitably careful planning and implementation is required to reduce the possibility of a *Furniss v Dawson* case and UK residence challenge by the Revenue.

PLANNING CHECKLIST — SELLING THE FAMILY BUSINESS OR COMPANY
Company • Corporate tax liability on asset sale may be reduced by sensible allocation of disposal proceeds — avoid creating 'wasted' indexation losses. • Balancing charge on sale of industrial building can be avoided by leasing the building instead.
Working shareholders • A share sale is generally preferred as this avoids double charge and enables retirement relief or reinvestment relief to be claimed. • Tax liability can usually be minimised by a pre-sale dividend and special pension contributions. • Can limit their exposure under the warranties and indemnities by disclosing all relevant details. • Consider using a pre-liquidation dividend for extracting all/part of the post-tax profits arising from an asset sale.
Other employees • Provides opportunity to realise gain on employee incentive scheme shares. • Employment contracts will continue to run on both asset or share sales.
Non-working shareholders • Should resist giving warranties and indemnities (as running of company is outside their control). • Individual tax position may be prejudiced by structure of deal — must analyse early as changes can sometimes be made.

Chapter 15

Winding Up the Family Company

Background

15.1 The shareholders of a family company may decide to wind it up voluntarily, perhaps following a sale of the assets and trade or a planned closure of the business. In such cases, there will often be a surplus available for distribution to the shareholders after the interests of the creditors have been satisfied. It will be essential to ensure that the surplus funds are distributed in a tax-efficient manner. Where a company is wound-up voluntarily, there may be time to implement appropriate corporate tax planning measures to increase the amount ultimately available to the company's shareholders.

15.2 If the company is wound up by a receiver or creditor, then the shareholders are likely to lose most if not all of their capital stake. It will then be necessary to consider what tax relief can be claimed in respect of their shares and any irrecoverable shareholder loans. If the company is insolvent, the actions of the receiver/liquidator will be dictated by commercial requirements but, where possible, these should be conducted on the most tax efficient basis to enhance the amount available for both creditors and shareholders. However, there is no point in planning to reduce tax liabilities that are never going to be paid due to insufficiency of funds.

Consequences for the company

Pension provision

15.3 Before the company ceases trading the proprietors'/directors' pension provision should be considered. Unless full provision has been made, there will be a tax advantage in making 'top-up' payments to an approved scheme. Provided the pension contributions are *paid* in the final CTAP, (i.e. up to cessation of trade) a trading deduction can be claimed with no spreading of special contributions. This will also reduce the funds remaining for distribution and hence the shareholder's exposure to tax.

Where a company has not made any pension provision for its proprietors/directors, it is possible for it to enter into a *Hancock*

241

Annuity arrangement. The company would purchase an annuity from an insurance company before the trade ceases. (Following the case of *Hancock v General Reversionary & Investment Co. Ltd (1918) 7 TC 358*, the purchase of an annuity to fund a future pension was held to be deductible against profits — it was not a capital payment.) The Insurance company would then be responsible for paying the pension (approval from the Inland Revenue Superannuation Funds Office would have to be obtained).

Termination of CTAP and closure costs

15.4 The company's trade will usually have ceased before it is wound-up and this will have a number of important tax consequences.

The cessation of the company's trade will bring about a termination of the company's current CTAP. [*ICTA 1988, s 12(3)(c)*]. Any unprovided expenses incurred after the cessation of trade (known as 'post-cessation' expenses) can only be offset against post-cessation receipts, which reduces the prospect of obtaining relief. [*ICTA 1988, s 105*]. In drawing up the tax computation to cessation, particular care must therefore be taken to ensure that specific provisions are made for all known trade expenses which have been incurred up to the date of cessation. This will include provisions for warranty claims and bad and doubtful debts.

The Revenue will disallow any expenses incurred in connection with the cessation of trade. However specific relief is given for statutory redundancy payments and any additional redundancy payments (up to three times the amount of the statutory redundancy payments). Such payments are treated as paid on the date of cessation if they are paid after the trade ceases. [*ICTA 1988, ss 90, 579(2)*].

Sale of assets

15.5 The cessation of trade will give rise to a deemed disposal of plant and machinery for capital allowance purposes, resulting in a balancing adjustment. [*CAA 1990, s 26(1)(e)*]. If the plant is sold either before or shortly after the trade ceases, the disposal value will generally be the net disposal proceeds. [*CAA 1990, s 26(1)(a)*].

The cessation of trade will not, of itself, trigger a balancing adjustment for industrial buildings allowances purposes, although no WDAs are available where the building ceases to be used for industrial purposes (unless temporary disuse can be argued). A balancing adjustment will arise on the disposal of the building, which will be recognised for tax purposes on the completion of the sale. [*CAA 1990, ss 4(1), 161(8)*]. Typically a balancing charge will arise on the disposal of an industrial building. Where the sale is completed after the cessation of trade, ESC

B19 enables any unused Schedule D Case I losses to be carried forward against such balancing charges (but *not* capital gains).

The sale of the company's chargeable assets may also produce capital gains, giving rise to a significant tax liability. The date of disposal for CGT purposes is the date of the unconditional contract. [*TCGA 1992, s 28*]. Frequently, the company's property will not be sold until after the trade has ceased and therefore the capital gain would not be covered by any trading losses generated in the final CTAP to cessation. In some cases, it may be possible for the property to be sold before the cessation (perhaps to the controlling shareholder) and then leased/licensed back for a short period. This will enable the capital gain to be triggered in the final CTAP and set-off against the current tax losses.

If the company's stock is sold to a UK trader, the actual sale proceeds will be credited in the trading account for tax purposes. In such cases, the Inland Revenue will find it difficult to impute market value. [*ICTA 1988, s 100(1)(a)(1A)(a)*].

Trading losses

15.6   The liquidator must consider how to make best use of any remaining tax adjusted trading losses. The main reliefs which are likely to be relevant are:

(*a*)   the offset of Schedule D Case I losses for the final CTAP to cessation against the company's other profits (before charges on income) of that period. [*ICTA 1988, s 393A(1)(a)*];

(*b*)   the offset of any remaining loss by carrying it back against the total profits (after deducting trading charges on income) for the previous three years. [*ICTA 1988, s 393A(1)(b)*]. Where a loss arises in the final period to cessation, any unrelieved trading charges on income can also be added to the Schedule D Case I loss figure to be carried back.

Close Investment Holding Company status

15.7   Where a close company ceases to carry on a trade or property investment business, it will usually be treated as a close investment holding company, 'CIHC'. [*ICTA 1988, s 13A*] (see 4.19). A CIHC cannot benefit from the lower small companies rate of corporation tax, nor can it claim marginal relief, whatever the level of its profits. In such cases, the company's post-cessation income and gains would be taxed at the main corporation tax rate of 33%.

If the company is not a CIHC throughout the CTAP which ended on the commencement of its winding up, it will not be treated as a CIHC for the next CTAP. [*ICTA 1988, s 13A(4)*]. However, where the company has ceased trading before it is wound up, this exemption is unlikely to apply. The company will normally have already become a CIHC before it goes into liquidation.

Pre-liquidation tax liabilities

15.8 The liquidator will need to take account of pre-liquidation tax liabilities as either preferential or ordinary claims. [*IA 1986, ss 175, 386*]. Broadly, preferential liabilities include unpaid PAYE including national insurance contributions etc. for the twelve months prior to the receiver's/liquidator's appointment, unpaid VAT arising within the previous six months and unpaid remuneration for the past four months. Assessed taxes are no longer preferred debts.

A practical approach will normally be required by the liquidator of the insolvent company when dealing with the company's tax affairs. He must inform the Revenue of his appointment and determine the outstanding corporation tax position. Where the company is insolvent or has substantial brought forward tax losses, the Revenue may be prepared to agree a 'nil liability' position without the need to submit detailed tax computations. However, if the liquidator wishes to agree an amount of trading losses for the purposes of a loss relief claim (see 15.6), the Inland Revenue will require detailed computations and accounts.

Post-liquidation tax liabilities

15.9 The commencement of a winding-up terminates the company's current CTAP and a new accounting period will begin. Each successive accounting period will last for 12 months, with the final accounting period ending on the date the winding-up is completed. [*ICTA 1988, s 12(7)*].

Corporation tax liabilities which arise during the course of the winding up (frequently only on interest received) would be treated as an expense or disbursement of the liquidation (see *re Beni-Felkai Mining Co. Limited (1933) 18 TC 632*). As a necessary disbursement of the liquidation, the tax liabilities must (together with any overdue tax) be met in priority to the claims of all creditors and the liquidators remuneration. However, where appropriate, the liquidator can apply to the Court for an Order of Priority to be made to ensure that his remuneration and expenses can be dealt with equitably.

Legal formalities

15.10 The shareholders of a solvent company can proceed to wind up the company voluntarily (a solvent company for these purposes is broadly one which is able to pay its debts within 12 months). A member's voluntary winding-up must be dealt with by a licensed insolvency practitioner. Quite often, the costs of a formal voluntary liquidation may seem relatively high compared to the value of the company's assets.

The alternative 'dissolution' route is often preferred to a liquidation. However, it should be noted that from 1 July 1995, *CA 1985, s 652A* imposes additional stringent requirements on the directors such as the need to notify all shareholders, employees, creditors etc., with tough penalties for non-compliance. Furthermore it is necessary to wait at least three months after the trade has ceased before an application can be made. A solvent company may be dissolved as a result of the company's name being struck off the register by the Registrar of Companies under *Companies Act 1985, s 652*. (This does not require a licensed insolvency practitioner.) In such cases, it is vital that any remaining assets must first be stripped out of the company, otherwise they will pass to the Crown under the '*bona vacantia*' rule in *CA 1985, s 654*. The Inland Revenue are prepared to treat a dissolution under *CA 1985, s 652* as a winding-up for tax purposes under ESC C16 (See 15.11 below.)

Dealing with surplus available to shareholders

Capital distributions

15.11   Where a company has surplus funds (i.e. after its creditors have been paid), it is necessary to decide how these can be extracted for the shareholders benefit in the most tax efficient manner.

Distributions made in the course of dissolving or winding up the company are treated as 'capital distributions' and are therefore chargeable to CGT. [*TCGA 1992, s 122*]. A distribution made to shareholders during the course of the winding-up does not count as an income distribution for tax purposes and does not therefore entail any ACT. The corollary is that no tax credit is available to the recipient shareholder. [*ICTA 1988, s 209(1)*].

Under Inland Revenue ESC C16, the Revenue will treat a distribution made prior to a dissolution as having been made under a formal winding-up, and therefore as a capital payment, provided certain assurances are given to the Inspector beforehand. Normally, the Inspector will require that any remaining tax liabilities will be settled and confirmation that, once the assets have been distributed, the company will request the Registrar to strike the company off the register (see 15.10).

A shareholder is treated as making a disposal for CGT purposes when he becomes entitled to receive the capital distribution from the company. [*TCGA 1992, s 122(1)*]. The commencement of the liquidation does not trigger any deemed disposal for the shareholder. The shareholder's capital gain or loss would be effectively computed as a disposal of his interest in the shares, as follows:

Example 1

	£
Capital distribution	X
Less Base value of shares	
Cost/Deemed March 1982 value	(X)
Unindexed gain/loss	X
Less Indexation	(X)
Indexed gain/loss	X

Multiple capital distributions

15.12 If a shareholder receives more than one capital distribution, all but the last one will be treated as a part disposal in respect of the shares. The normal

$$\frac{A}{A + B}$$

part disposal formula in *TCGA 1992, s 42* will be used to apportion the base cost of the shares where:

    A = the amount of the interim of capital distribution

    B = the residual share value at the date of the interim distribution.

The Revenue have indicated a relatively relaxed approach with regard to agreeing interim valuations of shares (for the purpose of calculating 'B') where the liquidation is expected to be completed within two years of the first distribution. For example, if all the distributions are made before the first CGT assessment is raised, the Revenue will agree that the residual share value at the date of any interim distribution equals the total amount of subsequent distributions, without any discount for the delay in the receipt of the subsequent payments (SP/D3).

It may be possible to reduce each shareholder's CGT liability by phasing the timing of the capital distributions over as many tax years as possible. This will enable the shareholders to benefit from more than one annual exemption. Although all parties may be anxious to conclude the liquidation as quickly as possible, by timing the liquidation shortly before the start of the tax year, it may be possible to pay capital distributions over three separate tax years (but paid over a period of only (say) 18 months). Where there are a number of shareholders, the benefits from using multiple annual exemptions may be considerable.

Example 2

Tax treatment of capital distributions

Brooking Ltd went into liquidation in March 1994. Mr Brooking formed the company in September 1989, subscribing for all the 20,000 ordinary £1 shares at par.

The liquidator made the following distributions to Mr Brooking (from the residual profits and initial capital).

	£
July 1994	15,000
August 1995 (final)	21,600

Mr Brooking's CGT computations would be as follows:

	£
1994/95 — July 1994	
Capital distribution	15,000
Less Part disposal cost	
$£20,000 \times \dfrac{£15,000}{£15,000 + £21,600}$	(8,197)
Indexation — £8,197 × 23.5%	(1,926)
Chargeable gain	£4,877

	£
1995/96 — August 1995	
Final capital distribution	21,600
Less Cost — £20,000 less £8,197	
used in 1994/95	(11,803)
Indexation — £11,803 × 28.6%	(3,376)
Chargeable gain	£6,421

Small capital distributions

15.13 The Inspector has the discretion to deduct 'small' interim distributions against the shareholder's base cost. [*TCGA 1992, s 122(2)*]. For these purposes, a distribution is treated as small if it does not exceed 5% of the value of the shareholding at the relevant date. The shareholder will obviously prefer to crystallise a chargeable gain if it can be covered by an otherwise unused annual CGT exemption (currently £6,000). Although the Inspector has the discretion, the Revenue have indicated that it would normally be exercised when required. (*IR Tax Bulletin, Issue 5, page 46.*)

Where the capital distribution exceeds the allowable CGT base cost, the 'small proceeds' rule does not apply. Instead, the shareholder can elect to offset the capital distribution against his base cost. [*TCGA 1992, s 122(4)*]. This means that any balance of proceeds and subsequent distributions will be fully chargeable to CGT.

Distributions in specie

15.14 If a liquidator distributes assets to the shareholders in lieu of their entitlement to a cash distribution, this will still constitute a capital distribution for tax purposes. [*TCGA 1992, s 122(5)*]. This will always be treated as a transaction at market value because the shareholders are connected with the company. [*TCGA 1992, s 17(1)(a)*]. In contrast to a capital distribution for cash, a distribution *in specie* involves two disposals — one by the company in respect of the asset disposed of and one by the shareholder in respect of his shares. As there is no tax credit available on a capital distribution, this gives rise to an acute form of the 'double charge' effect.

Pre-liquidation/dissolution dividend

15.15 It will often be beneficial to extract an income dividend before the company is wound-up (i.e. before the liquidator is appointed or dissolved). The optimum income dividend/capital distributions mix will depend on the shareholder's indexed based cost and the company's ACT capacity. These principles are illustrated in the following example.

Example 3

Planning a pre-liquidation dividend

Stiles Ltd sold its trade and assets as a going concern on 31 March 1995. It was then decided to put the company into liquidation and distribute the remaining cash to its sole shareholder, Mr Nobby.

Mr Nobby incorporated Stiles Limited in 1976. The March 1982 value of his shares has been estimated at £100,000.

Stiles Ltd's ACT capacity at 31 March 1995 is summarised as follows.

Year ended 31 March	Profits/ (Losses)	%	ACT Capacity	ACT already offset	Available ACT Capacity
	£		£	£	£
1995	222,400	20	54,480	–	44,480
1994	46,000	22½	10,350	(10,350)	–
1993	58,000	25	14,500	(6,000)	8,500
1992	(25,000)	25	–	–	–
1991	80,000	25	20,000	–	20,000
1990	(7,000)	25	–	–	–
					72,980

Stiles Ltd's current summarised balanced sheet is as follows:

	£
Current assets	
Debtors	28,000
Cash	500,400
	528,400
Less current liability	
Corporation tax	(55,600)
	£472,800
Financed by:	
Share capital	1,000
Reserves	471,800
	£472,800

(a) Capital distribution

If the reserves are distributed and share capital repaid to Mr Nobby after the commencement of the winding-up, this will be treated as a capital distribution, chargeable to CGT, as follows.

	£
Capital distribution	472,800
Less March 1982 base value	(100,000)
Indexation (say) 86%	(86,000)
Indexed gain	286,800
Less Annual exemption	(6,000)
	280,800
CGT thereon @ 40%	£112,320

(b) Mix of pre-liquidation dividend and capital distribution

If the reserves were paid to Mr Nobby before the commencement of the liquidation, this will be treated as an ordinary 'income' dividend in his hands, taxed at an effective rate of 25%. However, it would not be efficient to pay the full amount of reserves out as a pre-liquidation dividend. Ideally, a shareholder should receive a capital distribution on liquidation equal to the combined amount of his CGT *indexed* base value and any other CGT exemptions, since this part of the 'return' carries no CGT liability.

The 'excess' would carry CGT at a marginal rate of 40% and therefore only this amount should be extracted as an income dividend.

	£	£
Total amount to be returned		472,800
Less Amount to be returned as a 'capital distribution' with no CGT liability:		
March 1982 value	(100,000)	
Indexation	(86,000)	
Annual exemption	(6,000)	
		(192,000)
Therefore pre-liquidation dividend should be		280,800

A pre-liquidation dividend of £280,800 (paid after 6 April 1995) would involve ACT of £70,200 (i.e. 20/80 × £280,800), which can be offset under the six year carry back rule (the available ACT capacity being £72,980).

Mr Nobby's tax liability would then be:

	£
Dividend	280,800
Tax credit (20/80)	70,200
Gross dividend	351,000
Income tax @ 40%	140,400
Less Tax credit	(70,200)
Higher-rate assessment	£70,200

The capital distribution of £192,000 would be paid once the company is wound-up or after clearance has been obtained from the Inspector to dissolve the company under ESC C16 (see 15.11). No CGT liability would arise as it would be covered by Mr Nobby's indexed base cost and annual exemption. The tax saved by paying a pre-liquidation dividend is therefore £42,120 (i.e. £112,320 less £70,200).

Dormant company ACT trap

15.16 If a company has ceased trading and has no other income it is unlikely that it will have an accounting period for corporation tax purposes. [*ICTA 1988, s 12(2)(3)*]. In such cases the Inland Revenue take the view that ACT which arises in a *dormant* period (i.e. where there is no CTAP) cannot be offset or carried back. [*ICTA 1988, s 239(1)(3)*]. The Revenue has successfully taken this point before the Special Commissioners in *Aproline Ltd v Littlejohn* (HMIT) (1995) STI 969. Obviously, there is no problem if the company is a subsidiary as the dividend can be paid without ACT under the group income election under *ICTA 1988, s 247(1)*.

The risk of generating irrecoverable ACT can be avoided if the company triggers the start of a new CTAP (immediately after the trade has ceased) by acquiring a source of income — for example by opening a bank deposit account. [*ICTA 1988, s 12(2)(a)*]. In the *Aproline* case, the company started to charge interest on inter-company balances but this was not accepted as a source of income as there was not agreement to charge interest and no history of charges being made. The company will then be free to pay the dividend with the right to set off or carry back the ACT.

Retirement relief for capital distributions

15.17   In certain cases, a shareholder can claim retirement relief against his/her capital distributions. The special conditions which must be satisfied are as follows:

(*a*)   the capital distribution must be made within one year, extended up to three years by concession, of the cessation of trade. [*TCGA 1992, s 163(4)*];

(*b*)   the relevant date on or before which the individual must be 55 years old (or is retiring on ill-health grounds) is that date the trade ceases and the qualifying ten year period (see 14.20) is counted up to that date. [*TCGA 1992, s 163(6)*];

(*c*)   the chargeable business assets formula (see 14.22) is computed immediately before the cessation of trade.

Retirement relief is denied to the extent that 'chargeable business assets' are distributed *in specie* (see 15.14), which may significantly limit the relief available. [*TCGA 1992, 6 Sch 11*]. In such cases, it may be better to sell the assets to the shareholder first and then distribute the resulting cash by means of a normal capital distribution for which full relief can be claimed.

Relief for shareholders of insolvent companies

Negligible value claim

15.18   Where the shares are worthless, a shareholder can make a 'negligible value' claim. This will enable him to be treated as disposing of his shareholding for no or virtually no consideration. [*TCGA 1992, s 24(2)*]. Strictly, the deemed disposal does not take place until the claim is made (*Williams v Bullivant [1983] STC 107*). By concession, the capital loss claim can be backdated for up to 24 months (if required) provided the shares were also worthless at that earlier date (ESC D28). A claim made after 29 November 1993 to backdate a negligible value loss prior to that date under ESC D28 must be calculated on the basis of the post 29 November 1993 rules (see 10.8 above).

For disposals after 29 November 1993, indexation can no longer be used to increase or create a capital loss. This means that the allowable loss arising on a negligible value claim will, in most cases, be significantly reduced. However, there were important transitional rules to provide relief for indexation losses of up to £10,000 arising in 1993/94 and 1994/95. This relief could only be claimed by individuals and pre-November 1993 trusts.

Broadly, the transitional rules applied where the taxpayer had net chargeable gains for the year (after deducting his annual exemption). In such cases, the gain was reduced by any indexation losses, up to a maximum of £10,000. For these purposes, an indexation loss is simply the additional indexation element of the loss that would have been available under the old rules i.e., before indexation losses were restricted. The transitional relief for indexation losses must have been taken first in 1993/94. Any part of the £10,000 limit remaining unused in 1993/94 was carried forward for use on the same basis in 1994/95. The reduction for indexation losses is made before deducting any allowable losses brought forward from previous years.

ESC D28 provides that, where a negligible value claim is made between 29 November 1993 and 5 April 1995, an indexation loss (calculated to the date of the deemed disposal) of up to £10,000 can be established. This indexation loss can be used to reduce gains, arising in the year of the deemed 'negligible value' disposal and subsequent years, but it must be offset by 1994/95.

If a shareholder does not make a negligible value claim, his capital loss will then be deemed to arise when the company is finally dissolved, i.e., upon completion of the liquidation or when the company is finally dissolved. (A disposal arises for CGT purposes when the shares are finally extinguished. [*TCGA 1992, s 24(1)*]).

Example 4

Negligible value claim with transitional indexation relief

Mr Cohen's company, Craven Cottage Ltd, went into liquidation in July 1992. The liquidation was completed in July 1994 without Mr Cohen receiving any distributions from the liquidator.

Mr Cohen formed the company in June 1986 subscribing for 10,000 £1 ordinary shares.

A negligible value claim was made in March 1995, which backdated the deemed disposal of his shares to March 1994 (by virtue of ESC D28).

The calculation of the allowable loss (with transitional indexation relief) arising in 1993/94 is as follows:

	£
Capital distributions	
Less Cost	(10,000)
Indexation — transitional	
(June 1986 to March 1994)	
£10,000 × 45.7%	(4,570)
Allowable loss	(14,570)

Income tax relief for capital losses on shares

15.19   In certain circumstances, the shareholder may be able to make a claim to offset the capital loss arising on his shares against his other taxable income. [*ICTA 1988, s 574*]. This is particularly valuable as capital losses cannot be relieved unless and until the shareholder makes a capital gain (see 10.9 above).

In relation to liquidations, income tax relief can be claimed in respect of a capital loss arising on:

● a capital distribution during a winding-up; or

● a negligible value claim. [*ICTA 1988, s 575(1)(b)(c)*].

Strictly, *s 574* relief cannot be claimed for a capital loss arising on the dissolution of the company. However, by concession, *s 574* relief can be claimed where:

(*a*)   the company has no assets and is dissolved; *and*

(*b*)   the shareholder has not received a capital distribution in the course of the dissolution or winding up of the company *or* where an anticipated final distribution has not been made; and

(*c*)   a negligible value claim has not been made, (ESC D46). [*TCGA 1992, s 24(2)*].

If reliance cannot be placed on the concession to obtain relief on a dissolution, then a negligible value claim should be made while the shares still exist.

Where transitional relief for indexation relief is obtained (see 15.18), this can be incorporated into the allowable loss for the purposes of a *s 574* claim (ESC D28).

A shareholder can only obtain income tax relief under *ICTA 1988, s 574* if he originally subscribed for the shares. Therefore, relief cannot be claimed for shares acquired 'second-hand'. Furthermore, the then insolvent company must satisfy numerous conditions. In particular, the company must have been actively trading at some time within the three years prior to the disposal date (without subsequently becoming an investment, share or land dealing company). The company must also have traded for at least six years before it ceased trading, although a shorter period will qualify if the company did not engage in any of the above mentioned excluded activities prior to the disposal date. [*ICTA 1988, s 576*].

From 1994/95 *s 574* relief for disposals (or deemed negligible value disposals) can be claimed against the shareholder's income for the tax year of the disposal and/or the previous tax year — a claim for the year of disposal takes priority. [*ICTA 1988, s 574(1)(2)*].

For losses incurred in 1994/95 and subsequent years claims must be made in writing within two years after the end of the year of assessment in which the loss is incurred and for 1996/97 and later years the claim must be made within 12 months after 31 January following the year of assessment in which the loss is incurred. [*ICTA 1988, s 574(1)*].

Relief for shareholder loans

15.20   Generally, a simple debt is outside the scope of CGT and therefore if it becomes irrecoverable, relief would not be available for the creditor's loss. However, a shareholder (or indeed any other lender) can make a claim under *TCGA 1992, s 253* to obtain a capital loss equal to the *principal* element of his irrecoverable loan. The claimant will receive a capital loss equal to the amount which the Inspector has agreed is irrecoverable. It should be noted that the capital loss cannot be offset against income under *ICTA 1988, s 574* (as it does not relate to shares). See Chapter 10.

A number of conditions must be satisfied, the most important of which are:

(*a*)   the loan must be irrecoverable and the claimant must not have assigned his right of recovery;

(*b*)   the amount lent must have been used wholly for the purposes of the trade carried on by a UK resident company or another UK trading company in the same group to which the money is lent. The relief is not therefore available for loans to investment companies;

(*c*)   the loan must not constitute a 'debt on security' (broadly, a debt on security represents a loan held as an investment which is both marketable and capable of increasing in value). [*TCGA 1992, s 253(1)(3)*].

Loan capital loss relief cannot be claimed on intra-group loans, although group companies can obtain relief for payments made under guarantees given for group borrowing. [*TCGA 1992, s 352(3)(4)(c)*].

Strictly speaking, the capital loss does not arise until the date of the claim. However, ESC D36 enables a capital loss claim to be backdated to an earlier tax year or accounting period on a similar basis to negligible value claims. The concessionary backdating procedure will apply provided the claim is made within two years after the end of the tax year (or accounting period) in which the loss is treated as accruing. The conditions for relief must also have been satisfied at the end of that year or period. (See 10.8 and 10.9 above.)

Any subsequent recovery of part or all of the debt will be treated as a chargeable gain arising at the date of repayment.

Example 5

Capital loss relief for irrecoverable loan

Wright Ltd has traded profitably for a number of years. However, the company has experienced a downturn in trading during the last three years. In May 1992, Mr Billy the controlling shareholder had to make a cash injection of £80,000 to the company to ease its ailing finances. However, in December 1994, the company's bankers called in the receiver and the company was subsequently wound-up. No part of Mr Billy's loan account was repaid.

He can therefore claim under *TCGA 1992, s 253* for the £80,000 to be treated as an allowable loss for CGT purposes.

If Mr Billy realises a capital gain of £50,000 in 1994/95, he should be able to relieve it with his capital loss on the loan, provided he makes the claim by 5 April 1997. Mr Billy should be able to satisfy the Inspector that the full amount of the loan (or substantially all of it) was irrecoverable at 5 April 1995.

Converting loans into new shares

15.21   Given the potential advantages of income tax relief by making a claim under *ICTA 1988, s 574*, shareholders may be tempted to convert their loans by subscribing for further shares. However, where the company is insolvent the amount subscribed for the new shares is unlikely to be reflected as part of the shareholder's CGT base cost. This is because *TCGA 1992, s 17(1)* deems the shares to be acquired at their (negligible) market value, or if the share issue constitutes a reorganisation, *TCGA 1992, s 128(2)* effectively provides that the amount subscribed will only be reflected in base cost to the extent that the company's shares increase in value, which in such cases is unlikely.

Where the company has a deficiency of net assets, it will normally be disadvantageous to substitute share capital for shareholder loans. The shareholder should be able to claim capital loss relief for his irrecoverable loan under *TCGA 1992, s 253* whereas if it is 'converted' into shares there is unlikely to be any relief.

Losses incurred on Qualifying Corporate Bonds (QCBs)

15.22   In some cases, the shareholder may hold a loan note evidencing the debt. This will invariably constitute a Qualifying Corporate Bond (QCB). Even though the QCB will represent a debt on security, an allowable capital loss can still be claimed for the irrecoverable part of the debt under the provisions of *TCGA 1992, s 254*. However to qualify as a QCB the Bond must comply with the qualifying loan rules and the funds concerned must have been lent wholly for the purposes of a trade carried on by the borrower. It follows that if the holder received the QCB as consideration for the acquisition of shares relief will not be available. [*TCGA 1992, ss 253, 254*]. Under the Revenue's proposals to change the tax treatment of Gilts and Bonds, this restriction is likely to be removed (IR press release 10 July 1995).

PLANNING CHECKLIST — WINDING UP THE FAMILY COMPANY
Company   • Company must pay appropriate pension contributions before trade ceases.   • Specific provision should be made for all known costs and expenses in the final tax computation.   • Pre-liquidation dividend must be paid in a CTAP — (to avoid the dormant company ACT trap).
Working shareholders   • Tax liability may be reduced by paying an appropriate dividend before the liquidator is appointed.   • Maximise use of CGT annual exemptions by phasing capital distributions over more than one year.   • Capital loss on worthless shares can be triggered up to 2 years earlier by making a negligible value claim.

Other employees
* Opportunity to enjoy up to £30,000 in tax free redundancy/termination payments.

Non-working shareholders
* May also benefit from payment of a pre-liquidation dividend and staggered capital distributions (see above).
* Negligible value claims can be used to trigger earlier relief for capital losses (as indicated above).

Chapter 16

Passing On the Family Company

Introduction

16.1   Owners of most family companies either seek to pass the business on to the next generation or sell it to a third party, perhaps by means of management buy-out or straight sale. This chapter examines the tax and commercial implications of handing the business down to the next generation. In some cases the business will be handed on to the children for little or no consideration. Alternatively, the retiring shareholder may seek payment for his shares, perhaps by arranging a sale of his shares back to the company.

16.2   The current capital tax regime is probably as favourable as it is ever going to be in terms of providing for succession in the family company. When capital transfer tax (the predecessor of inheritance tax) was introduced in 1974, there was no relief for family owned businesses. Following the *Finance (No 2) Act 1992* changes controlling and substantial minority shareholdings in unquoted *trading* companies are normally completely exempt from IHT. Small minority holdings (25% or less) rank for a 50% reduction in the amount chargeable to IHT. Shareholdings in family investment companies will be fully chargeable to IHT.

16.3   March 1982 rebasing and business asset hold-over relief for unquoted (trading company) shares (see 12.8 above) usually make CGT on lifetime transfers of shares a manageable problem although the recipient will inherit the deferred CGT liability in the shares. However, the availability of a tax-free CGT uplift on death combined with the 100% IHT exemption often makes it attractive to retain the shares until death.

Relevant inheritance tax principles

16.4   It is helpful to begin with a brief review of the inheritance tax system, particularly as it applies to gifts of unquoted shares. The inheritance (IHT) tax regime taxes certain lifetime transfers of capital and estates transferred on death. IHT is calculated on the cumulation principle. Each chargeable transfer is added to the total of prior

258

chargeable transfers within the previous seven years to determine the rate of IHT. The current IHT rates on chargeable lifetime transfers (principally transfers to discretionary trusts and companies) are as follows:

Chargeable transfers within previous 7 years	Rate
Up to £154,000	Nil
£154,000 plus	20%

The nil rate band in existence for chargeable transfers after 9 March 1992 and before 5 April 1995 was £150,000.

'Loss to donor' principle

16.5   IHT is based on the 'loss to donor' principle. The measure of the value transferred is the reduction in the value of the donor's estate. [*IHTA 1984, s 3(1)*]. In relation to a transfer of shares, the transfer of value for IHT purposes would be computed as follows:

Value of shareholding before the gift	X
Less value of shareholding after the gift	X
Transfer of value for IHT purposes	X

The 'diminution in value' principle can mean that the 'transfer of value' for IHT purposes may exceed the value of the shares actually transferred. This would certainly be the case where a controlling shareholder transfers a small minority stake out of his holding but thereby loses control — the value of a controlling holding would be worth considerably more than the value of a non-controlling holding (discounted to reflect the lack of influence). This principle is illustrated in Example 1 below.

Since the IHT on a lifetime chargeable transfer is the primary liability of the transferor, the loss to his estate will also include the tax. Consequently, unless the transferee agrees to bear the tax the net transfer will have to be 'grossed' by the tax.

Example 1

Computing transfer of value

Keegan (Investments) Ltd is an unquoted investment company.

The shareholdings in Keegan (Investments) Ltd, together with their respective values were as follows:

16.6 *Passing On the Family Company*

	Number of shares	Value per share
Mr Keegan	51	£4,000
Mr Macdonald	30	£720
Mr Waddle	19	£180

In March 1994, Mr Keegan transferred 21 of his shares to a discretionary trust for the benefit of his family, leaving him with 30 shares.

The transfer of value for IHT purposes would be:

	£
Value of Mr Keegan's shareholding before the transfer — 51 shares × £4,000 per share	204,000
Less Value of Mr Keegans's shareholding after the transfer — 30 shares × £720 per share	(21,600)
Transfer of value	182,400

Note: for CGT purposes, the value of the shares transferred would be £180 per shares (being the value of a 21% holding) although hold-over relief would be available on a transfer to a discretionary settlement under *TCGA 1992, s 260*.

Related property

16.6   The related property rules prevent an individual fragmenting his shareholding by transferring some of his shares to a spouse or certain 'exempt' trusts. [*IHTA 1984, s 161*]. These provisions would require the transferor's shares *and* those held by his wife etc. ('related property') to be valued as a single asset (based on the degree of control etc.). Shares held by other members of the family and family trusts are not aggregated as related property and it may therefore be beneficial to spread the shareholdings, subject to optimising BPR (see 16.15).

The effect of the related property rules is illustrated below.

Example 2

Impact of related property on valuation

Assume that prior to Mr Keegan's transfer to a discretionary trust (in Example 1), the shareholdings were:

Mr Keegan	30
Mrs Keegan	21
Other shareholders	49

In measuring the value transferred (21 shares), Mr Keegan would be deemed to hold 51 shares before and 30 shares after the transfer *for valuation purposes*. Thus, the transfer of value would be as follows:

	£
Value of Mr Keegan's shareholding before the transfer — 30 shares × £4,000 per share (51% valuation)	120,000
Less Value of Mr Keegan's shareholding after the transfer — 9 shares × £720 per share (30% valuation)	(6,480)
Transfer of value	113,520

Main exemptions

16.7   Certain exemptions are available against transfer of value in arriving at the chargeable transfer for IHT purposes. The most important are:

(*a*)   annual exemption — £3,000 p.a., although one year's unused exemption can be carried forward to the next year. [*IHTA 1984, ss 19, 20*];

(*b*)   small gifts exemption — £250 per donee p.a.;

(*c*)   normal expenditure out of income — usually available for recurring expenditure met out of the donor's *income* provided he is left with sufficient funds to maintain his standard of income e.g. life insurance premiums, payments by deed of covenant. [*IHTA 1984, s 21*].

Transfers to a (UK domiciled) spouse are completely exempt. [*IHTA 1984, s 18*]. Business Property Relief is normally available for transfers of unquoted shares in trading companies and is discussed in detail in 16.15.

Potentially exempt transfer ('PETs')

16.8   Since 1986, most lifetime transfers are treated as potentially exempt transfers (usually referred to as 'PETs'). The transfer of shares to an individual, an interest in possession trust, or an accumulation and maintenance trust would, for example, qualify as a PET. [*IHTA 1984, s 3A(1)*]. A PET becomes permanently exempt from IHT provided the donor survives seven years from the date of the transfer. After seven years, the gifted shares would be excluded from the donor's estate (subject to the gift with reservation of benefit rules) and cannot be accumulated in calculating the tax on the donor's subsequent gifts and estate held on death. [*IHTA 1984, s 3A(4)(5)*].

If the donor dies within seven years of transferring the shares (under a PET), the value of those shares at the date of the original gift is included in his chargeable estate on death. [*IHTA 1984, s 131*]. If the asset has reduced in value the taxpayer may claim that the reduced value be used for the purposes of the calculation of the tax payable. A PET therefore has the beneficial effect of freezing the value of the gifted shares. Any subsequent appreciation in value would escape IHT. Business property relief ('BPR' — see 16.15 below) may be available to eliminate or reduce the IHT liability on a PET of unquoted shares becoming chargeable. However, there would be no BPR if the transferee disposes of the gifted shares before the transferor's death. [*IHTA 1984, s 113A(1)(2)*]. This would mean that the tax on the original gift of the shares would be calculated without regard to BPR.

IHT crystallising on PET

16.9 The calculation of IHT on the PET becoming chargeable involves adding the PET to the total *chargeable* transfers made within the seven years before the PET. The PET (after any available annual exemption etc.) is treated as the 'top slice' for the purpose of calculating the relevant IHT (which will be 40% after the donor's nil rate band has been used). Taper relief is available where the PET occurred more than three years before the donor's death, discounting the amount of IHT payable by the following rates.

Period before death	Reduction in IHT
3 to 4 years	20%
4 to 5 years	40%
5 to 6 years	60%
6 to 7 years	80%

This procedure is repeated for subsequent PETs. The tax on the PET would normally be borne by the donee (who can provide for the tax by taking out a decreasing term assurance policy).

Lifetime chargeable transfers

16.10 A transfer of shares to a discretionary trust, for example, would be a *chargeable* transfer and is not a PET. It would therefore be subject to a lifetime IHT charge of 20% if the value transferred (reduced by any BPR) exceeded the transferor's nil rate band (after allowing for any previous chargeable transfers in the previous seven years). Additional IHT may become payable if the donor does not survive seven years. The tax is calculated on a similar basis to a PET becoming chargeable (see 16.8). The IHT on the original transfer is calculated using at current death rates (i.e. 40% after the nil rate band has been used) which may be eligible for taper relief. Credit is then given for tax paid on the original transfer, (however, no repayment can be made if the lifetime IHT is higher).

Example 3

Computing IHT on lifetime chargeable transfer

Following on from Example 1 the IHT payable on the transfer to the discretionary trust by Mr Keegan in March 1994 (assuming the trustees paid the tax) would be as follows:

	£
Transfer of value	182,400
Less Annual exemption (1993/94)	(3,000)
Annual exemption (unused 1992/93 c/fwd)	(3,000)
Chargeable transfer	176,400

(Note: No BPR is available as the company is an investment company.)

	£
IHT thereon	
on first £150,000 @ 0%	–
on next £26,400 @ 20%	5,280
	5,280

If Mr Keegan died 3½ years later, the additional tax payable by the trustees (assuming current IHT rates applied) would be:

	£
On first £154,000 @ 0%	–
On next £22,400 @ 40%	8,960
	8,960
Less Taper relief @ 20%	(1,792)
	7,168
Less Tax already paid in March 1994	(5,280)
Additional tax	1,888

Transfers of death

16.11   On death the total value of the individual's estate (after deducting liabilities and funeral expenses) is chargeable to IHT. [*IHTA 1984, ss 5(1), 172*]. BPR and agricultural property relief may be claimed against qualifying assets (see 16.15). Various exemptions may be claimed for transfers to a spouse, charity etc.

The transfer on death is effectively treated as the individual's final transfer — the IHT payable must therefore take into account the total chargeable transfers (including PETs which crystallise on death — see 16.8) made within the previous seven years. After the £154,000 nil rate band has been used, IHT would be payable at the rate of 40%.

16.12   If the shareholder retains all or some of his shares until death, then the value of the shares at that stage would be included in his chargeable estate on death. However, if the shares carried more than 25% of the voting rights, they will normally be completely exempt from inheritance tax by virtue of BPR. In other cases, only 50% of the value of the shares would be liable to IHT. Consequently, if the family company shareholder plans to hold on to some shares, then he (perhaps together with his wife) should aim to hold more than 25% of the voting rights (see 16.15).

16.13   It is important to appreciate that, for CGT purposes, the shares will effectively be rebased to their market value at the date of death. [*TCGA 1992, s 62*]. Consequently, any capital gain in the shares will be 'washed out' on death; similarly there will be no relief for any loss.

The value 'ascertained' for IHT purposes on death would usually be taken as the CGT base value. [*TCGA 1992, s 274*]. The related property rules may therefore apply to give a higher base value for CGT. However, if the shares are completely exempt from IHT due to the availability of 100% BPR or otherwise, the value would not need to be 'ascertained' for IHT. This means that the value for the shares cannot be agreed until a subsequent disposal takes place. Furthermore, the SVD would argue that the shares should be valued in isolation under the normal CGT rules in *TCGA 1992, s 272*, without regard to related property. (*IR Tax Bulletin, April 1995, Issue 15, page 209*).

16.14   The prospect of obtaining 100% relief from inheritance tax combined with a tax free uplift in base value for CGT purposes will often discourage the controlling shareholder from transferring his shares before death. Whilst this stance is understandable (given the controlling shareholder's natural reluctance to give up his shares), it ignores the real possibility that the current liberal capital tax regime (and particularly the existing rates of BPR) may not survive a change of Government.

Business Property Relief for the family company

100% relief

16.15   100% Business Property Relief ('BPR') is generally available for unquoted shares in trading companies where the shareholder's voting power on all matters affecting the company exceeds 25%. Such shares are completely exempt from IHT, both on a lifetime transfer and on death. BPR operates by reducing the value transferred — in this case to nil. [*IHTA 1984, s 104(1)*].

The transferor must have the relevant 25% + voting control of the company. For these purposes:

(*a*)   voting rights exerciseable by the transferor's spouse (and other 'related property'); and

(*b*)   voting rights attaching to shares in a trust in which the transferor enjoys an interest in possession,

can be counted with the transferor's own votes in determining whether the 25% limit is exceeded. [*IHTA 1984, ss 104(1)(a), 105(1A), 161*]. It is sufficient that the transfer is made *out of* a 25% plus holding — it does not have to be a 25% + holding itself.

The relevant shareholding (or qualifying replacement property) must have been held for at least two years prior to the transfer/death to qualify for the relief. [*IHTA 1984, ss 106, 107*]. BPR relief is available to both working and passive shareholders — it is not necessary for the shareholder to be a director. It is important to ensure that shares carrying more than 25% of the votes are maintained or acquired (for at least two years prior to the IHT charge) to ensure complete relief.

Controlling shareholders in unquoted companies is another category which qualifies for 100% relief. [*IHTA 1994, s 105(1)(b)*]. This may seem superfluous in view of the 100% relief for '25% +' shareholdings. However, in this case the controlling (51%) interest does not have to be held throughout the two years prior to the transfer. Only the shares which are the subject of the transfer need be owned for at least the two previous years.

50% relief

16.16   Other unquoted shares (i.e. holdings carrying 25% or less of the votes or not falling within the special rule in 16.15) will qualify for 50% BPR against the value transferred. [*IHTA 1984, s 104(1)(b)*]. Once again, the shares must be held for at least two years before the relevant transfer. In certain cases, assets used in the trade but which are held outside the company also qualify for 50% relief (see 16.37).

It may be possible to defer any IHT liability on shares (e.g. on minority holdings in trading companies or shares in a family investment company) by electing to pay it over 10 years in equal instalments on an interest free basis — see *IHTA 1984, ss 227, 228* for detailed conditions.

Loan accounts

16.17   Family companies are often financed by loans from shareholders (which can be repaid more readily). However, loans, debts, directors current account balances etc. do *not* qualify for BPR. In appropriate circumstances, it may therefore be beneficial to capitalise such loans.

BPR on PET of shares becoming chargeable

16.18 Where a PET of shares becomes chargeable on the donor's death (within seven years of the gift), BPR will only be available if the donee has retained the shares until the donor's death and the shares still qualify for relief. [*IHTA 1984, s 113A*].

Binding contract for sale of shares

16.19 BPR will not be available if, at the time of the transfer/death, there is a binding contract for the sale of the shares (ignoring sales relating to certain reorganisations). [*IHTA 1984, s 113*]. Shareholders sometimes enter into agreements which require their executors to sell the shares to the remaining shareholders if they die before retirement. This is fatal as the Inland Revenue regard this as a binding contract for sale and therefore deny BPR (SP12/80). It is possible to avoid this problem by using put and call options which give the executors an option to sell the deceased's shares and the remaining shareholders the option to buy the same shares. Either party can therefore ensure that the shares are transferred without the risk of losing BPR (as there is no binding contract for sale).

Mortgaging shares

16.20 If shares (or other eligible assets) are mortgaged BPR would only be available on the *net* value (i.e. after deducting the mortgage). This problem could be avoided by giving any charges against non-business assets or collateral assets.

Excepted assets and non-qualifying activities

16.21 A close review of the company's activities and assets is necessary to ensure that the shareholder's BPR is not precluded or restricted.

BPR will be reduced if the value of the shares reflects any 'excepted assets' held by the company. [*IHTA 1984, s 112*]. An asset would be an 'excepted asset' if it was *not* used wholly or mainly for business purposes in the previous two years unless the asset was required for future use in the business. [*IHTA 1984, s 112(2)*]. Common examples would be investments, let property and substantial cash balances. For example business property relief has been refused for lettings of industrial units on three-year leases, (see *Martin and another (executor of Moore deceased) v CIR (1995) STI 491*) and furnished flats on assured tenancies (see *Burkinyoung (executor of Burkinyoung deceased) v CIR (1995) STI 492*). The restriction works by excluding the part of the value transferred which is attributable to the excepted asset. This is very much a question of negotiation and would, for example, depend on whether the valuation of the shares was based on earnings or assets (see 13.20 above).

The company's shares will not qualify for BPR if its business consists wholly or mainly in the dealing of securities, stocks, shares or land or buildings. Property development should however qualify as a trading activity. BPR is also denied if the company is an investment company which wholly or mainly makes or holds investments. [*IHTA 1984, s 105(3)*].

The holding company of a trading group will qualify for BPR although, relief will be restricted to the extent that the value of its shares relates to any non-qualifying activities carried on by members of the group. [*IHTA 1984, s 111*].

Relief will not be available if a company is in liquidation except where this is part of a reconstruction exercise. [*IHTA 1984, s 105(5)*].

Example 4

Calculation of IHT on death and BPR

Mr Matthews dies on 26 February 1996, leaving an estate summarised as follows:

(*a*)   family home valued at £160,000;

(*b*)   personal chattels worth £25,000;

(*c*)   200 ordinary shares in Stanley Ltd (representing a 20% interest), valued by SVD at £860,000. Stanley Ltd manufactures sportswear;

(*d*)   the entire share capital (1,000 ordinary shares) in Matthews Ltd, valued by SVD at £1,200,000;

Matthews Ltd trades as a retailer of sports merchandise through a chain of shops. The Capital Taxes Office have successfully contended that £200,000 relates to shops owned by the company which have been sub-let for many years and are not required for trading purposes;

(*e*)   bank balances and portfolio of investments valued for IHT purposes at £560,000.

Mr Matthews had made no gifts within the previous seven years.

Under Mr Matthews' will, the family home, personal chattels, bank balance and investments pass to Mr Matthews' wife. The shares in Stanley Ltd and Matthews Ltd pass to his son, who is a managing director of Matthews Ltd.

16.22   Passing On the Family Company

Mr Matthews' chargeable estate for IHT purposes is as follows:

		£	£
(a)	Family home		160,000
(b)	Personal chattels		25,000
(c)	Shares in Stanley Ltd	860,000	
	Less BPR (50%)	(430,000)	430,000
(d)	Shares in Matthew Ltd	1,200,000	
	Less Excepted assets	(200,000)	200,000
		1,000,000	
	Less BPR (100%)	(1,000,000)	–
(e)	Bank balances and investments		560,000
			1,375,000
	Less Spouse exemption (a), (b) and (e) (£160,000 + £25,000 + £560,000)		(745,000)
	Chargeable estate		630,000
	IHT payable		
	On £154,000 @ 0%		–
	On £476,000 @ 40%		190,400
			£190,400

Issues for the controlling shareholder

16.22   The controlling shareholder must really consider his basic objectives for the future development and running of the business before embarking on any serious capital tax planning. Once the commercial decisions have been taken, the relevant capital tax planning strategies can be implemented to meet those objectives.

The controlling shareholder will usually need to keep his options open (for example, his children may be too young to express any leanings or interest towards the business). The tax planning approach must be 'tailored' to his personal circumstances and ideally should not commit him to any particular course of action too early on. For example, the proprietor will (naturally) be reluctant to transfer any shares until he has decided that the shares will pass as a family heirloom and a sale has been ruled out. The unexpected may happen, e.g. premature ill-health or he may receive an offer to buy the company which cannot be turned down! All such eventualities must be catered for as far as it is practically possible. The main options available to the controlling shareholder are discussed below.

16.23   Ideally, capital tax planning should be considered when the company is incorporated, as the shares will then be of minimal value. Fragmenting the company's shareholdings amongst different members of the family, including family trusts, will have a beneficial effect on share value and perhaps more importantly will enable future appreciation in value to accrue outside the donor's estate. However, the proprietor will usually want to be in control of his own destiny and be able to exercise leadership. Consequently, he (perhaps together with his spouse) will normally require at least a 51% shareholding. If there is a possibility that the company may be sold in the future, the proprietor is likely to retain a substantial proportion of the shares. At this stage, the proprietor's children are likely to very young (or not even born!) and he will not know whether they will be interested and sufficiently competent to work in the company. Flexibility and effective control can be retained by placing some shares in an appropriate family trust e.g. a discretionary trust, a children's (accumulation and maintenance) trust (see 16.35).

The 25% + requirement for 100% BPR must always be kept in mind when framing the shareholding structure.

16.24 For the existing family company, the passing of shares and ultimately control to the next generation will depend upon whether the proprietor's children (or other members of the family) are interested in developing the business and, perhaps more importantly, have shown the necessary business acumen and expertise to develop it. (Entrepreneurial parents do not always have entrepreneurial children!) The proprietor should also pre-empt the possible risk of any key managers or employees who might leave the company if it was passed down to the next generation.

16.25 If the proprietor is financially dependent on the company, he is likely to maintain control of the company to secure a future income in retirement. He may not trust his children to provide him with a consultancy fee or an 'unfunded' pension from the company.

This is why pension planning remains an important part of succession planning (pension planning is considered in Chapter 9). The controlling shareholder should aim to build up a healthy pension and adequate savings over his working life from dividends and remuneration from the company. He can then be financially secure and independent in retirement, enabling him to surrender control of the company. The controlling shareholder may also be able to unlock capital from the company through a purchase of own shares perhaps benefiting from the generous levels of CGT retirement relief (see 14.19 above). The retention of trading property held outside the company might be used to provide rental income during retirement.

16.26 If the proprietor does not have a natural successor in the family, he may wish to sell his shares to a key employee, manager or management team. Soundings would need to be taken early on to see whether the employees/managers were interested in acquiring the company and if so, whether they could raise some personal finance and obtain the required bank institutional borrowing. It is also possible to structure a management buy-out through a company purchase of own shares (along the lines indicated in Example 5 in 12.27 above).

16.27   If the proprietor plans to realise his investment in the company via a 'trade' sale of his shares to a third party, this must be planned at an early stage. (The various implications of selling the family company were dealt with in Chapter 14.) In the writer's experience, the process of selling the family business can take several years before the 'right' deal is struck. Advanced planning reduces the cost and disruption to the business and gives time to rectify any weaknesses in the business, thus enhancing its value. It is often found that the value of the business is heavily dependent on the controlling shareholder. In such cases, the purchaser may (not unreasonably) require him to work in the business for the next two or three years to hand over the expertise and contacts etc., perhaps using an 'earn-out' arrangement (see 14.18).

16.28   If the proprietor can arrange for the sale of the business after his 55th birthday he will then be able to benefit from the generous levels of CGT retirement relief. Of course the sale of a company poses a potential IHT downside. Unless the proceeds realised on the sale of the company are reinvested in IHT exempt or favoured assets (for example, woodlands), then an IHT charge of 40% will be payable (whereas no IHT would have arisen if the company had been retained).

Passing shares to the next generation

16.29   If the controlling shareholder wishes to transfer shares to his children or other members of the family, this can basically be done in one of two ways. Shares could be transferred, perhaps on a phased basis, as he approaches retirement. Such transfers will qualify as PETs for IHT purposes and CGT business asset hold-over relief will normally be available (see 12.8 above). However, the effect of a hold-over election is to pass on the contingent CGT liability to the transferee shareholder(s). If the donor dies within seven years of gifting the shares an IHT charge will arise (subject to the availability of BPR).

The IHT transfer of value (based on the 'diminution in value' principle) may differ from the value used for CGT purposes (see 16.5). For CGT the value of the shareholding actually transferred is taken. Frequently, it will not be necessary to value the shares transferred if both parties agree to dispense with submitting a market value when making a hold-over election (see 12.9 above).

16.30   As it is now relatively easy to transfer ownership of a family trading company, the use of value freezing or value shifting schemes have declined in popularity. Such schemes might be considered if the proprietor does not wish to transfer his shareholding. There are many variations of the scheme, all of which involve various tax and valuation complications and professional advice should always be obtained. Generally, they would involve a bonus issue of new shares (which only participate in future growth and profits) which would be placed in the children's hands or the use of a parallel company for placing genuine *new* business.

16.31 The controlling shareholder could retain his shares (or most of them) until death. Normally, the shares would pass to the children etc. free of IHT due to the availability of 100% BPR. If it is considered inappropriate for the children to take the shares directly outright, for example if they are too young then an appropriate trust should be used. If the most desirable distribution of the estate is not clear at the time of the will, it is possible to use a discretionary will trust. Under *IHTA 1984, s 144* capital distributions made from the trust within two years of death are treated as made under the will. For example, a discretionary will trust could be created for the benefit of the surviving spouse and the children. This would ensure that the income and capital would remain available to the spouse when required.

It is usually preferable for IHT exempt shares to be passed to the children etc. at this stage to protect against any adverse changes in capital tax. Furthermore, the surviving spouse can take the *chargeable assets* free of IHT anyway under the spouse exemption.

If the surviving spouse is not left with a '25% +' holding, an appropriate increase in shareholding should be made. This will enable the surviving spouse to qualify for 100% relief in his/her own right (the related property holding would cease to be held on the death of the first spouse).

The children will inherit the shares at their market value at the date of death for CGT purposes (and do not therefore take over any contingent CGT liability in the shares which would have occurred had the shares been transferred before death). The combination of absolute exemption from IHT and CGT rebasing to probate value is particularly beneficial and indeed, provides a persuasive argument for holding on to the shares until death.

However, the potential downside with this strategy is the prospect of a more severe capital tax regime in the future. The Labour Party has indicated that the 100% relief for BPR is over generous; particularly for small shareholdings. The controlling shareholder may also be under some moral pressure to pass at least some of the shares to the children before death to provide motivation and maintain management morale.

16.32 It is important to get the basic aspects right, such as ensuring that a will is properly drawn up and is regularly reviewed to take account of changing circumstances. Appropriate life insurance arrangements should also be in place to cover potential IHT liabilities which cannot be mitigated by planning. Life insurance premiums can normally be paid for the benefit of the other members of the family free of IHT, usually under the 'normal expenditure out of income' rule or annual exemption. (The benefits of the policy should be held in trust for the beneficiaries so that they do not form part of the individual's estate.)

Using trusts

Benefits of using trusts

16.33   As already indicated, trusts can be used to shift value and future capital growth outside the proprietor's estate. Many family company proprietors are often sceptical about the use of trusts and it will be necessary to dispel their fears. Effective control can be retained over the shares if the proprietor or the proprietor's spouse acts as trustee. Although trustees have a duty to act in the interest of the beneficiaries, this should normally coincide with the proprietor's own wishes.

Trusts also enable the underlying income and capital value of the settled shares to be protected where the children are too young to handle capital properly or if there are concerns about the children's spouses or partners. By transferring shares into trust, the proprietor can defer his decision as to which children, grandchildren (or anyone else) should inherit and what stake they should have in the company. This decision will be easier to make as the children grow up as it is often the case that only some of the children seek involvement and responsibility in the business.

Use of discretionary trusts

16.34   Discretionary trusts probably give the greatest flexibility. The income (e.g. dividends on the shares) and often the capital would be held by the trustees to be dealt with at their discretion. The trustees (normally including the proprietor) will usually have the power to accumulate the income arising in the trust during the first 21 years and decide which interest each of the children will have in the trust's assets at a later date.

A gift of assets into a discretionary trust would be a chargeable transfer and is not a PET. Consequently, to avoid a 20% IHT charge, the value transferred should be kept within the transferor's nil rate band (allowing for annual exemptions) and subject to BPR consideration. CGT hold-over relief will be available for the transfer of shares etc. to a discretionary trust.

If the shares were originally transferred within the nil rate band, then no IHT arises on a subsequent appointment of the shares to the beneficiaries within the first ten years.

A discretionary trust is subject to a periodic IHT charge every ten years, which is broadly 30% of the rate applicable to a deemed transfer of the current value of the property held in the trust (taking into account the settlor's total lifetime transfers within the seven years prior to the creation of the trust).

The maximum charge is 6% (being 30% × 20%), but is usually lower, which is an acceptable price to pay for the privilege of placing the shares and other assets outside the settlor's and beneficiaries' estates.

If 100% BPR applied on the original transfer of the shares, there is no exit charge on the distribution of assets within the first 10 years or thereafter (provided the relevant BPR conditions are satisfied at each tenth anniversary). Furthermore, there is no periodic charge, provided the trustees satisfy the relevant BPR conditions at the tenth anniversary (and assuming any other trust assets are within the nil rate band).

It is important to note that the 50% BPR does not apply in computing the tax charge on distributions in the first ten years.

The reservation of benefit rules will apply if the settlor is able to benefit directly or indirectly from the gifted shares. If a benefit has been reserved, the shares would be treated as remaining within the proprietor's estate for IHT purposes. [*FA 1986, s 102*]. Although the continued receipt of remuneration from arrangements made prior to a gift of shares from the company by a proprietor/trustee might be regarded as a reservation of benefit, the Capital Taxes Office has confirmed this will not be the case where the remuneration received was 'reasonable'.

Accumulation and maintenance trusts

16.35 Accumulation and maintenance trusts may be appropriate for children/grandchildren (aged under 25), although at least one of the beneficiaries' interest in income must vest in them on attaining the age of 25, although it can be from as early as their 18th birthday. The children would then become life interest tenants if the shares are to remain under the control of the trustees. A transfer of shares to an accumulation and maintenance trust would be a PET for IHT purposes and CGT hold-over relief can usually be claimed under *TCGA 1992, s 165*.

Interest in possession trusts

16.36 The transfer of shares to an interest in possession trust is a PET and it is normally possible to hold-over the gain for CGT purposes.

Under an interest in possession trust, the beneficiary/beneficiaries (life tenant(s)) have the right to receive the trust income as it arises usually for life but it can be for a fixed period. The capital would then normally vest in someone else (the 'remainderman').

Although the life tenant has no right to the capital, the trustees could be given power to pay capital to him or he may become entitled to capital on reaching a specified age.

The life tenant is treated as owning the underlying capital of the trust for IHT purposes, even if he is never entitled to receive it.

Assets held outside the company

16.37 It is not uncommon for the company's trading property to be owned by the controlling shareholder with the property being let to the company. However, this is detrimental for IHT purposes. BPR is only available for land, buildings, machinery or plant used in the company's trade but held outside the company where the owner of the asset is a controlling shareholder (i.e. is in a position to exercise the majority of the voting rights; 'related property' shareholdings are also included for this purpose). [*IHTA 1984, s 105(1)(e)*]. In such cases, BPR of only 50% is available. [*IHTA 1984, s 104(1)(b)*].

However, if the value of the property was held by the company and therefore reflected in the value of the company's shares, 100% BPR would be available (provided the shareholder controlled more than 25% of the votes).

16.38 If it is feasible (and much would depend on the disposition of the other shareholdings), the asset could be gifted to the company, with hold-over relief being claimed under *TCGA 1992, s 165*. It should be noted that a gift to a company cannot qualify as a PET [*IHTA 1984, s 3A*] but, if the company is wholly owned by the transferor, there will be no reduction in value of this estate.

16.39 If the shareholdings are fragmented, then careful consideration will need to be exercised to ascertain the value of the transfer (particularly bearing in mind the discount attaching to minority shareholdings). Alternatively, a transfer of value or gift could probably be avoided by transferring the property in exchange for shares, (as there would be no 'donative intent'). However, a CGT liability might arise which may be held over under the reinvestment relief provisions (business asset gift hold-over relief would not be available as the full consideration is received in shares). Nevertheless, given current property values, there may not be any capital gain after allowing for indexation.

16.40 If the trading property is held by a non-controlling shareholder no BPR would be available. The property would then be fully chargeable to IHT, even if it was used for the purposes of the company's trade.

If the property is held by an elderly member of the family (perhaps the founder or founder's widow) and is particularly valuable, consideration may be given to transferring some additional shares to him/her so as to give a controlling holding, particularly if the shares and property will revert to the next generation on his/her death. Obviously, a considerable element of trust is required here!

PLANNING CHECKLIST — PASSING ON THE COMPANY
Company • Investment companies or trading companies which hold material investments frequently involve tax liabilities for the shareholders.
Working shareholders • Succession planning options should be kept open to deal with changes in circumstances and tax law. • Should retain more than 25% of the votes to obtain complete exemption from IHT on death (donees also inherit shares at market value for CGT). • Lifetime transfers to next generation (which may be necessary to preserve management morale etc.) are usually tax free; but donee takes on deferred CGT liability. • Trusts can be used to retain control over shares but enable value to be transferred outside shareholder's estate.
Other employees • Key employees should be involved in succession planning or they may become disenchanted and leave. • If there is strong second-tier management, consider an MBO if there is no obvious succession route.
Non-working shareholders • Similar considerations apply as for working shareholders, but IHT liabilities may arise (as only 50% BPR is available for holdings carrying 25% or less of the votes).

Index